The Developing Child

Bringing together and illuminating the remarkable recent research on development from infancy to adolescence, for students of developmental psychology, policy makers, parents, and all others concerned with the future of the next generation.

SERIES EDITORS

Jerome Bruner
New York University

Michael Cole
University of California, San Diego

Annette Karmiloff-Smith
Neurocognitive Development Unit, Institute of Child Health, London

Joseph J. Campos
University of California, Berkeley

Apes, Monkeys, Children, and the Growth of Mind

Juan Carlos Gómez

HARVARD UNIVERSITY PRESS

Cambridge, Massachusetts, and London, England

2004

Copyright © 2004 by the President and Fellows of Harvard College
All rights reserved
Printed in the United States of America

Library of Congress Cataloging-in-Publication Data

Gómez, Juan Carlos, 1959–
    Apes, monkeys, children, and the growth of mind / Juan Carlos Gómez.
    p. cm. — (The developing child)
    Includes bibliographical references and index.
    ISBN 0-674-01145-7
    1. Cognition in children.   2. Psychology, Comparative.   3. Primates—
Psychology.
    I. Title.   II. Series.
    BF723.C5G65 2004
    156.'5—dc22
    2004042433

To Triz,
who lived and loved through all that came

A Triz,
y lo que nació de nosotros

Contents

Preface

What can the study of monkeys and apes tell us about the developing minds of young human beings? This is the topic of this book, and the abiding interest of my academic career. My intention has been to write an introduction to this fascinating topic but at the same time, without losing readability, to discuss some of the deeper issues at the confluence of developmental and evolutionary cognitive sciences.

The argument is simple: our minds are part of a wider evolutionary pattern discernible in the minds of other primates. Its most characteristic feature is *development* as an adaptive strategy. In most primates infancy and childhood have been extended over an increasingly higher proportion of the life span. Characteristically, primates have prolonged infancies and a slowed-down process of development, as if there were special benefits to be gained from this otherwise risky beginning. One of these benefits is the ability to get to know their worlds—both physical and social—in better detail and greater plasticity, and consequently, the ability to produce more flexible and adaptive behaviors.

Primates evolved hands and sophisticated visual and tactual systems which have allowed them to discover and exploit a world made of natural objects. They also evolved a complex social life with intricate relationships and elaborate interactions in which others are singled out as agents and subjects of behavior. Most important, a trademark of primate infancies is the inextricable meshing of the social and the physical worlds.

These evolutionary trends have reached their extreme form in humans, but their origins are present in the minds of other primates. The human mind is the product of an evolutionary wave that favored cognitive development as a long-term adaptive strategy.

Other primates' understanding of the world is at times similar, at other times subtly or vastly different from our understanding, but even when the differences appear to be prominent, we can learn something about the origins and nature of our cognitive processes by looking at the broader landscape of primate minds, to which our mind naturally belongs.

One of the frustrations of writing a book, I have discovered, is the impossibility of covering all the topics and studies that one would like to. My apologies to all the authors whose work and views I didn't manage to incorporate or mentioned more fleetingly than I wished and they deserved. The other frustration is the impossibility of acknowledging all the debts and help I have received.

Jerry Bruner enthusiastically backed the idea of this book when it first came up. Annette Karmiloff-Smith helped to move me from idea to action, and, in coalition with Elizabeth Knoll, to take the action to a conclusion and produce a final manuscript.

More indirectly or farther away in time, but not for that less important, many names inevitably come to mind. To mention only a few, I wish to acknowledge Juan Delval, José Linaza, Sue Parker, Simon Baron-Cohen, the late Angel Rivière, and Encar Sarriá, all of whom had some decisive influence in my academic career and personal life.

Two anonymous reviewers offered a wealth of comments and advice that have contributed much to the final product. My gratitude to them, and to Anita Safran, who turned the final manuscript into a clearer and more readable version through her insightful and sympathetic editing.

My deep gratitude also to my colleagues in the School of Psychology and the newly established Centre for Social Learning and Cognitive Evolution; it is a privilege to be able to work in such an exceptional and stimulating environment.

Of course, and most excusably in a book about development, I am grateful to my parents for their patience and support throughout (even when my books and papers inundated our family home).

Finally, for all her help—reading more than one draft of all the chapters, bluntly speaking her mind about the shortcomings she detected, compiling the references, amending the figures, and managing to deal with everything that came to her hands, including a baby, during the difficult phases of the writing—I want to acknowledge and thank my wife and partner in life, Beatriz Martín-Andrade. This is her book (and, because she came in the middle of it, also the book of Nerea).

1

Hands, Faces, and Infancy: The Origins of Primate Minds

My daughter is nine months old. She is one of those babies who are not much interested in crawling and thus spends most of her time, when not in the arms of her mum or dad, sitting on the ground playing with every object she can get hold of. Her play is not especially sophisticated: she touches the toys (mostly with her index finger), holds them, and sometimes hits them against the ground or against other nearby toys. She is not very precise, and most of the time the toys roll away from her reach. Sometimes, though, she places one object in gentle contact with another, or appears to be trying to reconstruct a dismantled set by putting two of its pieces next to each other. Only a few days ago, when I played a favorite trick of developmental psychologists on her—I covered a toy she was about to grab with a cloth—she didn't try to take the cloth away and uncover the object. Now, however, she appears to begin to understand the trick and clumsily attempts to pull the cloth aside.

When she wants to approach an object, her helplessness is apparent: she struggles, leaning toward her target with one arm, then with another; sometimes, if she is lucky, she will somehow move herself (perhaps just by chance) toward the toy and finally get it. Only a few weeks ago, she was not able to do even this. She had to devote all her energy to balancing in a sitting position without falling to one side or backwards. And before that, during her first months of life, she just lay at the mercy of the adults around her, watching and listening. Once she learned to sit and her balance failed sometimes, she would cry in distress and wave her arms and there we came, dutifully, to take her in our arms and comfort her. She doesn't really know as yet how to request that we pick her up. She can of course cry and even wave her arms, but it is up to us to understand what she might want.

It will not take her very long to leave these particular expressions of her helplessness behind. She will soon crawl or find an alternative way of locomotion until she is ready to discover walking. She will devise gestures to make requests from us (she will, for example, point to the garden door to ask that we take her out on the grass) and figure out how to show us the things that capture her interest (like our neighbor's cat). Not much later she will discover words and the endless possibilities of combining them into sentences. She will certainly find new and increasingly skillful ways of manipulating objects, sometimes on her own, most of the time with the assistance of her parents and friends, who will help her to learn how to do things with objects. My daughter will become an adult member of the human species, with all our remarkable skills and knowledge.

I had learned my diaper-changing skills almost twenty years ago, when I had my first experience with a baby, but that was a very different baby—an orphan gorilla infant who was about the same age as my daughter is now and was being hand-reared in a zoo. Apart from the obvious differences in appearance, their behavior, at this particular period of development, was extraordinarily different. Muni—that was the name of this female gorilla—was perfectly able to move on her own, walking on all fours like adult gorillas. Even more, she could climb small trees, boxes, and other structures that offered some secure holds. She had little problem approaching on her own many of the objects she wanted. If she refrained from going places by herself it was out of fear, preferring the secure company of her surrogate human caretakers to the "dangers" of the surroundings populated by such unpredictable creatures as goats, zebras, and even—her worst nightmare—a baby elephant. Her attachment to adults was more limiting than her locomotion skills.

Muni was very interested in objects: she would grab them, watch them, and almost invariably take them to her mouth. Sometimes she could hit them against the ground, or explore them more gently with her finger, much as my daughter does today, perhaps a little more roughly and a little less imaginatively. When I played the trick of the cloth that suddenly covered an object, she had no problem pulling the cloth aside and recovering her toy.

When Muni the baby gorilla was frightened (as frequently happened when, for example, the baby elephant took a walk around the nursery area), she would not only cry and yell, but also very actively run toward us and, if we were not quick enough to take her in arms, she would literally climb up on one of us to the security of the chest.

Muni had an early playmate—Liu, an African patas monkey. He was much younger than Muni but clearly surpassed her in agility and locomotor skills. Liu would run and jump around the nursery rooms and garden area at high speed, making it impossible to catch him when he had grabbed something from us (as he was in the habit of doing, especially our pens and pieces of paper on which we were eagerly taking our precious notes of the gorilla's behavior). He was also attached to specific human caretakers from whom he would seek protection, and when we chased him to get our stolen pens, he would swiftly jump onto their shoulders. Like Muni, he was very fond of rough-and-tumble play, in which he eagerly engaged with the caretakers or with the baby gorilla. It was not always easy to play with him, for an important component of those playful fights and chases was biting. It was supposed to be mock-biting but it often hurt, given the sharp canine teeth of young patas monkeys. Liu, like Muni and my daughter, was interested in objects, although he rarely did anything with them other than take them to his mouth and crush them. (Alas, plastic pen caps were a favorite target of his teeth!) He very rarely took objects in his hands to examine them visually and discover what could be done with them, as Muni and my daughter did in their own ways. Liu was only a temporary playmate for Muni: like most monkeys, he grew very quickly into a young male patas. His impressive canines, his extraordinary agility, and his adult interests soon made him unsuitable for a zoo nursery environment.

Muni—an ape—grew more slowly, first into an adolescent gorilla, then into an adult one. Fortunately, very soon in her infancy she joined a group of other young orphan gorillas, and together they discovered the pleasures and conflicts of gorilla social life in captivity. Despite being reared without contact with adult gorillas (beyond their first six or seven months of life in the wild before being captured by furtive hunters), they all developed what appeared to be quite a complete repertoire of gorilla behavior: they had their gorilla vocalizations, their gorilla postures and expressions (for example, the characteristic chest-beating displays); they discovered gorilla social life, including sex and, to some extent, maternal and paternal behaviors. They also developed some special behaviors that are not usually seen in the wild, such as various curious gestures they used with their human caretakers and the ability to use tools.

My daughter will grow even more slowly than the baby gorilla. Eventually she will also discover the pleasures and pains of human social life and will learn about the world in her own human way. It will take years, but she will have to learn some very specific human things, like language (in her case, two languages at the same time!), human culture, how to use the impressive variety of human instruments and objects, and so on.

My daughter, Muni, and Liu are all young developing members of the same zoological group—the primates. They are *infants* that grow and learn to become adult, competent members of their respective species. This process of development occurs in different dimensions: physically, infants grow; behaviorally, they discover new patterns of action and interaction; and mentally, they acquire the view of the world that characterizes their species. They learn to attend to, pursue, and expect what is relevant to patas monkeys, gorillas, and humans, through one of the most enigmatic processes that have emerged in the course of evolution—cognitive development, meaning the progressive elaboration of a representation of the world. Cognitive development is the unique result of an extraordinary combination of factors operating from inside the individual organism and factors operating from outside—genes and environment, nature and nurture. These are two sides of a very special biological coin whose true nature lies in the intricacies that connect those sides: the interaction between the genetic setup selected by evolution, and the pressures and forces that each organism finds in its unique individual environment.

This book is about this process—about the development of primate minds; about how the unique styles of seeing the world that characterize primates are the result of the *evolution of their cognitive development*. Let us begin with a quick look at the primates and their distinctive characteristics.

Primates: A Family Tree

The primates are the subgroup of mammals to which we humans belong. There are about 200 different species of primates. Our closest relatives among them are the apes (see figures 1.1 and 1.2): chimpanzees, gorillas, orangutans, and bonobos, from which we separated about five to seven million years ago. More distant relatives (with about 20 million years of evolutionary distance) are the so-called Old World monkeys, for example, the different species of macaques, baboons, vervets, dianas, and others. Still more distant relatives are the New World monkeys (capuchins, squirrel monkeys, tamarins, and so forth), which branched off about 35 million years ago. Finally, another important subgroup of primates consists of the so-called prosimians, which separated from monkeys and apes about 50 million years ago, and which are considered to be very similar to the first animals (now extinct) that started the primate lineage about 60 to 70 million years ago (Fleagle, 1999; Napier and Napier, 1985).

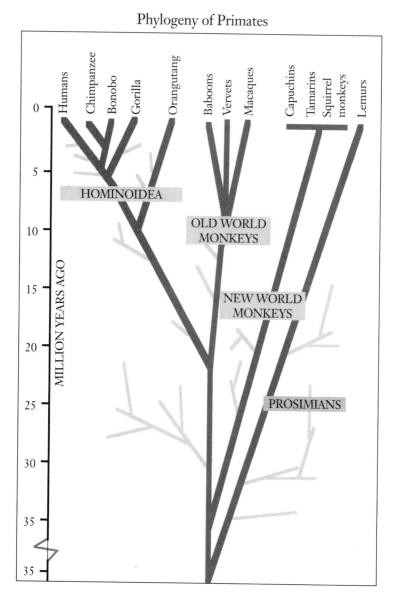

Figure 1.1. The primate family tree.

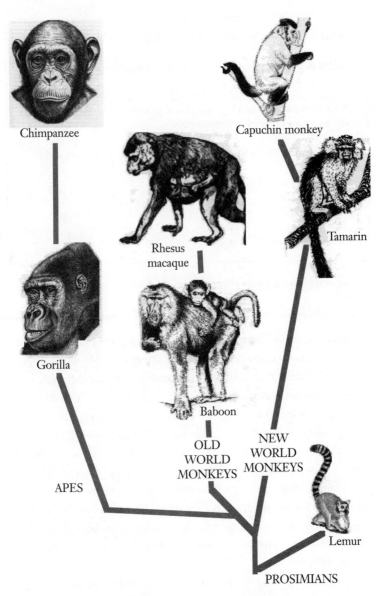

Figure 1.2. Some of the primates we will be encountering in this book (primate figures reproduced from Napier and Napier, *The Natural History of Primates*, 1983, with the permission of the M.I.T. Press, Schultz, *The Life of Primates*, 1969, with the permission of the Orion Publishing Group, and Hinde, *Biological Bases of Human Social Behavior*, 1974, with the permission of the McGraw-Hill Companies).

- **Frontal Eyes** with binocular—i.e., in-depth—and color vision

- **Faces:** Reduction of muzzle and increase of muscles in the frontal part of the head.

- Arms with **hands** (including free digits, thumbs, nails, sensitive pads) and legs with (generally) grasping feet

- **Bigger Brains** (especially enhanced visual areas and neocortex)

- **Infancy:** prolonged postnatal dependency

- **Behavioral flexibility**

- **Complex social life**

Figure 1.3. Major features characteristic of primates.

Primates are identified as a separate order of mammals because they possess a unique set of characteristics. The most important single factor that contributed to make primates different from other mammals was their original arboreal habitat. The first primates succeeded in making their living in the trees of the tropical forests which at that time extended over large areas of the Earth. In time they started to evolve features that allowed them to exploit further the opportunities offered by this singular habitat. Most of the features characteristic of primates are not absolute novelties in evolution (for example, social life or color vision). A few adaptations (hands) are unique to primates, however, and their combination in the same species certainly was an evolutionary innovation (figure 1.3).

Wild primates are still primarily found in the tropical rain forests where they initially evolved. These are very dense forests, with tall trees that make up a varied and complex vertical habitat where monkeys and apes can find a rich variety of fruits, leaves, and insects—the essentials of primate diets. But during their evolution many primates were successful in adapting to very different environments, such as dry forests or, to a lesser extent, the open savannah, or even to more hostile environments, very different from their original forests. For example, baboons can be found in some desert areas of Africa, and Japanese macaques are capable of surviving in the extreme winter conditions of high mountains.

Although the initial impetus for the evolution of primates came from their adaptation to arboreal life in tropical forests, those original adaptations enabled them to conquer other habitats and led to the eventual emergence of new primate species.

Eyes and Hands

Among the adaptations that allowed primates to master their life in the trees, two are of special interest to us for their cognitive implications: the growth and expansion of vision as a primary source of information about the world, and the anatomical differentiation between legs and arms that led to the emergence of grasping hands. Both evolutionary trends had profound consequences for the organization of the primate brain and for the development of primate mentalities.

Frontal Eyes and Color Vision

The evolutionary forerunners of primates are likely to have relied basically upon their senses of smell and touch to identify food, and on their mouths to snatch it (as most current mammals do). In mammals all these functions are located together—in the snout. In primates, these functions of the snout were divided and reallocated between the hands and the face. Primates essentially got rid of snouts and put their bets upon, first, visual perception, and second, manual grasping and tactual perception.

Primates have evolved a highly sophisticated sense of vision. Their two mammalian eyes converged to the front of their heads and they developed the ability to see in color (which is not unique in the animal world, but is a key feature of virtually all primates). Other animals, like herbivores, exploit their two eyes differently:

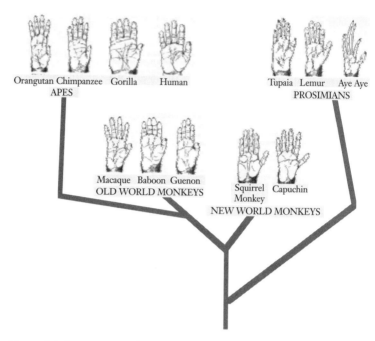

Figure 1.4. Some primate hands (hands reproduced from Schultz, *The Life of Primates*, 1969, with the permission of the Orion Publishing Group).

their eyes are located at each side of the head so as to maximize the area of simultaneous visual scanning when watching out for predators. In this arrangement each eye has its own visual field with only some degree of overlapping. In primates the eyes have converged forward, reducing the size of the area they can visually scan. This change makes primates look "twice" at the same thing, because to a great extent both eyes cover the same field of vision. But this visual redundancy has an important function: since the image registered by each eye is slightly different, their combination can create a stereoscopic or dual image of the world which captures with precision the dimension of depth in space. This is specially important for animals that have to jump from tree to tree or have to grasp fruits, insects, or branches with parts of their bodies (hands and feet) which are far away from their eyes.

The development of color vision further adds to the richness of the primate visual world. Seeing colors is very useful for animals that eat fruits and leaves, as color is a good indicator of ripeness or freshness. The primate eyes inaugurated a relatively new way of perceiving the world. The amount and complexity of information primates could gather through their sense of vision was essentially unprecedented in the world of mammals (Fobes and King, 1982). For a better understanding of the psychological consequences of this change, however, we must turn to another major complementary development of primates—the transformation of their forepaws into *hands*, organs specialized in grasping and manipulating things.

The Ascendancy of Hands

The hands of primates are exceptionally good instruments for arboreal locomotion. They provide a very effective way of grasping and holding branches for climbing, hanging, and moving around in the complex network of the tropical canopies. They are not the only possible solution to the problem of arboreal locomotion: squirrels, for instance, evolved claws that can be used as hooks to support climbing. But primates developed a "grasping" solution, and indeed their need for grasping can be so demanding that most have not only hands, but also prehensile feet with which they can grasp branches and even hold objects. In some New World monkeys (squirrel monkeys), the grasping function was further enhanced by the development of a fifth "hand"—a prehensile tail (Fleagle, 1999).

An interesting advantage of this grasping solution was that it is compatible with other functions not related to climbing. One other fundamental function of primate hands is their use as feeding instruments. Most primates use their hands to pluck fruits and leaves from the trees and then take them to their mouths, instead of approaching their mouths to the food, as most other mammals do. This is not a matter of evolutionary good manners, but an important adaptation that allows access to the fruits and leaves of branches that are too small to support the whole body of an animal.

Primate feeding usually is more complex than simply picking food and placing it in the mouth. For example, if fruits have hard shells, monkeys may have to use their hands to hold the fruit while they try to break into the shell with their teeth, or, in a more complex maneuver, they may use the hands to hit the shell against the ground.

Some lemurs of Madagascar feed upon a particular kind of millipedes that have developed a system of protection by secreting a highly disgusting substance to deter predators. Lemurs take these millipedes and roll them repeatedly with their hands. This makes the millipedes secrete copious quantities of their deterrent. The lemurs drop saliva onto the insects, and continue handling them (occasionally using their tails, guided by their hands, to further rub their victims). Only after this preparation do they eat the now (supposedly) better-tasting millipedes.

Similarly, when mountain gorillas feed upon nettles protected with dangerous spines, they have to engage in complex sequences of preliminary manipulations that are absolutely essential before they are able to take the edible part to the mouth (Byrne and Byrne, 1993).

These examples of primate feeding involve a lot of preliminary food manipulation and show how the hands of primates are not only a straightforward intermediary between the food and the mouth, but instruments that can fundamentally modify the state of the food before the animals proceed to its ingestion. Many food items could simply not be eaten without these preliminary manual preparations.

Some primate species have gone a step further in their food manipulation by developing the rudiments of tool use. For example, some chimpanzees take stones and use them as hammers to break nuts open, or extract termites by inserting stems into their nests (see Chapter 9). Humans are, needless to say, an extreme example of this manipulative trend of the primates. But uniquely sophisticated as we are, human manipulative abilities do not come out of the blue, but out of an ancient and well-established evolutionary trend toward object manipulation that is characteristic of the primates as a group.

The Versatility of Hands

The decisive evolutionary advantage of primate hands is their versatility. Although mainly evolved as instruments for feeding and arboreal locomotion, hands can also be used for other purposes, such as grooming, holding on to the body of the mother, controlling the excursions of youngsters by grabbing their tails, and so on. The primate hand is an organ *specialized* in having a *general* function—grasping—useful for a variety of adaptive purposes. The case of the hand illustrates an important feature of the primate order: primates specialize in not being too narrowly specialized!

The usefulness of hands, however, would have been very limited without the parallel changes in the visual system of primates. The combination of changes in the eyes and the hands makes very good sense. For effectively using hands to pick fruits (and even more so to capture flying insects) and grasp branches in the complex three-dimensional world of the tropical canopy, it is necessary to possess precise information about the location of the targets. This is provided by stereoscopic and color vision. The primate visual system allows a precise identification of the targets (palatable insects or ripe fruits) and an appreciation of their relative spatial position, so that effective reaching and grasping can take place (Napier and Napier, 1985). The primate forms of seeing and handling the world are the result of a co-evolution of the visual and limb systems—a partnership of the eye and the hand.

Finally, something that is easily overlooked is that hands are more than "executive" organs for grasping objects under the control of the eyes. Hands have their own ways of sensing the world: they are equipped with sophisticated organs of touch. Primate fingers possess highly sensitive tactile pads that provide the brain with precise and accurate information about the textures and shapes of objects. The hands, as arm extensions, can also provide information about other important features of objects, such as their weight, their flexibility, or their solidity. The coordination of rich tactual with rich visual information is, therefore, another crucial gain for primates—one that contributed decisively to the way in which they experience the world.

The Evolution of a World of Objects

My primary concern here is not with the anatomical features of the primates, but with their behavior and mentality—the way in which primates perceive and understand their worlds. Their new bodies came accompanied by new minds. The mental counterparts of primate bodies are reflected in a particularly interesting part of their anatomy—the brain. Primate brains have undergone a general increase in size in comparison to the brains of other mammals,* especially in the area known as "neocortex" (Falk and Gibson, 2001). The main function of this evolutionary operation of extension and refurbishment of the brain was to create the neural machinery necessary for the new ways of *representing* the world that came with the behavioral innovations of primates.

Psychologically, the main consequence of the rise of visually guided manipulation and handling was the evolution of *objects* as units of perception and action—trees, branches, leaves, fruits, bushes, flowers, shells, kernels, stones, rocks, insects, logs, and so forth. Although objects, broadly defined as "tangible and visible things" that are the targets of perception and action, are, phylogenetically, an old discovery (especially if we substitute "edible" for "tangible"), primates gained a peculiar way of dealing with environmental targets—manipulation. I will argue that manipulative behaviors co-evolved with a number of cognitive skills whose main function is to analyze and depict the world in terms of objects—not only detecting and perceiving objects as environmental units, but also detecting and using the relations between objects in space and their causal links.

The Evolution of Faces: A Society of Individuals

A fundamental part of the primates' world consists of the natural objects that compose their physical environment. But their world has another fundamental side—other primates. Most primates live

---

* This trait is not unique to primates, by the way. Aquatic mammals such as whales, dolphins, and porpoises have also developed big brains (Schusterman et al., 1986). This reminder helps us to picture evolution not as a ladder, but as a tree with the most surprising variations and coincidences.

in groups of varied composition and organization. Many of their morphological and behavioral adaptations have to do with social problems—how to identify and interact with their conspecifics in feeding, playing, acting aggressive, reproducing, and other social events. Of course, social life in itself is no novelty in evolution. Many other animals (lions, wolves, rats, dolphins) are social animals too, but primates are certainly among the most complexly organized social beings, and some of their more remarkable adaptations are of a social nature.

One such adaptation has been the evolution of *faces*—instruments specialized in the expression of individual identity and subjective states. A face is a truly unique set of visible and dynamic features located in the frontal part of the head. One of the reasons why primate faces are different from other animals' faces is the development of new facial muscles along with the differentiation of existing facial muscles, for the main function of facilitating facial expressions. In nonmammalian vertebrates, such as reptiles or birds, few head muscles go beyond the neck; this is why these animals look so inexpressive to a primate eye. In mammals, the subcutaneous muscles have started to invade the face, allowing the display of facial movements. Primates, expanding this trend, have developed many more facial muscles than any other animal. Among primates, apes and humans have the more complex facial morphology and musculature, the most complex network of facial muscles of the animal world (Huber, 1931).

Thus primates' faces have become a very special and rich source of social information: they may contribute decisively to announcing the identity of individuals, and simultaneously they convey information about their emotional states and dispositions, and about the targets of their attention. Faces do indeed play a central role in the social life of primates, and the primate brain seems to have developed mechanisms specifically devoted to dealing with the whole range of information that can be found in faces (Perret, 1999).

Another crucial component of primate sociality is the importance of *relationships* in their social life, that is, various types of bonds between individuals—a mother and her infant, two siblings, a male with another male, and so on. Each individual in a primate group has several relationships with other members, and they in turn have their sets of relationships. The result is an intricate network of bonds that makes the social life of a primate group complex and difficult to predict. For example, among primates a conflict between two individuals is an event of public interest in which other individuals usually get involved. Primates have, if not created, at least perfected the art of coalition formation—and with it, perhaps, the rudiments of politics (de Waal, 1982). This means that when individual A has a problem with B, he can rely upon the help of C, who happens to be his ally, but B, in turn, may have his own allies, so that a conflict between individuals becomes a more widespread social event.

Dramatic episodes of fight or threat are not the only social interactions. One of the most common and widespread social activities among primates is quite a peaceful and quiet one: *grooming*. When primates part the fur of other primates with their fingers, taking out skin parasites, small pieces of dead skin, or simply exploring, they are not merely performing a sanitary service; grooming is first of all a social activity, an affiliative behavior a primate performs with friends or with individuals he or she wants to be on friendly terms with—an activity which clearly involves the use of the fine grasping and exploratory abilities of the hands, turned in this instance into instruments of social interaction.

The second part of the book will be devoted to the analysis of primate social cognition—how primates perceive and handle communicative signals, the behavior of others, and perhaps more complex issues, such as the intentions and interests that motivate other primates' behavior. In essence, in the same way that primates have evolved cognitive mechanisms to perceive the world of objects, they have evolved mechanisms specialized in representing the world of *subjects*. The discovery of the complexity of the worlds of objects and individuals is made possible by a third characteristic of primates: infancy.

The Evolution of Infancy

The word *infancy* refers to the period of immaturity that most animals have to go through before becoming adult, breeding members of their species. What is remarkable about primate infancy is its extraordinary length. Although morphologically and physiologically newborn primates—as *precocial* mammals—are relatively advanced in comparison with *altricial* mammals (for example, their eyes are already open and functional, whereas the eyes of mice or cats are still closed), behaviorally they remain helpless for a longer period of time. Mammals that are born very immature grow up very quickly. Mice, say, or cattle start growing up in a steady way after birth and continue to do so until puberty, when their growth stops. For most primates, however, physical growth after birth is slowed down in a characteristic way and delayed until the onset of puberty. As a consequence, primates remain infants and juveniles for longer periods of time. This is especially so in apes, and even more marked in humans, who are considered by many as a mixture of *precocial* and *altricial* (Fleagle, 1999).

As a rule of thumb, monkeys such as macaques have a life expectancy of about 25 to 30 years, of which about 4 years are devoted to development; apes live about 45 to 50 years, of which 10 to 12 are spent in infancy and youth, and humans (in modern Western societies at least) live about 70 years, of which 16 to 18 correspond to infancy and youth (Jolly, 1972; Fleagle, 1999). Clearly, for primates there is something more important to do during infancy than growing physically. This more urgent task is behavioral and cognitive growth.

An immature organism is vulnerable to injury or destruction as soon as anything goes wrong. To compensate for this and ensure the viability of immature offspring, parents must make a considerable investment in the form of parental care. This is an evolutionary disadvantage for the parents themselves (in the primate world, especially for the mother). Energy and resources invested on the baby may increase the parents' risks of dying or being injured and prevent them from having more offspring. At first sight, a prolonged infancy seems to carry disadvantages both for the baby and for the parents. Why did primate infancy become extended in the course of evolution, then? A possible answer is that immaturity is an evolutionary strategy to promote the role of development in shaping the adult organism (Bruner, 1972). Instead of being completely pre-adapted by phylogeny, primates became more open to completing their behavioral adaptations during ontogeny. The benefits of this would be a higher plasticity in behavior and therefore a better ability to adapt to environmental challenges. An immaturity strategy can affect behavioral and cognitive development in two ways. We will consider these in turn.

Development Mediated by Parents

Most primates, including humans, usually have a single offspring at birth. This newborn is unable to survive by itself. For a long period of time it depends upon its mother for transport, body temperature, feeding, in short, everything except breathing and other elementary physiological functions.

The functions of such a close mother-infant relationship are not limited to physical nurturance. Infant primates also need social contact with adults for psychological reasons. This was most dramatically demonstrated by the well-known experiments of Harry Harlow (1971), in which he showed the devastating effects of providing macaque infants with all their physical and health needs while keeping them isolated from other macaques. The isolated monkeys became not only socially incompetent, but were also unable to properly explore and learn about the physical world. They were socially and psychologically inept, though in good physical health. This was also true, to a lesser extent, when the infant macaques were reared exclusively with other infants. The second experiment shows the importance of the *quality* of the relationship: social contact alone is not enough: a specific social contact with an adult is required for completely normal development.

A singular feature of most primate species is that they carry their offspring with them. This is quite unique to primates (although other examples with remarkable solutions, such as marsupials [kangaroos], can be found in the animal world). Primate newborns are equipped with reflexes to cling closely to the furry bodies of their mothers, who then can walk or climb with their babies safely secured—the first adaptive function of having grasping hands. Primate infancy, therefore, is fundamentally social from the very beginning. The infants' discovery of the physical and social worlds takes place from the secure base provided by the mothers. Thus primate infants are with their mothers when the adults are feeding. They are therefore exposed from the very beginning to the right feeding places and the right feeding items. They are also exposed to the feeding techniques used by their mothers. For example, chimpanzee infants can watch as their mothers perform the elaborate patterns involved in termite fishing. How much they can learn from this is a disputed matter. But the fact is that from the beginning primate infants are selectively exposed to certain objects and events of the environment by their mothers. They do their apprenticeships riding on their mothers backs in more than the literal sense of the sentence.

Behavioral and Cognitive Flexibility

A second, and perhaps less obvious benefit of prolonged immaturity is that it may have the important consequence of fostering the flexibility of behavioral adaptations to the environment. Instead of being born with a well-established repertoire of behaviors or with a set of dispositions to learn very quickly the species' life essentials, primates engage in a prolonged period of development during which they slowly acquire and deploy their characteristic behavior patterns. The fact that they have to build or assemble these patterns favors their plasticity and therefore makes them more versatile and adaptive. Take, for example, the case of species recognition. Many birds are born with the ability to learn their species identity in a quick, highly channeled way: this is the phenomenon known as imprinting. But this quick learning has the disadvantage of its inflexibility: it is virtually irreversible. Birds that become imprinted to the wrong object cannot rectify this ontogenetic misunderstanding, and during the rest of their infant lives they will follow a "mother" as odd as the ethologist Konrad Lorenz (1981), who famously discovered and exemplified this phenomenon. In contrast, primates, including humans, need a longer period of time to learn the identity of their conspecifics. Face recognition, although highly channeled from the very beginning, is a relatively slow learning process in comparison with imprinting (Johnson and Morton, 1991). The result is the formation of a flexible representation of what a face is and the ability to categorize new individuals at any point in development.

This leads us to one of the crucial tenets of this book. The behavioral flexibility associated with prolonged development is the result of flexibility in forming *representations* of the world. My argument is that a crucial characteristic of primates is their ability to construct representations of the physical and social world and mediate their behavior by means of those representations. This is where their behavioral flexibility comes from—the representations they have built during their prolonged infancy. And this is why this book is about the evolution of cognitive development: my aim is not simply to describe the intelligent and flexible behaviors characteristic of primates, but to try to understand the sorts of representations that make possible such behavioral flexibility. An advantage of having one's behavior mediated by representations of the environment is that it allows for behavioral innovations in response to changing environmental conditions. For an illustrative example, consider the following experiment.

A squirrel monkey infant, like most primate babies, usually clings to its mother's fur to facilitate its transport. What would happen if an infant were suddenly unable to cling? Would the mother go away without him? Would the whole sequence of maternal behavior be disrupted? The psychologist Duane Rumbaugh (1965) decided to answer this question in an experimentally straightforward way. He rendered a monkey infant temporarily unable to cling to her mother by the rather crude (but easily reversible) procedure of carefully tying his hands with tape on his back. The mother's reaction was first to invite his infant to cling to her by pressing her belly against him; she even "cued" the infant into the right action by slightly lifting him with one hand toward her belly. When this also failed, she finally solved the problem by picking up the baby with both hands and walking upright while holding him! This was probably the first time she carried her infant in such a way. However, she produced this innovative action almost spontaneously, without having to learn it from scratch by pure trial and error. Similar behaviors have been observed in natural conditions when babies were seriously ill or, sadly, dead, yet their mothers still carried their bodies.

To be sure, the mother would have shown a more advanced degree of flexibility and understanding of the world if she had examined her baby and had understood the reason why he could not respond to her demands, and then removed the tape that tied his hands. This sequence would have shown causal understanding of the reasons why the baby was unable to behave as usual. This degree of intelligence may be observed in some primates. For example, Dian Fossey (1983) reported observations of adult gorilla leaders trying to gnaw through the wire that clamped a baby in a poacher's trap.

Such anecdotal reports illustrate the flexibility and creativity of the behavioral repertoires of primates. Ethologists—scientists who study the behavior of animals from an evolutionary point of view—usually begin their studies of a species by compiling its *ethogram* a list of the different behavior patterns characteristic of the species. In the case of primates, it is difficult to provide complete and accurate ethograms. A better description of the behavioral repertoires of primates would be an *ethogrammar:* a set of rules or schemes that can generate relatively varied and innovative behavior sequences. These "ethogrammars" are formed by the representations that primates acquire during their lives and that mediate their behavioral flexibility.

Representations, Development, and Evolution

Implicit Representations and Practical Intelligence

The term "representation" is fundamental in current cognitive and developmental psychology. It refers to the ways in which brains are capable of picking up, storing, and manipulating information about the environment. Yet despite its importance, this term is far from having a precise and generally accepted meaning. Moreover, some cognitive scientists vigorously oppose some implications they attribute to the notion of representation (Still and Costall, 1991), such as the idea that behavior mediated by representations must be entirely explained by information stored inside the brain of an organism. This restricted sense is not the one in which I will be using the notion of representation in this book.

Humans are used to a particular kind of representation: explicit descriptions of the world ("propositions") that can be expressed with words or other symbols and that we handle in our minds like some sort of mental objects that reflect the external environment (Fodor, 1979). However, there are other kinds of representations, less explicit and not symbolic, in the sense that they do not *stand for* aspects of the world nor are handled like objects in the mind.

Many of the representations used by nonhuman primates (and human infants) appear to be practical and implicit; rather than symbolic *descriptions* of the world, they are more like *instructions* about what to do and what to expect in different situations. The usefulness of these representations may crucially depend upon their interaction with incoming information from the environment and also their online combination with mental processes like intentions and motives. They are "practical" or "implicit" representations that probably cannot be recovered off-line to ponder and brood over the past and the future in the way humans can with their explicit representations.

Implicit knowledge is an essential component of any mind, including the human mind. Children appear to start their representational careers with implicit or practical representations of the world that only progressively may be converted into more explicit knowledge (Piaget, 1936; Karmiloff-Smith, 1992), but the later emergence of explicit representations is not at the expense of practical ones. Rather, they coexist and, crucially, they interact in a person's mind. There are probably different kinds of explicit and implicit representations, and nonhuman primates might be capable of making some explicit representations.

One of the benefits of studying cognitive development in nonhuman primates is that it may help us to gain a better understanding of the phenomenon of implicit knowledge and implicit representations, and perhaps to learn about the origins of more explicit forms of knowledge. Fundamental as they are, these notions are far from being well defined in developmental psychology and cognitive science. Hence studying animals that lack language may teach us much about the nature of implicit knowledge.

Comparing Human Minds with Other Minds

A central point of contention in the study of primate cognition has always been the comparability of primate minds with human minds. Some scientists believe that there must be continuity between the human and other primates' minds, as there is continuity between the human and other primate bodies. Others believe that although there may be continuity between humans and other primates in some basic cognitive processes (perception, attention, perhaps even memory), one of the landmarks of humans is the evolution of new forms of cognition—a unique set of cognitive organs or functions that do not exist in other primates. Language is a clear example: although communication is pervasive among all primates, humans appear to have evolved a unique way of performing this old function, and in so doing they may have introduced levels of cognitive complexity that are completely alien to nonhuman primates (Pinker, 1994). Cognitive functions like thinking, reasoning, consciousness, imitation, causal understanding might be exclusively human or might have attained a qualitatively new level of functioning in humans (possibly through the operation of language as a cognitive amplifier, as Vygotsky first suggested, 1930). The study of nonhuman primates would show us, then, in what way the human mind dramatically departs from the primate mind.

The debate about continuity of human and nonhuman primate cognition critically hinges on the notion of representation. Some discontinuity advocates believe that although nonhuman primates produce behaviors that look similar to human behaviors (tool-use, social transmission of habits, strategies of deception), the comparable human behaviors are generated and controlled by (partially or completely) different cognitive mechanisms. Humans could have evolved completely new forms of representing and understanding the world which we simply do not find in other primates (Povinelli, 2000).

Precursors or Co-Cursors?

Continuity advocates argue that even when a particular ability appears to be exclusively human (language, for example), it may still be possible to find an evolutionary connection, in the sense that nonhuman primates may exhibit *precursors* of that ability. An evolutionary precursor is a forerunner, an early form of an organ or a structure from which another, more complex or simply different form is derived. For example, morphologically the paws of the earliest primates were precursors to the many different kinds of hands found among current primates. An interesting issue is whether simpler forms of cognition found among other primates (the communicative calls of monkeys and apes) are precursors to higher cognitive abilities in humans (speech).

Strictly speaking, however, it is misleading to apply the notion of evolutionary precursor to compare humans with other *living* primates. Is the face of a chimpanzee a precursor to the human face? We have no reason to believe that the human face evolved from a chimpanzee face, or a chimpanzee face from a rhesus monkey face. The real precursor of the human face was also the precursor of the chimpanzee face: it was the face of the common ancestor we shared some 5 to 7 million years ago, from which human, chimpanzee, gorilla, and other ape faces are all derived. In this sense, rather than forerunners or precursors, we should speak of evolutionary *co-runners* or *co-cursors*.

The popular tendency is to assume that in the domain of cognition current ape characteristics may have changed less than human characteristics, and therefore they might bear a closer resemblance to the features of our extinct common ancestors. This assumption is not always well founded, but even where it may turn out to be true, we should not lose sight of the fact that apes are not direct reflections of our common ancestors, but reflections that are refracted by their own 5 to 7 million years of independent evolution.

Nature, Nurture, and Evolutionary Developmental Psychology

Given that the topic of this book is the development of cognition in monkeys, apes, and human infants, we will confront from the beginning some of the central issues of developmental psychology. To return to the beginning of this chapter, why is the development of the gorilla Muni, the monkey Liu, and my daughter so similar and so different at the same time? Where do these differences and similarities come from? Are they purely genetic, or are they the result of learning and experience?

These two extreme interpretations illustrate the two opposite views about the nature of cognitive development that traditionally dominated human developmental psychology. *Empiricist* approaches hold that the essence of human intelligence is that it got rid of any "instinctive" or predetermined ways of acting and thinking, and has become predominantly sensitive to environmental variations. If anything, humans have replaced inherited adaptations with cultural adaptations that must be learned during development. What is innate is only this unlimited ability to learn beyond biological adaptations. *Nativist* approaches, in contrast, claim that the structure of the mind is as genetically determined as the structure of the body, and that the mind is best described as a collection of instincts (Pinker, 1994). Thus the human mind is constitutionally able to learn language, to develop very abstract representations of the world, and to learn by imitation from others, in the same way as the human body is able to walk bipedally. The environment plays a mere triggering role—as cognitive food that allows the predetermined structures to grow and thrive.

One would expect an evolutionary perspective to favor such a view of cognitive adaptation as a product of genetic selection. But when the evolutionary approach is merged with the developmental approach, it is possible to integrate nativist and empiricist factors in the explanation of cognition (Parker and MacKinney, 1999). Such an integration is known as "constructivism," and it has its roots in the work of Jean Piaget—a trained biologist who turned into the most influential developmental psychologist of the twentieth century with his studies of the origins and nature of cognition.

It is difficult not to sympathize with an effort to integrate rival views, to find a middle ground where the best of each view can be put together. Yet it is not easy to be a constructivist. In deciding what is genetically determined and what emerges (and how) out of the interaction between the organism and the environment, constructivists tend to swing in the direction of nativism or empiricism, so that the classical debate between nature and nurture is frequently repeated within the supposedly integrative framework of constructivism.

Another major issue of current developmental science is the conflict between domain specificity and domain generality. Is the mind a general-purpose cognitive mechanism that we use to solve different kinds of problems (for example, acquiring language, learning to use tools, learning mathematical concepts; Piaget and Inhelder, 1966), or is it rather a collection of specialized mechanisms, each specifically adapted to a particular kind of problem (Pinker, 1994)? Or, alternatively, is the mind a combination of both domain-specific mechanisms and at least one domain-general ability, some sort of generalized central executive skill (Fodor, 1983)? In the last years, some brands of evolutionary psychology have become associated with a domain-specific view of the mind as a collection of "mental organs"—the so-called "Swiss army knife metaphor" of the mind (Barkow et al., 1992). Yet I will argue that describing cognitive specializations is not incompatible with understanding organisms at the more global level of how those mechanisms are *articulated* together, in the same way as describing the organs of the body is not incompatible with describing their higher-order articulation into an *organism*.

An Invitation to Cognitive Development

In summary, the prolonged immaturity of primate infancy is an adaptive "strategy" that can be best summarized as an invitation to cognitive development. The environment of the adult primate is made of objects and persons—a physical and a social world. The task of the young primate is to discover and find its way into this world of objects and persons, learn their interrelationships, and, occasionally, even go beyond the skills and knowledge of adults by discovering new objects, new ways of dealing with them, or new ways of interacting with their conspecifics. This voyage of cognitive discovery is supported by and results in representations, ways of perceiving and being in the world.

2

Perceiving a World of Objects

One old philosophical question is whether newborn babies can see objects from the very beginning of their lives, or do they slowly sort them out of the primordial confusion that inundates their senses at the beginning of life? Do newborns see their environment as segregated into independent units, or are their first perceptions confusing aggregates of light, sound, and texture that only little by little get organized into distinct patterns?

Spotting Objects

Recent research in developmental psychology suggests that human babies possess quite sophisticated abilities to analyze the visual world and very quickly see their environment in terms of objects. At the beginning, babies may not perceive exactly the same things as we adults do, but very quickly they develop representations that separate visual scenes into figures and backgrounds, and figures into individual units that correspond to objects (Slater, 2001; Rochat, 2001). This extraordinary ability appears to be the result of a number of specialized cognitive mechanisms. Are these mechanisms specific to humans, or are they part of a shared primate way of seeing the world, evolved in parallel with eyes and hands to facilitate the representation of the environment in terms of objects? Although studies with nonhuman primates are still scarce, the available evidence suggests that at least the basic mechanisms of object perception may be a shared primate heritage.

For example, Robert Fantz (1956, 1965), one of the pioneers in the study of early perceptual abilities in human babies, conducted studies with chimpanzee and monkey babies as well. He invented a simple but effective method of studying the perception of very young primates that cannot give distinct locomotor or manipulatory responses—the method of differential fixation or visual preference. One of the things very young monkeys, apes, and humans can do well is to look or not look at a stimulus placed at the appropriate distance. Fantz showed his young subjects pairs of different stimuli (cards with different colors, shapes, or patterns, and real three-dimensional objects), and measured how long they looked at each stimulus. If they showed a consistent preference for looking at certain stimuli over others, this demonstrated, first, that the subjects were capable of seeing some differences between them, and secondly, that their perceptual system was attuned to attending to and processing certain kinds of information over others.

Fantz discovered that in their first weeks of life rhesus monkeys, chimpanzees, and human babies all tended to look at *patterns* (elaborate shapes or complex visual textures like checks or stripes) over simpler but physically more intense stimuli, such as very bright colors. This preference for patterns became stronger over time.

Using more sophisticated recordings of eye direction, he was able to determine that one-week-old chimpanzees visually explored simple shapes: their eyes followed the contours of horizontal or vertical lines. At one month of age, chimpanzee babies could discriminate between different shapes (they looked at a cross more than at a circle) and they seemed to prefer looking at more complex or elaborate patterns. Interestingly, this development of a preference for increasingly complex patterns was also found in visually deprived chimpanzees, that is, infants who were kept in complete darkness during their first weeks of life except for the testing sessions. This experiment strongly suggests that the progressive preference for visual complexity is a robust property of the primate visual system that needs very little experience to manifest itself (Fantz, 1965).

At the end of their second month of life, chimpanzees' perceptual preferences had become more sophisticated. They looked more at three-dimensional stimuli with complex surface patterns and pronounced contrasts in color and brightness—features commonly present in ordinary objects. The deprived chimpanzees did not demonstrate this preference so clearly, however, a finding which suggests that this developmental step is more dependent on acquired information—the building of incipient representations of objects.

Fantz found essentially the same pattern of early visual development—progressive attention to increasingly complex displays culminating in a preference for solid objects—in human and in rhesus monkey babies. Like chimpanzees, visually deprived monkeys showed the progressive preference for more complex patterns, but failed to develop a preference for three-dimensional objects. It was only when they were moved to a normally lighted environment that they eventually developed a preference for looking at solid objects.

Fantz (1965) interpreted his findings as indicating that primates are born with certain perceptual predispositions that allow them to start having a selective, highly organized experience of the world of objects before being able to act upon them. These predispositions are innate and relatively resistant to early deprivation, but they do not remain static. Monkeys who were tested after 8 weeks of being reared in complete darkness no longer showed an ability to look at patterns. Their attention was captured by nonconfigurational stimuli, such as bright colors and intense lights. After being transferred to normal light conditions, these animals found it very difficult to develop visually guided behaviors. Interestingly, during their confinement in darkness some individuals had developed compensatory patterns of perceptual behavior, such as using their hands and arms as "tactual eyes," moving them in an arc in front of them to feel their way while walking. Sometimes this method of orientation persisted for a long time after they were transferred to a normally lighted environment. They had learned to guide their behavior with nonvisual representations and could not straight away adjust to visual representations. But although their visual development was arrested by light deprivation, the monkeys were still building a "view" of the world with their available sensory modalities; they had started to learn about objects and space in a tactual-kinesthetic format.

The spontaneous tendency of the visual system to attend to complex configurations rather than to isolated features has been confirmed by studies of discrimination learning in monkey babies. In discrimination learning, a monkey receives a reward (a piece of food, say) if he responds to a particular stimulus over another (for example, a triangle over a square). By the time they were ten days old, infant rhesus monkeys (which were already capable of some degree of locomotion) could learn to discriminate among particular targets by their brightness or even by their shape (triangle versus circle) if big enough figures were used. However, the monkeys found it easier to discriminate among stimuli that differed in several dimensions at the same time (color + size + shape) (Zimmerman and Torrey, 1965). Although they could be taught to attend to isolated dimensions of objects, their spontaneous tendency was to attend to the complete stimulus—the whole object.

Sackett (1966) confirmed these conclusions by measuring the spontaneous visual preferences of infant rhesus monkeys when he presented them with patterns of varying complexity that were projected on a wall in their cages. Although initially, at 10 to 14 days of age, the baby monkeys addressed their attention equally to all patterns except the plain black, very soon they started to devote progressively more attention, first to the patterns of middle complexity, then to the more complex patterns. By 35 days of age, there was a perfect correspondence of amount of attention and complexity of pattern. Exactly the same developmental trend of progressive preference for complexity has been found in human infants with the same patterns (Brennan et al., 1966).

An interesting finding of Sackett's study was that manual and oral exploration usually accompanied visual attention. The monkeys approached and tried to touch the patterns projected on the wall with their hands and mouths. However, since they did not

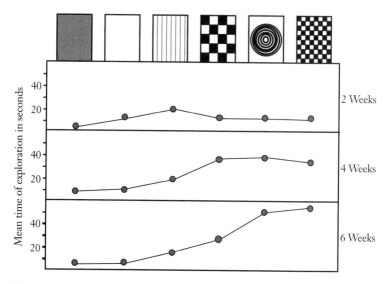

Figure 2.1. Time spent by rhesus monkeys paying attention to each pattern projected on a wall at different stages during their first weeks of development. Patterns are arranged from left to right in order of increasing complexity (defined as number of unit changes per unit area). (Adapted from Sackett, 1966).

get any differential tactual experience from each pattern (the projecting surface was the same) nor receive any other differential reinforcement, we must conclude that the progressive preference for visual complexity grows on its own (Fantz, 1965). Sackett's experiment also confirms earlier findings that rhesus monkeys start spontaneously touching and exploring with their hands the objects they see during their first or second week of life. Interestingly, even when the objects placed at their disposal are food items, often the monkeys do not consume them directly but spend some time manipulating them (Zimmerman and Torrey, 1965).

Monkeys thus seem to have a natural tendency to touch what captures their visual attention—namely, a stimulus with the sort of complex perceptual properties that correspond to an individual solid object. This tendency shows up at different ages in different species: rhesus and other monkeys approach and touch objects when they are only a few weeks of age; human babies, in contrast, start touching the objects they see much later (4 to 5 months), and they cannot actively approach them until even later than that (see Chapter 3).

An interesting consequence of this tendency of primates to touch what they see is that their visual representations are very soon coordinated with patterns of tactual-kinesthetic information arising from the same targets. This results in complex cross-modal or multisensory representations of objects.

Attending to New Things

In addition to the progression of preference from simpler to more complex visual stimuli, another important dimension controls attention slightly later in development—novelty. As early as at two weeks of life, both human and rhesus monkey infants have been reported to show some preference for new stimuli (Pascalis and Bachevalier, 1999). A reliable and well-established preference for looking at novel over known stimuli has been definitely found in human infants at four months of age. This means that they can not only discriminate among stimuli, but also remember which objects they have seen before and then attend to whichever is new.

Gunderson and Sackett (1984) explored the development of this ability in pigtailed macaques. Pigtailed macaques' basic visual system follows a developmental pattern virtually identical to that of human infants, except that it happens four times faster; one week of development for the monkey is roughly equivalent to one month of development for the human infant.

These scientists used exactly the same methodology that had been used with human infants. Given the rule of the 4 to 1 ratio of development, the authors expected macaque monkeys to show a preference for novelty at 4 weeks. This is exactly what they did find: after repeatedly showing, for example, a pattern of concentric circles during the familiarization period, the four-week-old monkeys preferred to look at a new stimulus (a checquered circle) when simultaneously shown the old and the new pattern. Younger monkeys showed no preference; their looking patterns appeared to depend more upon what side the stimuli were shown than upon their identity. This side bias has also been reported in human babies younger than 4 months when tested with this procedure.

Similar principles appear to guide infant perception across the few primate species studied so far: one, operating in the first weeks of life, makes infants attend to increasingly complex patterns over simpler stimulations; the second, operating later in early life, makes infants attend to new over known things. This implies an emerging ability to form and keep in mind representations of perceived objects that in turn influence subsequent perceptions. The development of these early object representations seems to follow a similar pattern in monkeys and humans, which suggests a similarity in basic aspects of cognitive functioning among primates.

Exploring Objects as a Function of Experience

Preference for relative complexity is not limited to visual perception. Sackett (1965a and b) found that when wild-born rhesus monkeys were given the opportunity to explore and manipulate three objects offering different degrees of movement complexity (a chain, a T-shaped bar that could only be moved downward, and a nonmovable bar, all hanging from the ceiling of the cage), they clearly outperformed monkeys reared in captivity in the number of manipulations of any of the objects. This was especially true of the chain, the object that offered a potentially wider variety and complexity of movement. The relatively deprived captive-born monkeys (reared in dull laboratory cages) touched the chain only 57 times during a 12-hour period of exposure (producing an average of 6.5 minutes of manipulation time); in contrast, the feral monkeys touched the chain 2,010 times, each spending more than 4 hours with it). Severely deprived monkeys (reared in isolation) only made 8 contacts with the chain altogether. The captive monkeys showed much more interest in the T-bar and especially the unmovable bar, with which they spent 47 minutes on average. The isolated animals found the static bar more attractive, but even so they only made 36 contacts (5.8 min.) on average.

When given standard discrimination learning tests, however, the socially deprived monkeys and the feral monkeys did not differ in their ability to learn these laboratory tasks (Sackett, 1965a). The deprived animals performed well in highly constrained and passive learning tasks, but they were deficient in their ability to generate knowledge about the world of objects in spontaneous exploration. What young primates develop during infancy is not simply an accumulation of object representations, but a cognitive and motivational base from which they actively organize their exploration of the surroundings. Initial limited experience may have a cascading effect by further limiting what can be learned from new experiences.

Representing Scenes and Events

Primates appear to be predisposed from very early on to discover objects as units of perception and attention. So far, we have been focusing upon how inherent properties of individual objects attract the attention of young primates. In natural conditions, however, primates usually have to deal with large arrays consisting of many objects and substrates (think, for example, of the dense vegetation of a rain forest), not with single objects or displays artificially selected and presented by the experimenter. How do primates deal with complex displays of objects?

Marc Hauser and his collaborators (Hauser and Carey, 1998; Hauser, 2001) have recently explored some principles of object individuation in nonhuman primates, drawing on experimental procedures originally used with human babies. Consider, for example, the following experiment (Xu, Carey, and Welch, 1999). Babies are shown a yellow duck standing on a red toy truck. In terms of their spatial disposition, they could be one single object, because they constitute a single continuous mass. But we adults tend to see them as two different objects because of their visual features: the shapes are different, the colors are different, and our mind simply ignores the spatial continuity and registers (*represents*) them as two different objects that happen to be in contact. We would be surprised if we tried lifting the duck and discovered that the truck moves up with the duck as a single unit. Along with adults, twelve-month-old babies (as indicated by their prolonged looking times) also find this event surprising. They represent the duck and the truck as separate objects despite their superficial appearance as a single continuous mass. However, ten-month-old babies, when confronted with the same scene (a hand lifting the two objects as if they were a single entity), do not show any surprise. Apparently they do not as yet spontaneously represent the display as two separate objects. At that age their mind is paying more attention to spatial continuity as a criterion to sort out the environment into objects.

In a version of this experiment adapted for nonhuman primates, Hauser and Carey (1998) found that adult tamarin monkeys behave like ten-month-old human babies. The experimenters used a piece of monkey chow resting on a marshmallow instead of ducks and trucks. The tamarins showed no surprise when the experimenter lifted both pieces together. But adult semi-free rhesus monkeys (phylogenetically closer to humans) behaved like twelve-month-old babies: they were surprised (looked for longer) when a pepper and the sweet potato on which it was placed moved up together as a single object (Munakata et al., 2001). The rhesus were representing them as separate objects that happened to be in contact. Since these food items were previously unknown to the rhesus monkeys, they must have been using the featural differences between sweet potatoes and peppers to represent them as different objects despite their spatial continuity.

Hauser and Carey (1998) believe that this experiment may be tapping upon something truly fundamental in object cognition. The ability to see *one* three-dimensional entity with two distinct sets of features as *two* individual objects instead of a single object, without having any other information about their individuality, might be a milestone in the development and evolution of object cognition. Old World monkeys may have acquired this discrimination, and it may reflect an ability to perceive the world with a classificatory attitude; not only in terms of objects, but also in terms of *kinds* of objects. Of course, more studies with other monkey species are needed to test this interesting hypothesis.

Inferring Objects

Sometimes we must decide about the identity of objects not only on the basis of perceptual information, but also by making inferences. For example, if I see a green apple in the drawer of my desk, and then, after closing the drawer, I discover an identical green apple beside my computer screen, I assume that they must be two different apples. In this case I am using a spatio-temporal principle to distinguish the otherwise identical apples: I know that the same object cannot be in two different places at the same time and there is no way in which the apple might have traveled from the drawer to the side of my computer screen (it would be a different matter if I had left the room and found the second apple upon my return; then, having lost the spatio-temporal track, I would not know whether it was the same or a different apple). We use these principles so automatically and effortlessly that it may even sound strange that we refer to them as "principles." But do young infants understand object identity in the same way?

In a situation similar to the two apples example, when ten-month-old babies are shown first one toy moving behind a screen and then an identical toy moving behind a second screen, when both screens are lifted they expect to see two objects, and they are surprised (look for longer) if only one object appears (Spelke et al., 1995). In their minds there are two different objects of the same kind, one behind each screen, even though they have not seen the two simultaneously.

If, however, we show our subjects how one toy is placed behind the first screen, then how the toy leaves that screen and moves behind the second screen, when the two screens are lifted, babies only expect to see *one* object. Babies assume that the object that moves to the second screen is the same that had gone behind the first. In this, they behave like adult humans who also assume that there is only one object moving from one place to another (Spelke et al., 1995).

Adult rhesus and tamarin monkeys have the same expectations as human babies when confronted with similar situations: they show surprise (look for longer) if only one object appears in the condition where two objects were placed behind separate screens, or if two objects appear in the scenario where a single object is moved from one screen to another (Hauser and Carey, 1998).

It would seem, therefore, that one-year-old human babies and at least adult rhesus and tamarin monkeys have a basic ability to identify and keep track of objects in relatively elaborate scenarios that require some sort of inferential representations (representations that go beyond the information perceptually given). This way of representing objects could be relatively old in primate evolution, as it is present in adult members of both New and Old World monkeys. It remains to be tested at what age it appears in monkey infants. Preliminary evidence suggests that at least in one Old World monkey species (pigtailed macaques) this ability is already present by 5 weeks of age (Williams and Carey, 2000).

So far, so good: monkeys and human one-year-olds represent object events as do adult humans. But perhaps things are not so simple. The developmentalists Carey and Xu (2001) proposed an intriguing possibility. In a situation like the above, young human infants may indeed be representing two objects, but not necessarily two "apples" or two "balls"; that is, the young infant mind may initially represent objects within spatio-temporal parameters ("there are two things behind the screens"), but not yet on the basis of featural or property representations of the same objects ("there are two apples"). Young babies may represent that there are two objects behind the screens but not *which* objects, despite having seen them a few moments before.

Carey and Xu make this suggestion from the following evidence. They let ten-month-old babies observe that a truck appears from behind a screen and returns behind the screen; and then a ball appears from behind the same screen and returns behind it. When the screen is lifted, the babies are not surprised if only *one* of the objects is revealed (the other having been surreptitiously withdrawn by the experimenter). They react exactly in the same way as if, instead of two different objects, the same object had appeared twice from behind the screen. It is not that they cannot perceive the featural differences between both objects (as we saw in the previous section, babies can discriminate among different objects from very early on), and they have no problem anticipating two different objects when two different screens are used (even as early as at 4 to 5 months of age).

Babies have no perception or memory problems, but a *representational* limitation—one that prevents them from integrating what they have seen into a coherent, adult-like picture of what is going on. These young infants cannot keep mental track of the identity *and* the location of an object at the same time, as we adults do. They appear to be able to keep in mind the existence of *an* object behind the screen, but they cannot connect this representation with that of the identity of the object.

The investigation of this issue (known as the problem of "object individuation") began with early primate psychologist Tinklepaugh's work with primates (1929). He was interested in determining whether adult rhesus monkeys did or did not have any ability at all to represent things in their minds. He showed his subjects that he placed a piece of banana inside a container, and then allowed them to look for it. The catch was that in some trials the identity of the food was surreptitiously changed; for example, the piece of banana was replaced by a piece of lettuce. He discovered that adult rhesus monkeys "looked surprised" when they found a different piece of food in the container (at least if the unexpected item was not a preferred one, such as lettuce instead of banana), and they looked further in the hiding place as if in search of the missing item. Tinklepaugh's conclusion was that monkeys kept in their minds a representation not only of the existence of food but also of the identity of the food.

When given a similar test in which the identity of a hidden object is surreptitiously changed, human babies engage in this sort of prolonged search for the original object only from 18 months of age onwards. As Xu and Carey suggest (1996), it is one thing to figure out that there is an object behind a screen, and a very different (and developmentally later) thing to figure out what that object is. In a modified version of this test, in which two different objects are taken out and put back into a bag in succession (but then one of them is surreptitiously withdrawn), twelve-month-old babies look for longer inside the bag, as if in search of the two objects. Ten-month-olds are content when they find one object, seeming not to understand that there must be two objects. Santos and colleagues (2002) have recently adapted this paradigm to test semi-free rhesus monkeys, and found that when they see that two different pieces of food are placed in succession inside a box (but one is surreptitiously removed), the monkeys search longer inside the box than when they see that only one piece was placed there.

This finding is confirmed by another study (Uller et al., 1997) with the same free-ranging group of rhesus monkeys. This time, the researchers measured the amount of time the monkeys spent watching possible and impossible events (the procedure used by Xu and Carey); for example, they saw a carrot placed behind a screen and then a piece of squash. When the screen was lifted, they looked longer at the impossible event of seeing only one item (only the piece of squash). They behaved like twelve-month-old human babies, not like ten-month-olds.

Moreover, Hauser, Carey, and Hauser (2000) found that free-ranging rhesus can perform simple subtraction operations. When shown two different numbers of food pieces placed behind two different screens (3 behind screen A and 2 behind screen B), they normally went first to the screen behind which they saw more food being placed. But then, if after observing how many pieces are placed behind each screen they see someone taking away some of the pieces from behind one of the screens, they appear to be able to adjust their mental representation of the hidden quantity. They still choose the screen with more food, even if now this is the one that originally contained less food. Rhesus monkeys can therefore calculate mentally the amount of food when items are taken away from behind a screen—but they can do this only for numbers smaller or equal to three. This again coincides with the constraints within which twelve-month-old human babies also operate when they are given similar tests.

Hauser and Carey (1998) believe that these findings reveal that both prelinguistic human infants and adult monkeys "represent number as one dimension of their experience of the world" (p. 82). By "number" they don't mean the ability to count systematically or to use symbols to represent quantities, but rather a more basic and primitive ability to construct representations, not only of objects of different types, but also of different objects of the same type.

According to them, this evidence may be relevant to an ongoing debate in cognitive science about the ways in which humans identify and keep track of objects. Studies of perceptual abilities in human adults suggest that in object perception we may be using two very different systems that work so tightly together that normally we don't realize their singularity: one system is specialized in ascribing an identity to the object on the basis of its "features," namely, the cluster of visual characteristics that, for example, distinguish an apple from an orange; the second system is specialized in detecting the mere fact that there is an object (*any* object) in a particular location in space. We are usually not aware of this plurality of systems in our everyday object cognition. However, ingenious experiments show that both can be dissociated even in normal human adults (see Carey and Xu, 2001). (A simple way of experiencing something similar to this dissociation is when you see with the "corner of your eye" that something is moving on your right but you are unable to tell what or who it is until you use your focal vision capable of processing the features that identify the object).

Carey and Xu's idea is that in ontogeny the first system—detecting and tracking objects as unidentified units—appears before the second—identifying the features of the objects. This would explain why infants who are 10 months of age fail to infer that there must be two items in the experiment where two objects appear and disappear behind one screen in succession: they keep mental track of the existence of an object there, but cannot figure out which object.

A less radical interpretation would be that both systems are at work in young infants, but they cannot yet be coordinated into a single representational framework of the sort adults have, especially when babies have to use their representations to solve problems or make sense of what is going on. This would also explain recent results according to which it is possible to find some evidence of object individuation with featural information in babies younger than 10 months of age if simplified testing procedures are used (see Santos et al., 2002, for a brief review).

As Hauser and Carey (1998) point out, these findings may have interesting consequences for developmental psychology. The ability to separate objects according to their featural properties rather than responding to spatio-temporal cues appears in infants at about the same time as their first words for identifying types of objects (it is even possible to find some correlation between passing the Xu and Carey tests and the emergence of the first words). This led to the idea that language might be responsible for the development of that new way of representing the world—a case of language changing cognition. The findings with rhesus monkeys suggest that this hypothesis is mistaken: the ability to represent individual objects by their features was already established in primate evolution well before human language emerged. It is a generalized primate adaptation for representing the world of objects, which allows primates to form representations of things they have not actually seen, like the two pieces of food behind a screen. They appear somehow to be able to imagine what they are going to find by mentally updating the representations they have formed of separate events.

Primate and Other Animals' Ways of Perceiving Objects

Many indications suggest that the primate cognitive system in general is geared toward the perception and representation of objects in the world. Are there differences in object perception among different species of primates or between primates and other animals?

One important feature of object perception is known as "visual completion," or the ability to represent a complete object when only a part of it is visible (because, for instance, it is partially con-

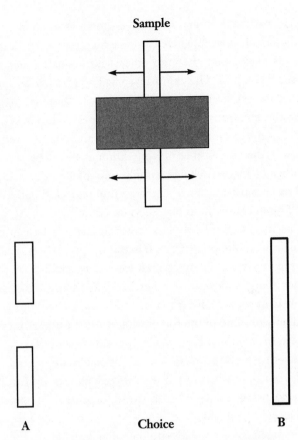

Figure 2.2. Which option corresponds to the sample? Chimpanzees, like 4-month-old babies, chose option B (a complete rod) when the two ends in the sample moved in unison, but they chose A if the ends moved separately.

cealed by another object). We can do this even with relatively new objects: our visual system is designed to complete objects when certain display conditions obtain. In human babies this ability can be detected as early as at 4 months of age (Kellman and Spelke, 1983), and it has been recently demonstrated in an adult chimpanzee using an adaptation of the same test as used with humans (Fujita, 2001). The chimpanzee first learned to select on a computer screen an image that matched another image shown as a sample. Sometimes the sample image depicted a single long rod; other times two short rods placed one after the other with a small gap between them (see figure 2.2). The chimpanzee had no problem learning to match the images, even with the stimuli moving from left to right.

Then the chimpanzee was tested with the same moving stimuli, but this time a small part of the central area was covered up in such a way that the visible moving stimulus could be consistent with either of the two choice stimuli: one long rod or two short rods. The chimpanzee, however, chose the single-rod option in almost 100 percent of the trials. She was assuming that the central screen partially occluded a single object, exactly as human babies do from around 4 months of age. It is as if the perceptual systems of the chimp and the child are geared toward assuming a single object when there is movement coherence between visible parts. Indeed, the chimpanzee chose the two-rods option when the stimulus showed only one end of the rod moving while the other end stayed stationary, or if both ends moved in opposite directions.

Baboons have also shown some ability for "assuming complete objects," but only when tested with three-dimensional cardboard stimuli, not when presented with two-dimensional computer displays (Deruelle et al., 2000).

When pigeons were tested with the same paradigm as the chimpanzee (using computer screen displays), they failed to show any evidence of "object completion": they rather appeared to perceive two short rods all the time (Fujita, 2001). This suggests that the primate perceptual system is adapted for "picking out" solid objects from perceptual arrays, whereas the system of other species phylogenetically distant to primates may not be so designed. As yet we have no data about the performance of mammals other than primates in tests like these. Hence we don't know if object completion is a primate trait or a mammalian adaptation upon which primates capitalized. Nor do we have data about the *development* of object completion in chimpanzees or monkeys. We don't know therefore if human infants are precocious in the development of this skill or if they just follow a general primate pattern.

Tomonaga (2001) conducted extensive experiments comparing

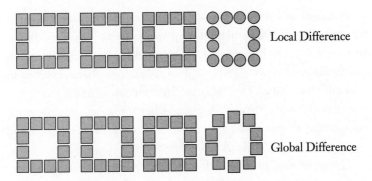

Figure 2.3. Examples of visual stimuli that differ either locally (one global square made of small circles) or globally (small squares compose a global circle).

certain aspects of the perceptual systems of humans, chimpanzees, monkeys, and pigeons. The results suggest that primates share many basic properties that are not seen in pigeons, as if there were a common plan for primate perceptual cognition that differs from that of phylogenetically more distant species. (Of course, the same caveat about the lack of studies with nonprimate mammals applies here.) Despite these basic commonalities, however, some differences appear among primate species.

Experiments have shown that human adults typically tend to perceive first the global outline of a stimulus and only secondarily its local details (Navon, 1977). For example, when it comes to composite figures like the big square made of small squares or the big square made of small circles (figure 2.3), we are usually quicker and commit fewer errors identifying the global shape than the component figures. Also, if people are asked to identify a particular shape among several in a display, the total number of items present increases their response time when they have to identify the component figures, but no extra time is needed for identifying the global figures. This has been interpreted as an indication that in humans global figures are processed in an automatic, parallel way, whereas the component figures are processed in series and with a special effort of attention. Global processing takes precedence in humans.

Fagot and colleagues (1999) studied this phenomenon of "global precedence" in baboons, chimpanzees, and humans, using exactly the same stimuli and a methodology as similar as possible with the three species. The human subjects behaved as expected from previous findings: they were faster and more accurate when they had to find a global shape. The baboons, by contrast, behaved exactly in the opposite way: they were faster when they had to find small component shapes and took longer and made more errors when they had to focus on the global shapes.

The experimenters tried different ways of facilitating global processing for the baboons (Fagot and Deruelle, 1997): linking the component elements with lines to underscore the global shape, decreasing the spacing between the components, keeping the sample on the screen during the response period .. all to no avail—the baboons consistently showed an inclination to local processing. Only extremely reduced distances between components had some effect in overcoming the local precedence of baboons (Fagot et al., 2001).

The chimpanzees, on the other hand, showed no preference at all. They performed equally well with the global and the local cues, as if they had some sort of intermediate processing style between that of baboons and that of humans, not specialized either in detail or global processing.

In another experiment (Fagot et al., 1999, 2001), the subjects had to detect a target that differed from others either globally or locally. For example, in a display of big squares made of small squares there was one big square made of small circles (local processing required), or there was one big circle made of small squares (global processing required).

Again the humans showed a global advantage. They found the odd stimulus much faster when it was a global figure than when it was the small component shapes. And again the baboons showed the opposite pattern: they were faster with the local shapes. By the way, it is not that they were better than humans in dealing with the local shapes. Baboons and humans solved the local trials practically with the same speed; the difference was due to the humans' unusual celerity in detecting global figures, which the baboons found especially difficult. Interestingly, the baboons could perform at the same speed as humans with global figures in a control condition in which they were shown defined squares and circles made with continuous lines. This demonstrates that the difference between baboons and humans does not lie in the readiness to perceive squares and circles as such, nor is there a problem with the absolute size of the figures, but rather in the ability to sort out the higher-order figures in the arrays of small figures.

The two chimpanzees tested in this task each behaved differently: one was equally fast with global and local figures, showing again an intermediate processing style. The other chimpanzee was faster with the local figures (the baboon pattern).

Hopkins and Washburn (2002) have recently reported an advantage with global over local figures in 5 chimpanzees, whereas rhesus monkeys tested with exactly the same stimuli showed a local figure advantage. Capuchin monkeys also have been recently reported to show a local processing bias (Spinozzi et al., 2003).

These results are potentially very important. They point to the possibility of different "cognitive styles" present in different primate species otherwise endowed with essentially similar perceptual abilities. Different species may be attending to different aspects of one and the same scene and, as a consequence, may end up representing them in different ways. It is important to note that the monkeys in these experiments are in fact able to see and respond to the global figures (with some attentional effort), but their natural tendency was to process the parts of a whole first and faster. In contrast, the chimpanzees either showed no definite tendency or, in Hopkins's studies, showed global precedence like humans. Research suggests that some developmental conditions such as autism may be related to an imbalance in the typical human tendency to process globally. The unusual skills for local processing of some individuals with autism may be the source of some of their problems, but also of some of their remarkable talents or islets of ability, such as "photographic" drawing or prodigious rote memory (Frith, 2003).

To summarize, primates' visual perception is designed for organizing the world in terms of objects. Beyond the basic task of parsing scenes into their component units in the immediate environment, primates can also create more complex representations in which they keep track of individual objects by integrating spatio-temporal and featural cues, including a primitive sense of number. We know that some aspects of this basic object individuation system may be different from those of other phylogenetically distant species like pigeons, but we don't know yet how originally "primate" they are, or if instead they reflect more primitive mammalian adaptations. In fact, a recent experiment by Uller and colleagues (2003) suggests that a primitive numerical representation of objects may be present in salamanders, an amphibian species! Salamanders showed a significant tendency to choose the tube containing more flies (an important element of their natural diet) when quantities like 1 against 2 or 2 against 3 were contrasted. They failed, however, to notice the difference between 3 and 4, like macaques and human babies. This suggests that the "numerical" individuation system used by primates to deal with objects may indeed have older phylogenetic antecedents.

Cross-Modal Representations

Objects can be known through various sensory modalities: you see an orange, you take it and feel its skin and weight and shape, you smell it, and finally you may taste it, while hearing its peculiar crunching (so different from that of a nut or an apple) in your mouth and feeling the texture of its flesh. One object is the source of an extraordinary variety of sensations picked up by our different sensory modalities. Indeed, it has been suggested that the very notion of object arises out of the unified coordination of collected sensations that tend to cluster together. Philosophers and early students of human infants such as Piaget (1936) thought that to understand that the sensations coming through different modalities actually correspond to one and the same object is a progressive cognitive achievement that takes a considerable time to emerge.

A way of measuring the ability to represent objects "cross-modally" is to ask subjects to identify an object in one sensory modality, for example, visually, after having experienced it through a different modality, for example, tactually. This test is specially stringent when the objects presented are completely new, since this procedure would exclude the possibility of using previously acquired associations. Can primates anticipate the appearance of a novel object in a different modality from that in which it was first experienced?

For a time it was thought that only humans were capable of cross-modal knowledge, and that probably this ability was mediated by language, so that words would act as some sort of central abstract code capable of putting together the information coming from each sensory modality (Lewkowicz and Lickliter, 1994). It has been demonstrated, however, that monkeys, apes, and human infants are all capable of cross-modal cognition without language.

Bryant and colleagues (1972) demonstrated that human infants as young as 9 months could recognize shapes across sensory modalities. The experimenters first made infants touch one object that emitted a sound when squeezed (a feature that makes objects more interesting to young children), but without allowing them to see the object they were touching. Then the infants were offered two objects at the same time which they could see—a completely new one and the noisy one they had just touched. These infants showed a clear tendency to take and manipulate first the interesting object they had touched before, as if they were able to conceive the visual appearance the noisy object should have. The rate of preference was virtually identical to that of infants who were shown the noisy object to begin with and then allowed to make their choice.

This surprising result was extended even more surprisingly by Meltzoff and Borton (1979). One-month-old babies were given one of two pacifiers: one in a perfect spherical shape, the other with a dented form. After allowing them to mouth one of these, a visual image of both shapes was projected simultaneously on a screen in front of the babies. Infants preferred to look at the visual shape that coincided with the one they had just explored with their mouths. Cross-modal integration of information is not only independent of language, but is also probably an innate, hard-wired property of the human brain (Lewkowicz and Lickliter, 1994).

In 1970 Davenport and Rogers demonstrated that chimpanzees

and orangutans also have the ability to transfer information from one modality to another. They first trained their subjects to make what is known as a match-to-sample test: the subject is shown an object (the sample), and then she is given a choice between two objects, one of them identical to the sample; the other different. The subject is rewarded by choosing the identical one. Typically, this is a visual test: the sample and the choices are placed in front of the subject. Davenport and Rogers had the idea of presenting the sample visually but making their subjects choose among two objects presented tactually—the apes had to introduce their hands into a box to touch the choice objects. It took the chimpanzees relatively long to learn this procedure—above 500 initial trials with a few training objects, and then another few hundred to ensure generalization to other objects. This, on its own, does not demonstrate cross-modal perception, because the objects used for this prolonged training were the same, and the apes might have learned to associate a particular tactual sensation with a particular visual configuration in order to obtain the reward without realizing that the objects are the same. The crucial test was to offer the apes completely new objects in each trial, so that they could not use any learned association. When this was done, they were capable of recognizing the new objects in a significant number of trials. The conclusion was that they were really identifying the objects on the basis of two different sources of information. And they could do this going back and forth: from seeing to touching and from touching to seeing.

Moreover, these authors demonstrated that the chimps could do the cross-modal transfer even when the visual stimuli were not the corresponding objects themselves but photographs, or even, in some cases, altered photographs and line drawings of the objects, although in the latter cases their performance was worse and some subjects could not solve the problem.

When Davenport and colleagues (1973) tried this procedure with monkeys, they could not complete their study because the monkeys refused to reach and touch objects inside a box without seeing them. Another group of researchers—Weiskrantz and Cowey

(1975) and Cowey and Weiskrantz (1975)—found a suitable procedure to investigate cross-modal matching in rhesus monkeys: instead of offering them objects to be explored manually, they gave them pieces of food (some cookies made with powdered monkey food) cut in distinct shapes (star, circle, cube). Some shapes had been consistently dipped in a quinine solution so that their taste was extremely sour and disagreeable to the monkeys, whereas the other shapes had their normal taste. The monkeys were given these pieces of food in total darkness, so that they had only tactual information (manual and oral). After that, the monkeys were shown a pair of shapes, one sour, the other of normal taste. After a few seconds of visual contemplation, they were given a choice. Would they choose at random or would they be able to use the tactual information about shape they had gained in the dark to guide their choice, now on the basis of exclusively visual information? The monkeys chose the good-tasting shapes in a percentage of trials (67 to 79%) that was practically identical to those reported for apes and human infants with the other procedures. They were able to integrate tactual and visual information, either by translating from one modality to the other or by generating a multimodal central representation of the objects.

An unexpected but very interesting finding happened when the monkeys were given a control task in which the shapes they were shown visually did not coincide with those they were given tactually. The aim of this test was to check that the monkeys were not giving the correct matching responses by some means that had escaped the experimenters' controls. The prediction was that if they were engaging in true cross-modal matching, they would find it impossible to choose one cookie over the other when there was no shape correspondence. Surprisingly, their responses were not random: they were biased toward a particular testing shape, which often happened to be the "wrong" cookie, the one that had a sour flavor. The explanation is that the monkeys were engaging in "local matching"; they were detecting local similarities between the stimuli. For example, the animals that had experienced a "key" shape as positive in the tactual phase, tended to choose round cookies in the visual phase, whereas animals that had received a tactual rectangle as positive showed a strong preference for a visual star. The key and the circle had in common their round portions; the star and the rectangle, the sharp edges.

This finding is important because it confirms that the monkeys are engaging in genuine translation of shape information from one modality into another (actually, there was a correlation between the degree of matching ability of individual monkeys in the normal task, and their tendency to deviate from chance in the control task). But it also raises the question of whether they are constructing a representation of the global shape and using this global representation to guide their choice of the whole object in the new modality, or are they guided by local cross-modal correspondences. That is, do they recognize visually the object they touched with their hands and mouths, or do they recognize merely some isolated features?

The high level of performance in the original task (where many different shapes sharing features such as round versus sharp edges were contrasted) suggests that the monkeys pick up more information than just an isolated feature, but a more conclusive experiment remains to be conducted to determine if they truly generate global representations of whole objects.

A second implication from this finding is that rhesus monkeys are clearly conducting a local analysis of the objects, similar to that reported by Hopkins and Washburn (2002) in a unimodal visual task. It would be interesting to see if local matching in cross-modal conditions is equally present in apes and humans, or is more common among primates with a local-precedence perceptual style.

Gunderson (1983) carried out the pacifier study with pigtail macaques 1 to 4 weeks of age, finding that they are indeed capable of the same discrimination as one-month-old human babies. The baby monkeys, after mouthing the two different kinds of pacifiers in the dark, showed a clear preference for looking at the corresponding pacifier when both were shown to them. Even the few one-week-old macaques that were tested showed evidence of this cross-modal ability. As the author pointed out, this is to be expected if one takes into account that the general ratio of sensorimotor development between macaques and humans has been estimated to be 1:4; thus behaviors tend to appear in human babies 4 times later.

Recently, Gallese (2003) has reported the discovery of neurons in certain areas of the rhesus monkey neocortex that have the ability to respond to different sensory manifestations of the same event: for example, they can respond to the sight of a hand tearing a piece of paper, to the same action performed and therefore proprioceptively perceived by the monkey himself, or to the *sound* of the paper being torn. This supports the notion that primates construct rich multisensory representations of events that can be activated by the information incoming from only one modality, for example, a nut-cracking sound may activate in the mind of the monkey the representation of someone cracking a nut.

The conclusion of these studies with human and other primates appears to be that one crucial, and probably hard-wired feature of the primate brain is the ability to put together information from different modalities into cross-modal representations of objects and events. The primate mind appears to be configured to create the basic and powerful notion of multidimensional objects as soon as possible, and to use it to organize their knowledge and behavior. This capacity does not appear to be an absolute novelty in evolution, but the extension of a trend already present in mammalian brains (Lewkowicz and Lickliter, 1994).

Contemplating Objects and Events

Many experiments with monkeys and apes are typically carried out in the form of problems which primates have to solve and are then rewarded with a piece of food. Usually monkeys and apes are not willing to respond at all in these experiments unless they receive the food or some other extrinsic reinforcement. This may lead one to assume that primary needs like food consumption are the only thing that motivates nonhuman primates to act. This is not the case. Primates do spontaneously look at and explore the objects in their environment. Objects need not be food or be associated with food or any other reinforcement for them to be looked at and touched. Exploration itself appears to be an important *motive* in the regulation of primate behavior, and one that could have important consequences for their cognitive and behavioral development. Although their explorations often take the form of manipulations, primate exploration can also be merely perceptual or contemplative.

A number of classical studies (Butler, 1965) demonstrated experimentally the importance of contemplation as a primary motive in primate behavior. For example, both rhesus monkeys and chimpanzees will learn to press levers or pull other devices when the only reward they obtain is the opportunity to look through a window or through a hole or to listen to some sound (such as other primates' vocalizations). Interestingly, whereas in standard experiments where primates are reinforced with food the performance of subjects rapidly deteriorates as their hunger gets satiated, the effectiveness of contemplation rewards remains essentially constant (Butler, 1965). Curiosity becomes satiated only very slowly (especially if you are a laboratory primate kept in a relatively boring environment).

Careful experiments have shown that primates are really motivated by the visual scenes themselves and not merely by the action of opening a window or activating a mechanism. For example, when they have a choice, monkeys clearly prefer looking through a hole in front of which slides or films are projected (Butler, 1965).

What do monkeys and apes *see* when they watch a scene? Are they obtaining information by analyzing in some way the scenes they are contemplating? Do we have any evidence that primates are really attending to the contents of the scenes, and not just interested in the light and indiscriminate movements of the stimuli? Butler (1965), using a precursor of the preferential looking paradigm, was able to demonstrate years ago that the contents of the scene do matter to monkeys. He measured how long rhesus monkeys would keep a window screen open to look into a room that offered them different shows. The most effective displays were either another monkey or an electric train running. Food was a much less interesting visual spectacle for the monkeys.

Using movies depicting other animals as the stimulus scenes, Butler also demonstrated that monkeys are sensitive to the clarity of the pictures, and that they preferred films projected at normal speed over slow motion, color over black and white, and normal orientation over upside-down. In summary, monkeys prefer conditions of maximum visibility and perceivability, which suggests they are really watching the contents.

What information can primates extract from watching? Darby and Riopelle (1959) carried out an ingenious experiment in which they allowed rhesus monkeys to watch other rhesus' performance in a typical discrimination learning problem, in which the subjects had to pick the correct object out of a choice of two. The question was: could the observer monkeys learn which was the correct object from seeing the others dealing with the problem? To answer this question, each observer monkey was allowed to respond to exactly the same problem after watching the other monkey's response. It turned out that the observers did learn which was the correct choice from watching the others. Moreover, they learned to select the correct object even more efficiently when the demonstrator monkey made the wrong choice out of the two alternatives. In this case, when his turn came, the observer monkey chose the opposite object, thus gaining the reward. Note that this suggests that the observer is not just imitating the demonstrator, nor is he simply paying attention to the same object that the first monkey manipulated. Some sort of simple reasoning on the basis of the observed information appears to be going on. We will return to the topic of what primates can learn from watching others in Chapter 9.

More recently, Dunbar and O'Connell (Dunbar, 2000) reported an intriguing result. They gave chimpanzees, orangutans, and preschool children a series of "puzzle boxes" containing a reward, which they could get only if they could undo the different mechanisms locking each box. The participants were allowed first to observe the boxes but not to manipulate them. For example, the boxes were left lying outside the apes' cages for a 24-hour period, during which the animals could neither touch the box nor observe anybody else doing anything with it. The experimenters found that contemplating the box had a significant effect upon the speed with which chimpanzees, orangutans, and children were capable of opening the boxes. Dunbar (2000) suggests that this improvement could be attributed to some form of "mental rehearsal" of the actions to be performed. Whatever the explanation, the primates appeared to be extracting some useful information from the simple contemplation of a static display. In sum, the available evidence suggests that even for adult primates capable of manipulation, the mere contemplation of objects and events is highly motivating, and they appear to be able to analyze what they contemplate and extract information that can be used later on.

The World of Objects

All available evidence suggests that the perceptual system of primates is geared toward the representation of sensory stimulation in terms of objects. Monkeys and apes are born with adaptations that make them selectively attend to sources of stimulation that correspond to individual objects. For example, a monkey baby in the arms of her mother will attend to a plant, a fruit, or another monkey rather than to the bright sky or the undifferentiated ground. These adaptations, however, are not ready-made templates: they appear rather to be facilitators that focus the attention of the primate on the right source of stimulation from which to start building more detailed representations of what will turn out to be objects. The way in which this stimulation is processed is constrained by further adaptations in the young primate brain: visual scenes are analyzed in units following certain segregation rules (so patterns moving together or pattern continuity tend to be represented as single objects). These visual representations are very soon coordinated with tactual and kinesthetic information, as visual attention guides the hands and mouths of primates toward the objects they see. The result is the elaboration of complex multisensorial representations of objects, events, and scenes in which the actions of the primates themselves may play an important role.

This early organization of perception around the unit of objects may be broadly similar across species of monkeys and apes, including humans (and to some extent perhaps common to other mammals). The early focus on patterns and solidity, the progressive preference of complexity and novelty, the object-completion effect, the early ability for cross-modal integration, the primitive system of object individuation, all appear to be present in all primates studied so far. Other features of object perception, such as the relative weight of global versus local attention or the inferences that can be made about invisible object events, may vary among different species of primates.

Yet all these adaptations are invitations to *develop* object representations. Objects as units of perception, far from being a ready-made adaptive feature of primates, are developmental products obtained under relatively constrained developmental recipes.

3

Practical Intelligence: Doing Things with Objects

People tend to think of objects as artificial things made for specific purposes: a pencil, a cup, a shoe, a hammer, tables, chairs, books, stone axes—examples are endless. Objects are not an invention of humans, however: the world is full of natural objects—stones, water, trees, sand, leaves, fruits, mud, branches, carcasses. The typical primate environment is a three-dimensional arrangement of shapes, volumes, colors, and textures that correspond to distinct entities. Primates perceive these entities in their environment as objects. But objects are much more than visual displays: they are solid entities that can be touched and handled, notably through that most relevant innovation of primates—the hands. In this chapter we will learn how primates develop their manipulative abilities to act upon the world of objects and to what extent they have evolved a corresponding set of representations for acquiring and storing knowledge about objects as manipulable fragments of the world.

Objects in Action: A Piagetian View

Naturalistic observations of primates show that the manipulation of natural objects is a crucial component of primate lives, from simple food-gathering procedures such as taking a piece of fruit or an insect to the mouth, to complex sequences of manipulation, as when mountain gorillas process thistles to gain access to their edible parts (Byrne, 1995), or, most remarkably, the use and preparation of objects as tools to manipulate other objects, as in the case of chimpanzees fishing for termites with sticks or cracking nuts with stones. But what do these behaviors reveal about the cognitive abilities of primates? Are they just elaborate habits or instincts without any supporting representations worth the attention of the cognitive scientist, or are they based upon some degree of intelligent understanding?

One of the best descriptions of the development of object manipulation as the development of intelligence was provided by Jean Piaget, with his epoch-making studies about the first two years of life of three young primates—his own children (Piaget, 1936, 1937). He believed that beside simple behaviors—instinctive reflexes or habits acquired by associative learning—on the one hand, and the symbolic, abstract thought of adult humans on the other, there was a third type of intelligence, in the very essence of which were the notions of action and object. He called it sensorimotor or practical intelligence and devised a detailed developmental chart of its emergence in the human infant, as a system that understands the world in terms of objects, causal connections, and spatial and temporal relations.

Piaget's ideas about practical intelligence have proved of special interest to primatologists because they characterize a kind of intelligence that is independent of language or any other explicit symbolic abilities, and therefore is in principle applicable to the study of other primates (Parker, 1977; Parker and MacKinney, 1999).

Piaget thought that the notion of "object" and related notions like "space" and "causality" are initially "sensorimotor" or "practical" in the sense that they remain linked to the representations of actions ("schemas" in Piagetian terminology), rather than being thoughts or explicit mental representations; they are produced by and used for doing things in the world rather than for thinking about it. In Piaget's theory this is a first, foundational phase in the development of the more abstract forms of human intelligence that appear later in child development (Piaget, 1936).

His conviction that intelligence is built through action led Piaget to believe that in their first 4 to 5 months, before they are able to manipulate objects, babies have a very limited understanding of the world. They don't have a notion of *objects* as solid, unified, independent, and permanent entities "out there" that are responsible for the variety of sensations they experience. They will attain this notion during their first two years of life through the progressive creation and coordination of *schemas*—what today we would call implicit representations—of their actions with objects.

Research conducted after Piaget has shown that this conclusion of his may be erroneous. As the experiments discussed previously have demonstrated, the perceptual system of humans and other primates appears to be set from the beginning in such a way that objects are units of perception before they are units of action (Fantz, 1965). But Piaget's description of the development of intelligent *actions* in babies has proved to be extremely accurate, and is a powerful tool to probe the development of intelligence in primates other than humans.

How Human Babies Begin to Use the World of Objects

Piaget described sensorimotor development as a sequence of stages that emerge as infants' actions come to be organized into progressively more complex systems of practical intelligence. We have summarized these stages in figure 3.1. In the first stage of development, newborn babies have a rather limited collection of reflex actions that are automatically triggered by very specific stimulations: for example, the suckling reflex, triggered by anything that gets into the baby's mouth, or the reflex of closing the fingers over anything that touches the palm of their hands. When pediatric tests originally developed for assessing the repertoire of reflexes in human babies have been applied to newborn monkeys and apes, they were found to possess a very similar repertoire of innate reflex actions at the beginning of life, with some minor differences, like the absence of a "walking" reflex (present in humans) and strong cling-

Stage 1 (1 month)
Babies' reflexes are activated in contact with objects in the world,
e.g., suckling, clinging (in non-human primates), grasping.

Stage 2 (2–4 months)
From reflexes to simple acquired behaviors, such as different forms
of suckling and mouthing, different forms of grasping.

Stage 3 (4–8 months)
Schemas of action are coordinated into more complex units:
taking grasped things to the mouth, grasping things seen, etc.
New actions upon external objects emerge mainly by chance, but
babies can repeat them and keep them in their repertoire (so-called
"secondary circular reactions").

Stage 4 (8–12 months)
Schemas are coordinated in means-ends sequences: e.g.,
pushing aside an object that is blocking the way to another.
New objects are explored by trying different known schemas on them.

Stage 5 (12–18 months)
Objects are used as tools to manipulate other objects.
New objects are explored by trying new actions with them and
by combining them in different ways.

Stage 6 (18–24 months)
New forms of tool use and other intelligent actions are generated
without having to try them out first; now babies seem to have some
form of symbolic thinking that allows them to figure things out in
their heads.

Figure 3.1. Stages of sensorimotor or practical intelligence and some of
their landmarks according to Piaget (1936, 1937).

ing reflexes (absent or weaker in humans) (Bard, 1992; Redshaw,
1989). For monkey and ape babies the reflex of clinging tightly to
their mothers' fur is very adaptive indeed, when your mother might
be moving on a tree several meters above the ground!

These reflex actions may seem "clever" in the sense that they serve some functions fundamental for the survival of primate new-borns; but of course they are not really intelligent because babies have no control over them. They are automatic reactions that happen to them, a prolongation of their morphological adaptations (like having hands or eyes). Nonetheless Piaget suggested that these automatic responses are the jumping board from which babies will build new schemas of action. For example, from the suckling reflex babies eventually develop different ways of suckling: some better adapted to extract milk from their mother's breast, others modified to suck a pacifier or their own fingers, perhaps others to explore the texture of objects. Reflexes start the cognitive machinery of new-borns by making them act and store their first sensorimotor representations of their own actions. These are "practical representations," that is, neural records of how to do something in response to a stimulation and what to expect after that. But limited and eminently practical as they are, these first acquired actions constitute the first steps toward intelligence.

According to Piaget (1936), during their first 2 to 4 months of life babies build an increasingly varied collection of simple action schemas differentiated from their initial reflexes (stage 2 of figure 3.1). Then something important happens: instead of remaining as a collection of independent behaviors, the sensorimotor schemas start to be *coordinated* into longer and more elaborate sequences of action. For example, babies begin taking to their mouths things that they happen to grab with their hands; or grasp something they see, or look at what they have grasped (stage 3).

This is a crucial process in the development of intelligent behavior. Babies not only acquire new kinds of actions, such as ways of grasping, hitting, crawling, or climbing; they also develop the ability to create more elaborate sequences of behavior by combining simple actions in meaningful ways. These coordinations are initially modest (seeing and grasping an object and taking it to the mouth), but soon (between 8 and 12 months of age; stage 4) they become more complex and bear the flavor of genuine intelligence. Babies can now combine different actions in novel, well-adapted ways; if, say, they try to reach an object that they have seen and it happens to be too far away, they can stop the reaching action, crawl toward the object, stop, and then reach again. Or if they are trying to get an object and find an obstacle in their way, they can first push the obstacle aside and then reach for their target. This is one of the first signs of genuine intelligence—the baby is able to interrupt something she was trying to do, and carry out a different action that puts her in a better position to do what she wants. She has solved a simple problem, not by blind trial and error, but in an intelligent way. There is here a nascent ability to keep a goal in mind while executing an intermediary action that allows the goal to be achieved.

In a further step, around one year and a half (stages 5 and 6), infants become capable of using objects as tools to act upon other objects, for example, using a toy rake to collect the ball that is outside their playpen. Tool use is one of the crowning achievements of practical intelligence and one of its more significant "symptoms," because it appears to require a sophisticated understanding of the world of objects.

Piaget's view was that new actions are not simply acquired and stored by babies as a collection of separate schemas: they are represented neurally as part of a complex network of schemas organized according to an implicit logic of principles like the following: there is an external world of objects that can be perceived through different modalities; objects can be touched and moved (but only if one applies a force to it; otherwise, someone else or some other force has to move the object); to apply a force to an object one must usually first establish contact with it; objects exist continuously, even if one is not perceiving them all the time, and so on. But this is a *sensorimotor* or practical understanding, not the verbal formulation of the principles we have just enunciated: those principles *describe* well what the babies know, but they *are not* what they know—at least not thus far.

Yet this coordinated system of implicit representations has the property of being able to generate new behaviors in response to environmental challenges. Practical intelligence is a problem-solving device and, as such, a powerful source of quick and productive adaptation. From an evolutionary point of view, the practical systems of intelligence described by Piaget could constitute the cognitive counterparts of the anatomical adaptations primates evolved to manipulate the objects of their environment.

Object Permanence

One of Piaget's most famous and seminal discoveries (1937) was the unexpectedly complex sequence of development of an apparently simple ability—retrieving objects. Piaget studied this ability extensively because he thought it was a key index to how a baby understood a fundamental property of objects: namely, that they exist independently of our perceptions and actions. Babies follow a remarkable number of steps in the process of learning to retrieve objects when they disappear from their view.

According to Piaget, during their first 4 months of life babies simply perfect their ability to follow moving objects with their gaze, literally keeping track of targets that otherwise would disappear. But if they lose perceptual contact with an object, they don't appear to be able to resume it. They behave as if the object has disappeared and nothing can be done to find it.

From 4 to 8 months babies discover the manipulability of objects. They eagerly grasp any object they see (at first only if they can see their hand at the same time; later also when their hand is out of sight); they can hit or shake objects to provoke sounds (a rattle); and if they hear a sound, they turn around, apparently with the expectation of seeing its source. Babies now appear to understand that objects exist out there and can be contacted through different means. This coordination of different sensations and actions around a particular object as the *invariant* that they have in common is a crucial part of what is involved in the practical notion of object.

However, if babies are about to grasp an object in front of them and someone covers the object with a cloth, they stop their attempt and look puzzled, as if the object had suddenly disappeared in mid air. This is exactly what Piaget believed infants of 4 to 8 months of age were experiencing: their practical knowledge allows them to retrieve an object as long as they have an ongoing perceptual connection with it (by sight, sound, or touch), but as soon as this perceptual connection is lost, they act as if the object were gone or, at least, as if they had no idea of where it could be, even when they saw the object being slowly covered in front of them.

At 8 to 12 months, coinciding with the emergent ability to engage in means-ends coordination of actions, babies react to the test of the object that disappears under a cloth in a new way: they now take hold of the cloth, move it aside, and retrieve the object. If we repeat the experiment, the baby will retrieve the object again as many times as necessary (unless she gets bored!). She now appears to understand, first, that objects continue to exist after her perception of them is interrupted, and secondly, that they are underneath the cloth. This would appear to reflect an impeccable notion of object permanence—but that's not quite the case yet. After hiding the object a couple of times under the same covering we now change the hiding place and put the object under a different cloth, all this under the baby's attentive gaze. Surprisingly, she will turn to the original cloth, raise it, and look as if she expected to find the object there! Again, this is not a mere coincidence: babies all around the world commit this surprising error at around this age, of searching for an object where they found it before, not where they have seen it placed last. This is such a typical and robust finding that it has come to be known as the "typical stage-4 error" (in reference to the Piagetian stage in which it occurs) or the A-B error, where A and B designate the two alternative locations (Bremner, 2001).

This finding reveals that infants still have a lot to learn about the way in which the space is organized and how objects exist in it. Their typical error is, on the one hand, a good error: they clearly are able to remember where objects used to be or anticipate that objects will be found beneath or behind another object. On the other hand, this extended knowledge betrays them because they cannot handle it well as they cannot integrate it with new pieces of information. In this case, they fail to update the cue of the whereabouts of the disappeared object; for some reason the old cue wins out and they search in the wrong place. Piaget thought that this illustrates well the practical and action-bound nature of sensorimotor knowledge. Visual information about where the object is remains subordinated to the practical, action-related knowledge of how it was retrieved previously, so there is a failure in coordinating the information in an adaptive way.

At 12 to 18 months, infants appear to overcome this limitation and stop committing the A-B error. They are no longer fooled by the change in location: they always search for the object in the place in which they have seen it disappear last time. They apparently have no problem updating their sensorimotor knowledge and making their way through the world of permanent, but not always visible objects. But Piaget discovered that one crucial piece was still missing from the child's understanding of objects. If, instead of putting the object under the cloth in full view of the child, the experimenter closed his hand on the object, then put the hand under the cloth, left the object there, and took the hand out, then the child would examine the hand of the experimenter and remain puzzled by not discovering the object there. At no point did the child look for the object under the cloth. He was apparently unable to *infer* or *imagine* that the object must have been left under the cloth. At this stage of growth infants can only understand events that are fully or partially perceivable by them. Once an event occurs completely out of their sight, they, apparently, are at a loss. According to Piaget, their intelligence is still linked to sensorimotor representations that depend upon direct perception: they are not yet able to use independent *symbolic* representations.

From 18 to 24 months the baby begins to work out what happens in the invisible displacement test: she is now able to realize that the object must have been left under the cloth. Children have started to use symbolic representations and they can now figure out what has happened outside their perception. This remarkable developmental sequence, Piaget believed, was a direct reflection of the growing complexity of babies' practical understanding of the world of objects.

Gorilla Babies, Monkey Babies, and Object Permanence

It took almost 40 years for primatologists to realize the potential of Piaget's work in relation to their own (Jolly, 1972; Parker, 1977). What they found when they decided to compare human infants with other primate infants was an essential similarity in the general pattern of sensorimotor development, as if Piaget had described the ontogeny of practical intelligence not only for humans, but for primates in general.

One of the earliest studies of nonhuman primates from a Piagetian point of view was Margaret Redshaw's (1978) work with gorilla babies, using a set of standard developmental tests based upon Piaget's ideas. She found that gorillas followed very similar steps in the development of their ability to do things with objects, for example, in their ability to retrieve objects when they disappear from sight. When tested with a battery of Piagetian object-permanence tasks, baby gorillas go exactly through the same steps as human children in exactly the same order, although at a slightly accelerated rate. For example, gorilla babies started to be able to retrieve covered objects when they were 5 months old, whereas human babies—whom Redshaw herself tested as a comparison group—did so at 8 months; the gorillas stopped making the typical A-B error at 8 months, whereas the human babies overcame this at 10 months. Gorillas understood very simple invisible displacements for the first time at 9 months; humans at 10 months.*

But beyond these slight differences in timing, what is extraordinary is that exactly the same sequence of development of object retrieval occurs in two different primate species.

Similar studies with other monkey and ape species (chimpanzees, orangutans, capuchin and rhesus monkeys, among others; see Tomasello and Call, 1997; Doré and Dumas, 1987; and Parker and

---

* The ages reported by Redshaw for human babies are lower than Piaget's. Some landmarks of sensorimotor intelligence do appear to develop on the average slightly earlier than he found, but even with his three children he found considerable individual variation in the rate of development.

McKinney, 1999, for detailed reviews) have confirmed that the sequence of development of object permanence is exactly the same in all primates. All species initially fail to search for an object when it is completely covered; later in their development, when they start passing this test, they all commit the typical A-B error of searching in the old place when the hiding place is changed; and when they overcome this, they are still unable to understand invisible displacements. What is different is how soon they pass through these stages. Chimpanzees and orangutans, like gorillas, tend to reach stages slightly earlier than the average human infant. Monkeys, in contrast, are decidedly much quicker than either humans or apes; they show the ability to retrieve hidden objects for the first time at around 1 to 2 months of age, whereas gorillas and chimpanzees do so at around 7 months, and human infants at around 8 to 9 months. Cats and dogs achieve this skill in a record 2 weeks! Monkeys, therefore, show the same "four-times-faster" advantage we already observed in the earlier discussion of perceptual development.

All apes and monkeys studied so far reach at least stage 5 level of object permanence. Chimpanzees and orangutans, like gorillas, understand invisible displacements too, completing the whole sequence as described in human babies. But the monkey species tested so far have mostly failed to show a systematic understanding of invisible displacements* and their understanding of object permanence seems to remain at a lower level of complexity than that of apes and humans.

When animals other than primates (notably cats and dogs) were tested with adapted versions of object permanence tasks (they were not required to grab objects and care was taken to avoid olfactory cues), they were found to develop like monkeys, with one potentially crucial difference.** Cats and dogs that reach stage 4 of object

---

* Only one capuchin monkey has been reported to pass a stringent test of object permanence (Schino et al., 1990). Some authors remain unconvinced that this is conclusive (Doré and Goulet, 1998).

** Again there is some controversy on this score. Some authors have claimed to have found a degree of invisible displacement understanding in dogs, but others doubt the stringency of the testing procedures used (Doré and Goulet, 1998).

permanence (searching for completely hidden objects) do not commit the typical A-B searching error, which is one of the defining features of this stage (Doré and Goulet, 1998). It is as if they reached stages 4 and 5 of object permanence at the same time!

This developmental anomaly in relation to the typical primate pattern suggests that the representational basis for dog and cat performances might be different from that of primates. Careful tests reveal that, in dealing with visible displacements of objects, cats and dogs attend to the relative position of the hidden object in space, but not to the identity of the container or the screen that is hiding them. Thus, if the containers are moved sideways after the object has been hidden, so that an empty container now occupies the place where the container with the target stood before, typically cats and dogs look for the target in the empty container (Doré and Goulet, 1998). This could be an indication that rather than establish the relationship of occlusion between the two objects ("the target is *inside* the green cup"), cats and dogs represent only a relationship of spatial location ("the target is *there*").

Finding hidden objects may be such a pervasive function for successful adaptation in nature (finding food, keeping track of prey, predators, or conspecifics) that it may have been implemented by different neural systems during evolution, each system having different properties. Indeed, Etienne (1976) has described object-permanence algorithms in insects, which remain oriented for a few seconds, keeping still, in the direction where a potential prey has disappeared (a way of maximizing the probability of finding the potential prey again); if after that period the "object" has not reappeared, a program of spatial reorientation is activated and the insect turns around, as if "forgetting" about the lost target and looking for new potential prey. Chickens, by contrast, appear to depend upon trial-and-error associative learning to deal effectively with disappearing pieces of food (Etienne, 1976).

Primates may have evolved a more complex representational system for dealing with object location through integrating different subsystems of object representation (remember our discussion of Carey and Xu's [2001] ideas in Chapter 2). The typical A-B location error could be an unavoidable step in the developmental path of this more complex system of object representation. Object-permanence tasks, then, may be tapping a distinctive aspect of primate cognition—a set of abilities to deal with objects in a primate-specific way.* The top skill of this primate view of objects would be the understanding of unseen changes in object location, which Piaget found in the last stage of sensorimotor development and which, in his view, involved some sort of ability for explicit symbolic representation.

The Invisible Life of Objects

Current evidence suggests that the crowning achievement of object understanding described above may develop fully only in the ape and human lineage. Some controversy continues regarding the ability to understand invisible object displacements in monkeys.

Fillion and colleagues (1996) created a series of imaginative tasks to reassess the understanding of invisible displacements in monkeys and humans. Their participants were trained to use a computer game in which they had to intercept with a cursor targets moving on the screen. Monkeys and humans had no problem learning to do this. The invisible displacement tests consisted, first, of trials in which an area of the monitor appeared as an opaque shield behind which the moving target could disappear during a part of its trajectory. From the beginning, monkeys were capable of moving the cursor toward the point at which the target should reappear after traversing the shield (which was impenetrable for the cursor). This shows that they were able to somehow calculate or extrapolate the invisible part of the displacement of the target.

In a "laser-gun" version of the game (as the new task was colorfully explained to the human participants), a piece of opaque card-

---

* Some birds have been shown to possess complex notions of object permanence (Pepperberg, 1999). This may or may not be supported by representations similar to those of primates. The bird brain is so different from the primate brain that birds' object-permanence representations (or, more interestingly, the ways in which these representations are supported) are most probably different.

board was placed over part of the monitor screen, so that the missiles shot by the subjects could hit the target when it was out of sight. Would the subjects (monkeys and humans) take this opportunity or would they only shoot when the target was visible? Both humans and monkeys shot at the invisible target when it moved behind the piece of cardboard. The authors concluded that their subjects, both humans and monkeys, were representing the invisible displacement of the object, and they did so from the beginning of testing, as if this were a natural capacity, not a learned skill.

Does this finding contradict the apparent inability of rhesus monkeys to understand the invisible displacement of an object in the standard Piagetian task? A closer look at each type of task suggests that in fact they involve very different kinds of invisible displacements. The typical Piagetian test is administered in two versions. In one, the experimenter closes his hand upon a small object, then moves the hand underneath a cloth, leaves the object there, and takes the hand out. The movement of the object under the cloth is completely invisible *from the beginning*, and to solve this task it will not help to represent the precise trajectory followed by the object. What a successful subject has to do is to figure out the invisible *change of location* rather than the invisible *trajectory* of the object.

The second procedure for the Piagetian task is even more telling. A small box lies hidden under the cloth; the experimenter takes the object under the cloth as the subject looks on and then hides it, out of sight, in the box under the cloth. When the subject lifts the cloth in search of the object, he finds the box instead: he has to figure out that the object *must* have been placed in the box, independently of the trajectory or the way in which it was put there.

What is at stake in the Piagetian invisible displacement tasks is not the ability to represent a given invisible trajectory, but the ability to *infer* an unseen past event (where the target object must have been placed) on the basis of the present available evidence, and the ability to reorganize one's search strategy accordingly. In contrast, the object-tracking tasks of Fillion and colleagues just require the continuation of an ongoing tracking, something similar to representing an object that is partially occluded (which human infants do at around 5 to 6 months of age even with a manual search task). This is cognitively very different from having to activate a representation of a completely absent object without any direct cue—and inferring its whereabouts. The merit of Fillion and colleagues' studies is to call attention to the misleading label of "invisible displacement" for the Piagetian task: the essence of this task is not an unseen movement in itself, but the invisibility of the object-placement event and the need to represent it by inference.

Indeed, Doré and Goulet (1998) suggest that the crucial demand of these displacement tasks might be the ability to *explicitly* represent the object *behind* a screen. That is, organisms that systematically pass the simpler visible displacement tasks (stage 5 of object permanence) may be retrieving hidden objects under the guidance of procedural representations ("the object will appear behind this screen") in which information about the position of the object remains implicitly embedded in a search procedure, rather than being freely available as a separate piece of information. The passage from stage 5 to stage 6 of object permanence could therefore signal the emergence of more explicit ways of representing objects and events. In Piagetian theory, this is the culminating achievement of sensorimotor intelligence, but it is at the same time the beginning of a new developmental avenue for representing the world of objects, at least for human children. We will discuss later to what extent nonhuman primates reach higher forms of Piagetian intelligence beyond the sensorimotor level. For the moment, it suffices to conclude that primates may have a special way of representing the whereabouts of objects, and among primates apes may eventually use more explicit and flexible representations of object location that are less dependent upon direct perception and impending action.

All the same, monkeys do demonstrate some understanding of the invisible life of objects. Rhesus macaques, for instance, can understand the accumulation of objects behind a screen when they are moved one by one. They can translate several visible displacements into the representation of an invisible collection of objects, and they can guide their search behaviors with such representations (see previous chapter). Southgate and Gómez (2003) have found some preliminary evidence of rhesus monkeys' understanding of certain classes of invisible displacement. In one demonstration we turned one cup over another so that the contents of the first fell into the second. Some macaques searched correctly in the second cup, although the target was never seen falling into the lower cup. Unlike the traditional Piagetian tasks, however, here there is a direct cue to the whereabouts of the target—the overturning of the cup and the consequent activation of a mechanical force to which monkeys appear to be specially sensitive—gravity. In fact, monkeys (and children) are so sensitive to gravity that they can overestimate its influence, disregarding other physical variables.

For example, Hauser (2001) found that a *gravity bias* may overcome rhesus monkeys' understanding of the solidity of objects. The monkeys were shown a small table, then a screen was placed in front of the table and a piece of food was dropped, so that the monkeys could see that it started to fall behind the screen. The screen was then withdrawn and the monkeys were allowed to search for the food. Most of them looked first on the floor in the area *under* the table, although logically the food would have dropped and stayed *on* the table. Interestingly, if in a similar setting the food is thrown rolling on a horizontal plane, the monkeys never look for it beyond a solid barrier. This suggests that the misunderstanding applies only to events in which objects fall by the force of gravity.

A similar gravity bias has been found in adult tamarins, rhesus monkeys, and human children through other experimental tasks (Hood et al. 1999; Southgate and Gómez, 2003). In children the gravity bias persists until relatively late in their development, but they overcome it at around 3 to 4 years of age (Hood, 1995). Monkeys, in contrast, appear to retain it all their life. Does this mean that the gravity bias is a permanent feature of the nonhuman primate mind (at least the monkey mind, as we don't have yet any data about how apes might behave in this test)?

All in all, according to the evidence we have discussed so far, object-permanence tasks might appear to provide an accurate reflection of the growth of representational complexity in the primate mind. But some scholars disagree.

Knowing before Acting: Post-Piagetian Object Studies

The idea that Piaget may have been wrong in linking action and knowledge (in assuming, for example, that successful object retrieval reflects a more accurate object knowledge) has been central to developmental psychology in the last decades (Bremner, 2001). When one tests very young babies with purely perceptual tasks, in which they just have to watch what happens to objects, they appear to know more about object permanence than they can show with their hands. For example, the central milestone of object permanence—realizing that an object continues to exist when covered by a screen—has been found in human babies at around 4 to 5 months (or even earlier) in a variant of Piaget's experiment; instead of measuring their ability to retrieve a hidden object manually, we just measure their reaction when someone else lifts the screen where the object was hidden and the object (surreptitiously withdrawn) fails to reappear. If four or five-month-old babies were really unable to represent a hidden object, they should not be surprised at all. However, they systematically look for longer (are surprised) at puzzling displays in which objects hidden behind a screen fail to reappear or, more complexly, other objects freely move through the space where the hidden object should be (Baillargeon et al., 1986; Bremner, 2001). They appear to *know* that covered objects continue to exist, although they are as yet unable to retrieve them.

We don't know yet if very young monkeys and apes show a similar gap between perception and action in object permanence. We do know that *adult* rhesus monkeys may show such a looking/searching dissociation in object retrieval tasks involving gravity (Santos and Hauser, 2002). These are adult monkeys, and therefore their perception/action gap would not be a developmental transition, but a permanent feature of their cognition. Even so, this suggests that perception/action dissociations are not exclusively human, but a cognitive phenomenon that should be understood in an evolutionary framework (Hauser, in press). The developmental findings with human babies strongly suggest that their sense of objects might be more independent of action than Piaget thought, and much more precocious. One possibility is that this knowledge is innate. Evolution might have provided humans and other primates with a series of mental tools and representations such as object permanence to complement their anatomical adaptations for object manipulation. Sensorimotor development would consist of activating and deploying these latent representations and providing their specific contents (the sort of objects that each individual encounters in its environment), but not of creating the basic cognitive notions themselves.

But, if this were the case, why do infants fail to use their precocious knowledge of object permanence until 8 to 9 months of age (in the case of humans) and, even then, why they commit such serious mistakes as the A-B error, acting as if they did not know the whereabouts of objects? A straightforward explanation would be that infants lack the necessary motor skills to implement their knowledge: they might know where the object is, but they don't know how to retrieve it. A merit of the motor immaturity hypothesis is that it could explain why monkeys demonstrate object permanence much earlier than apes or humans. Their motor development rate is quicker, and thus they can make use of their innate knowledge much earlier. Unfortunately, perceptual tests of object permanence have not been carried out with infant monkeys and apes, so we don't know if they would show a similar mismatch between watching and acting in their own developmental time scale.

The inability of young babies to retrieve hidden objects does not appear to be a simple matter of motor clumsiness, however. Babies of about 6 to 7 months of age lift a transparent cup in order to regain possession of a toy. But when an identical, but opaque cup is used to cover the toy, then they do not go ahead with the same retrieval action that they so easily performed with the transparent cup (Bower, 1974). This shows that the baby's failure cannot simply be a matter of lack of motor skill.

A more interesting hypothesis is that what babies have to develop is the ability to elaborate and carry out a plan of action—an executive ability. Perhaps seven-month-olds cannot combine their knowledge that the toy is under a particular cup with their skill of lifting a cup in order to get the toy. Indeed, when the toy is covered by an opaque cup, they have to keep in mind the location of the toy while they put together and execute their plan of action. This might prove to be too demanding for their emerging planning abilities; conversely, when the toy is visible under a transparent cup, its location can be kept *in the eye*, not in the mind, and this may free the brain to work on planning the appropriate retrieval action.

It is therefore likely that the "working memory" of seven-month-old babies is not powerful enough to handle all the pieces at the same time, at least not when the crucial one—the whereabouts of the object—has to be handled as a mental representation.

Human Babies, Rhesus Babies, and Object Retrieval

Adele Diamond (1990a, 1991) discovered that both human and rhesus monkey infants' performance on A-B tasks is affected by the delay between the hiding of the object and the start of the search. When infants are allowed to search as soon as the object disappears (or if they remain oriented toward the correct screen before starting their search), they are much more likely to search correctly. Once they have started to solve the task with, let's say, 4 seconds of delay, it is enough to increase the delay to, say, 6 seconds to make them commit the error again. The amount of delay infants can tolerate increases with age in humans and rhesus monkeys alike, but in monkeys this development occurs in their own, faster developmental time scale. In rhesus, changes in the delays they can tolerate occur almost from one day to another, whereas in humans they occur almost from one week to another. We may speculate that some fundamental capacity for "keeping in mind" the representation of the new location matures at different rates in each species.

Yet the A-B error cannot simply be a matter of weak short-term memory. If longer delays caused babies to forget where the object was, they should be searching randomly. But the essence of the A-B error is that the infants systematically look in the place where the object was found *before*. This is a paradoxical combination of bad shorter-term memory and excellent longer-term memory!*

Diamond (1990a, 1991) proposed that there was a second crucial cognitive factor at work—the inability to *inhibit* prepotent or dominant responses. The idea is that in the A-B task, looking in location A has just been reinforced by the discovery of the desired object and has therefore become specially salient in the mind of the baby. When tested at the critical delay, infants cannot keep in mind the new location of the object, and crucially they cannot inhibit the repetition of their previously successful action of searching in A. Moreover, Diamond suggests that at least in some cases the infants who search in A might in fact remember that the object is actually in B, but they simply cannot prevent themselves from executing the dominant action of looking in A. Indeed, she observed a few infants clearly looking at B while their hands went to A! Infants may have a transitory conflict between knowledge and action, one in which action—far from being the source of knowledge, as Piaget argued—would actually be interfering with it.

Diamond suggests, therefore, that overcoming the typical A-B error does not reflect the development of object knowledge, but the development of an executive ability to inhibit inappropriate prepotent responses.

Development as the Mastery of Inhibition: The Box Task

Diamond (1990b) further investigated the importance of inhibition in the development of primate actions with a simpler task inspired by another discovery of Piaget's (1937). Infants over 4 to 5 months of age have no problem reaching for objects they can see in full view. Sometimes, though, if one places the object they are interested in on top of another object, babies may behave as if the top object had suddenly disappeared. Although the target object is still in full view, they reach toward the other object or simply do not

---

* Random searches can occur with longer delays (see Bremner, 2001).

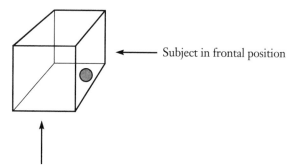

Subject in lateral position

Figure 3.2. The transparent box task (Diamond, 1990): babies have to retrieve the object from inside the box. Only one side is open. Babies can be placed right in front of the opening or to one side. The object's position also varies: it can be close to the opening or deeper inside the box.

reach at all. Piaget's interpretation was that the object notion at that age was still too fragile: infants did not understand that two objects may be contiguous in space without constituting a single entity and got confused.* Diamond's interpretation, however, is that infants know only too well that the target object is there on top of the other, but they cannot reach with enough precision to grasp it without accidentally touching the other object, and, when this happens, they cannot inhibit a reflex reaction of grasping the wrong object or withdrawing the hand in response to the unexpected collision. Again, the idea is that there is not a cognitive deficit in the babies' representation of objects, but a problem of coordination and inhibitory motor control.

For evidence to support this view, Diamond studied the development of the ability to take an object from inside a transparent box (figure 3.2) in human and rhesus monkey babies. She found a fascinating series of intricate developmental steps for dealing with this apparently easy task.

---

* Some evidence for this interpretation has been found in the experiments of Carey and Xu (2001) discussed in the previous chapter.

Initially (at 5 to 6 months), human babies can take the toy only if it is partially outside the transparent box, but if it is inside, they fail to do so even if the opening is just in front of them—their clumsiness makes them hit the edges of the opening and this makes them interrupt their search. Later (at 6.5 months), babies can retrieve the toy from inside the box whenever they happen to be looking at it straight through the opening. Their problem is that when they reach, they follow their line of gaze directly; as a result, if they are looking at the object through one of the transparent walls of the box, they try to reach directly through the wall and hit their hands repeatedly. They are unable to maneuver their hands around the wall toward the opening of the box.

Later on (at 7.5 months) babies continue to reach following their direct line of gaze, but they solve the transparent wall problem by bending their head and body forward toward the aperture, so that they can look at the object directly through it and then reach successfully. One month later (at 8.5 months), infants bend and look through the opening, but then return to their original position and reach correctly through the opening while looking through the transparent wall. However, if the opening is placed sideward at an angle of 90 degrees in relation to the babies (see figure 3.2), they reach only while bending again, this time sideways, to look through the opening. The infant leans on the same-side hand and reaches with the other hand, in what Diamond called the "awkward reach" strategy.

At 9.5 months, babies have mastered the problem when the opening is in front of them: they can now reach successfully without having to look first through the aperture. But if the opening is to one side, they have to look first through it, but then they sit straight again, and reach with their hand while looking through the transparent front wall (no more awkward reaches).

Finally, at 11 to 12 months, babies can control their reaching without having to look directly through the opening at any time. Their indirect visual information is now enough to guide their manual search.

Diamond found essentially the same developmental sequence in rhesus monkeys when she confronted them with the transparent box task, but in a "condensed" version. Not only did rhesus infants progress more quickly (from 1.5 to 4 months of age), but they also concentrated the human stages into three super-stages. They never went through the first human phase of retrieving the target only if it was partially outside the box; from the beginning monkeys were capable of retrieving the target even from slightly inside the box. Also from the beginning, they were able to move around the box to look and reach for the food through the available openings. This was crucial for their success, because initially they showed the same limitation found in human infants of reaching only along their direct line of sight. Sometimes, in their attempts to retrieve the food they accidentally pushed the food very deep inside the box. Then, like human babies, monkeys would try to retrieve it through the nearest transparent wall, unable to resist the appeal of the visible target. When monkeys overcame this problem, they went through a phase of "awkward reaching" like that of human infants, before achieving sufficient control of reaching through "indirect" vision.

Hence the performance of monkey babies was comparable to that of human babies, though their sensorimotor organization allowed them to succeed from the very beginning of their reaching careers—provided the target was not too close to a transparent wall.

Diamond's interpretation of these results is, again, that what human and rhesus babies develop is not a better understanding of objects, but a better ability to control voluntary hand movements in relation to environmental obstacles, especially a better ability to inhibit reaching in response to direct stimulation.

Since the ability to inhibit direct reaching into the box appears more or less at the same time as babies become able to overcome their errors in the A-B task—toward 12 months of age in humans, toward 4 to 5 months in rhesus—Diamond (1990b) concluded that a fundamental inhibitory ability must be developing in the infant brain by a process of maturation that follows different rhythms in different species. She suggests that this fundamental development occurs in a particular region of the prefrontal cortex, because rhesus monkeys who are lesioned in that area never overcome the typical A-B error and systematically fail indirect reaching tasks (Diamond, 1991).

Inhibition and Representational Development

It is tempting to conclude from this remarkable piece of research that Diamond is right in suggesting that the correct object representations are available in the minds of primate infants from very early, but they lack the executive machinery necessary to make good use of these representations. This would fit well with the finding that human babies under 5 months of age show signs of understanding object permanence if their testing involves looking instead of reaching.

An alternative interpretation is that the development of executive abilities is in fact the development of the capacity to control behavior with increasingly complex *representations* and, therefore, is based upon genuine changes in the way infants understand the world. Think, for example, of the transparent box task: success requires that the information that is visually available be *re-presented* in a more functional way. To begin with, primate infants develop the ability to change their view of the problem by changing the position of their body, so that they can see the target directly in their line of reach; here we have a literal sensorimotor *re-presentation* of the relevant information. Later on, infants acquire their new representation of the situation by looking through the side opening, but instead of reaching immediately, they keep this representation in mind while returning to their original position, from which they finally execute the action. Eventually, they can form the correct representation of the situation without having to look directly through the target opening. These representations are described as "sensorimotor" in that they represent the object from the point of view of the action to be performed.

The A-B and the transparent box tasks illustrate the importance of *representing* information for one's practical purposes even when this information is apparently given, whether openly present in the environment or covertly present in the subject's mind. Indeed, skills such as inhibiting actions or putting together and keeping in mind pieces of information (working memory) must play a fundamental role in allowing infants to achieve better adapted plans of action. In this sense they are some of the cognitive tools by means of which more complex object representations are attained in development. The point is that motor, memory, and inhibitory development cannot occur without change in the way in which infant primates see the world.

This interpretation is reinforced by a recent experiment by Hauser (1999) using the transparent box task with tamarin monkeys. He found that even if his monkeys were adults, they initially engaged in the sort of direct reaching against the transparent wall that Diamond described as characteristic of immature brains. A possible interpretation would be that the inhibitory abilities necessary to solve this task are a conquest of the Old-World primate brain. This interpretation might appear to be confirmed by the fact that the tamarins did well when an opaque box was used, which, according to Diamond's original idea, removes the need for inhibition. But Hauser found that after their experience with the opaque box, the tamarins became able to solve the problem when they confronted the transparent box again. If their brains were incapable of direct-reach inhibition, they should have continued to fail with the transparent box. Hauser suggests that the tamarins' initial problem was a lack of understanding of the nature of plexiglas—which after all is quite an unnatural material. The experience with opaque boxes helped the tamarins acquire a more correct understanding (*representation*) of the plexiglas box, which eventually led to a solution of the problem. In fact, tamarins also found it easier to solve tasks with transparent boxes with a pattern of lines on their walls, which could help them understand the solid nature of the plexiglas.

In sum, although looking-time experiments and inhibition and working-memory studies may reveal early forms of object knowledge in young babies, they are not incompatible with the idea that performance in object-permanence tasks reflects the growth of object understanding. Rather, the growth of working memory, in-hibition, and the combination of separate pieces of information may be tools for carving more complex, better-integrated represen-tations of objects. Whatever the ultimate explanation of the A-B error (and a final explanation must be able to integrate a complex body of apparently inconsistent findings; Bremner, 2001; Bogartz et al., 2000), it appears that, to some extent as Piaget originally sug-gested, the phenomenon has to do with the development of a more complex and coordinated way of representing objects in relation to space, action, and other objects. Thanks to comparative research, we know that this way of representing objects may be a primate cognitive universal that in some respects may differ from the way in which other mammals represent objects; and that among primates some, like apes and humans, may achieve more elaborate levels of object representation.

Practical Intelligence: Solving Problems with Objects

Object permanence is only one aspect of Piaget's description of sensorimotor development, but one in which several crucial fea-tures of practical intelligence are evident—among them its nature as a problem-solving device. Sensorimotor intelligence is an adap-tive system with the ability to generate appropriate responses to challenges in the environment without having to go through the relatively slow process of blind trial-and-error and associative learning. Tracing the whereabouts of objects is just one kind of practical problem.

When Piagetian observations with nonhuman primates were car-ried out in areas other than object permanence, it emerged that in general they followed Piaget's developmental schedule, but again at very different rates and extents. Crucially, the developmental rates and extents were not necessarily the same within each domain of practical intelligence even for the same species. The sensorimotor development of human infants, far from being a golden norm of what any system of practical intelligence should be, is just one par-ticular case, much as the human body, far from being the golden standard for primate bodies, is just one of the many shapes within the primate pattern.

For example, in her study with gorilla and human babies, Redshaw (1978) found that the very act of grasping objects (which, as we saw in the previous section, is far from straightforward behavior) is seen in gorillas at 3 months, whereas in human babies it happens at 5.5 months. More complex acts like pulling a support or a string to get an attached object within reach occur at 6 months in gorillas, and at 8.5 months in humans. A particularly striking difference between gorillas and humans occurs in their ability to approach distant objects, for example, crawling to a distant toy in order to get hold of it. Gorilla babies did this as early as in their fourth month of life, whereas human babies did so only at around 10 months of age. Macaques can clumsily crawl toward an object as early as at 1 to 2 weeks of life (Zimmerman and Torrey, 1965).

If, in a more challenging situation, the movement toward the target requires a detour around some obstacle (for example, avoiding a chair that is interposed between the baby and a toy), gorillas performed the roundabout walk at 8 months or earlier, whereas human babies were successful only at around 12 months.

In fact, in the sensorimotor scales used by Redshaw, human babies developed only one item faster than gorillas—the use of a stick to obtain an object out of reach. Human babies started to use the stick at 12 months of age (roughly the same age at which they could get around obstacles); in contrast, only one of the four gorillas showed any ability to use sticks at all during the period of study, and that was at 26 months of age, more than one year later than human babies!

Other studies (Parker and MacKinney, 1999) confirm that gorillas and other great apes are late in using sticks in comparison with human babies. In my own longitudinal study of the development of young gorillas in a zoo nursery, the earliest appearance of stick use as a hand extension was recorded at around 22 months of age and in very simple tasks, such as picking up yogurt from a cup (Gómez, 1992). In most monkey species, stick and other forms of tool use may remain completely absent from their repertoire throughout their lives. In the rare cases when stick use has been described in monkeys, it is generally in adult individuals. Capuchin monkeys may be the exception, in that they show some stick use as early as at 18 months of age (see Parker and MacKinney [1999] for this and other possible instances of early tool use in monkeys).

Nonetheless young gorillas are able to use tools in a different way at almost exactly the same age as the human infants that Renshaw studied used sticks (10 to 12 months). At that age one of the subjects of our longitudinal study, a female gorilla called Muni, was able to move boxes and other objects such as broomsticks to particular places in order to use them for climbing and reaching elevated targets. She used boxes as a stool and broomsticks as a ladder or climbing pole. For instance, when trying to open a latch fixed on the higher part of a door, she would go in search of a broom, carry it with her to the door, lean it against the door frame, and then climb up the broom until she could reach the latch (Gómez, 1999).

A broom is a stick (longer and probably more difficult to handle than the shorter sticks used to reach distant things), but instead of using it as an extension of her hands to manipulate the target, the young gorilla uses it as a way of extending her locomotor reach (figure 3.3). A human baby would find it difficult or impossible to use a broom in a similar way even much later in her development, given her own sensorimotor constraints. Are these constraints purely physical (lack of the necessary strength for moving boxes and the skills for climbing up poles) or are they also cognitive—a consequence of a different way of thinking about practical problems? Perhaps human babies do not think of this kind of practical solution until much later in their development, as gorillas, in turn, don't think of using sticks as hand extensions until later.

Is the use of boxes and poles to extend locomotion simpler than the use of sticks as hand extensions, and therefore is human practical intelligence more sophisticated from very early on? Raking an object with a stick requires placing the tool's end in a particular relation to the target, and then dragging in while keeping the two in contact in that position. Climbing on a box or up a pole may seem

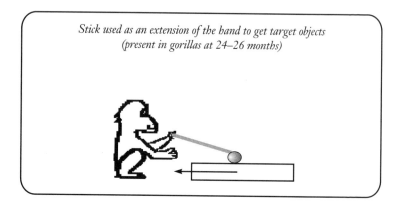

Stick used as an extension of the hand to get target objects
(present in gorillas at 24–26 months)

Stick used as an extension of the body to reach target objects
(present in gorillas at 10–12 months)

Figure 3.3. Gorillas use tools to extend their body reach (climb) (10–12 months) before using tools to extend their hand reach (24–26 months), whereas human infants do it the other way around.

to be in itself a less precise action, but climbing is only the final part of the solution. The gorilla first had to find the box or pole (sometimes in a different room), then move them to the target area and, more importantly, place them in the right location—in the case of the pole leaning against the door frame, place it in a particular position so that it stood firmly in place while she climbed up. These actions, therefore, may not be cognitively less demanding than the use of a stick to drag an object toward oneself. If anything, actions like using a stick to pick up yogurt from a cup would appear to be cognitively less complex, yet they appeared much later in our gorillas.

A possible explanation is that the early locomotor maturity of gorillas, combined with other features such as their greater physical strength and their feet with opposable thumbs, takes them along a somewhat different pathway of sensorimotor development when compared with human babies. Shortly after they have started to grasp and explore objects (at around 3 to 4 months), gorillas are able to approach them by walking or climbing. At around 8 months of age, they can engage in complex detour walks or detour climbs in order to reach objects of interest—provided a detour route is already available. At around 12 months, gorillas become capable of creating roundabout "bridges" by arranging objects in appropriate positions.

Gorillas' sensorimotor way of representing the world appears to be initially organized around the powerful attractor of goal-directed locomotion. Locomotion—both horizontal and vertical—is a dominant component of the sensorimotor world of ape and monkey infants from very early on. This dominance is relative and may be transitory—tool use as an extension of the hand eventually emerges in apes as well—but it may have important consequences in the way in which apes, monkeys, and humans get to represent some aspects of the world of objects during their development. For one thing, using tools as a hand extension requires an explicit, external projection of an otherwise straightforward action (reaching). This sort of projection is among the most difficult demands apes find in a problem-solving situation. For example, once they are able to use a stick to bring an object into reach, chimpanzees find it extremely difficult to solve the problem if an obstacle lies in the way of the object, such that they must initially push the object away in a detour trajectory instead of directly pulling it in (Köhler, 1927; Guillaume and Meyerson, 1930).

The different ways in which human and gorilla babies initially use stick-like things is a good example of how one category of objects can be known in different ways by different sensorimotor systems. Human babies are directed toward the use of tools as hand extensions, whereas gorillas may be initially more directed toward using objects as props to extend locomotion. These constraints or orientations need not be absolute determinations—in time both ape and human youngsters become capable of both kinds of tool use, although perhaps their underlying representations have been decisively affected by their developmental history.

There is a final developmental puzzle in relation to the solving of practical problems by means of tool use. Gorillas have almost never been observed using tools (either as hand extensions or as supports for extended locomotion) in the wild. As far as we know, gorillas develop tool use only in captivity. Something similar happens with other apes and the few monkey species that have been observed using tools.* Chimpanzees (and some orangutans; see van Schaik et al., 2003) appear to be the only nonhuman primates that routinely use tools in the wild. This discrepancy between what in more technical terminology we would call sensorimotor "phenotypes" of wild and captive apes constitutes an interesting problem for developmental and evolutionary cognitive science to which we will return later in the book.

Discovering How to Do Things with Objects: Primate Exploration and Investigation

Because primates learn to use objects to solve problems, it is tempting to think that this problem-solving power is the fundamental design feature of primate practical intelligence. It is again to the credit of Jean Piaget (1936) to have noted and systematically described another aspect of intelligent sensorimotor systems that tends to be easily overlooked—their ability to generate actions with

---

* With the possible exception of capuchin monkeys.

objects outside problem-solving contexts, in a playful or exploratory mode. Not only do primates like to watch and touch things for their own sake, but they are also interested in manipulating them outside problem-solving situations.

Sue Parker, another early Piagetian student of primates, discovered an interesting difference between rhesus macaques and human babies. When young rhesus monkeys start manipulating objects, they do so in single-shot style: they will hit a wheel in their enclosure or a branch in the wild, provoke an effect, and that's it (Parker, 1977). In contrast, human babies from around 4 to 5 months of age show considerable interest in the effects their actions provoke on objects, so much so that they usually repeat the actions several times while watching those effects intently. Piaget called this pattern of repeated actions "secondary *circular* reactions"; Parker called her macaques' actions "secondary *linear* reactions." Superficially, they may look very much the same—doing something to an object to provoke an effect—but the repetition and observation of the actions may have consequences regarding what representations young primates acquire about objects and actions. Thanks to those circular repetitions, human babies might develop more detailed representations of the sort of effects their actions have upon objects and how the two are connected. Moreover, Piaget noted that in the course of those repetitions babies frequently ended up provoking new effects by chance. For example, while hitting toys against the ground, a baby may make a rubber toy emit a curious sound by accidentally squeezing it; this may lead him to repeat his squeezing action, eventually incorporating it into his repertoire of "things one can do with objects." Thus, circular reactions may be an important mechanism not only for learning about existing actions and objects, but also for discovering new types of actions (Parker, 1993).

This may sound like what the behaviorists called operant learning by blind trial and error—keeping in one's repertoire actions that by chance provoke rewarding effects. Note, however, that the baby's reward is not food or comfort or praise by adults (although the latter may occasionally be obtained too): the execution of the actions themselves and the contemplation of their consequences upon the objects are rewarding enough for young human babies. Curiosity or, in more technical terms, the intrinsic motivation of actions is an important characteristic of practical intelligence. And secondary circular reactions are only the beginning of it.

According to Piaget, toward 8 to 12 months of age infants engage in systematic explorations of what can be done with an object by applying to it a selection of their schemas of action one after another (hitting, biting, squeezing, and so forth). At 12 to 18 months of age they not only try different known schemas upon new objects, but also introduce purposeful modifications of their known actions, as if trying to challenge the new object in new ways. Piaget described this as performing little practical experiments; hence babies may systematically drop an object from different heights or throw it with different force as if trying to observe how variations in action produce variations in the object's reaction. Also typical of this age group is the production of elaborate combinations of objects: putting objects one into another, or one on top of the other; pushing one object with another, and more. Piaget called these "tertiary circular reactions"—a sort of playful or exploratory counterpart of tool use.

Few researchers have explored this side of sensorimotor intelligence in nonhuman primates (as indeed few developmentalists have replicated or extended Piaget's early observations with human infants). The results of some of the early studies with primates suggested that in the area of spontaneous object exploration, monkeys and apes may lag well behind human babies—complex object manipulation outside a problem-solving context may be specific to humans (Vauclair, 1996). Indeed, as Parker pointed out, rhesus monkeys fail to show even simple secondary circular actions—they just have linear actions. Moreover, they may execute their single-shot actions upon objects and pay little attention to the consequences, as if they were more interested in the action itself and perhaps its proprioceptive and auditory consequences than in its visible effect upon the object. This may affect the type of object representations the monkeys elaborate and their understanding of how objects and actions are connected. For example, a macaque's representation of the links between actions and objects may be focused upon the basic connection between its hand and the object, but miss the details of the object's behavior, especially how it may affect other objects. This might explain why tool-using behavior is so infrequent among macaques, and why it takes them so long to acquire any tool-using behaviors at all.

Apes (and perhaps a few monkey species, specially capuchins) may be different from macaques in this respect. Although some authors working from a Piagetian perspective initially reported that they found little in the way of spontaneous object manipulations in gorillas and chimpanzees (Vauclair, 1996), more recent studies suggest that the apes do engage in circular explorations of objects. In our longitudinal study with hand-reared gorillas, for example, we found that they would repeatedly hit an object, scratch a surface, make noise by hitting two objects together, spray water by obstructing the water dispenser with a finger, repeatedly open and close doors, repeatedly turn the light in a room off and on, and so on, always paying attention to the consequences of their actions (Gómez, 1999).

They also explored objects by sequentially applying known actions to them. For example, at 12 months of age, one of our gorillas, Nadia, explored a plastic toy drum by mouthing it, looking at it while holding it in front of her eyes, rubbing it upon her chest, hitting it on the floor, and again mouthing it, always looking at the object after doing something with it.

Some gorillas go on to tertiary circular reactions and constructive object combinations. For example, after Muni watched how a human lifted the lid of a box, she started a series of opening and closing actions with the same object. The lid fitted very narrowly, so that it was difficult to close it again. She tried in different ways until she succeeded in closing it; then she immediately reopened the lid and started the cycle again. Her actions were not simple repetitions: she changed her movements (perhaps in search of effectiveness), but over and over again she would undo the result—the closed lid—she had worked so hard to obtain and try again.

These exploratory actions were *intrinsically* motivated. The gorillas explored the objects in themselves, not because they were needed to solve any problem. Even some food manipulations appeared to be directed at exploring the physical properties of the food item (for example, using an apple as a bouncing ball). Many of these exploratory actions may be organized around a particular goal, like closing the lid of the box. Yet the repeated undoing of the accomplished result indicates that this is not a simple problem-solving activity, but an exploration of the actions and the objects themselves.

The repetitive nature of the manipulation suggests that the goal is not simply success or mastery but "studying" the procedure itself. One possibility is that the aim of these manipulations is to achieve some form of practical understanding rather than effectiveness (Karmiloff-Smith, 1992). This ability to focus attention on the actions themselves may help to create more explicit representations of the structure of actions and their causal relation to objects. According to Karmiloff-Smith and other developmental theorists, the ability to generate increasingly explicit representations is one of the crucial features of human cognitive development. The evolutionary origins of this important human feature may be reflected in the repetitive exploratory manipulations that some primates work at with concentrated attention outside problem-solving situations.

The exploratory or investigative manipulation of objects (that is, not subordinate to feeding, fighting, or other primary functions) appears to be a characteristic of primates, much as their curiosity or desire to contemplate things is. Within this general primate trend there are differences among species, both in the quantity and quality of the explorations (Torigoe, 1985). A common joke of primatologists, especially in laboratory contexts, is that primates are interested in three things only: food, food, and more food. In fact, outside artificial laboratory tasks, this joke is fundamentally misleading about the nature of primate motivation—and therefore about the nature of their cognition.

Conclusion

For primates objects are units of action, environmental elements that can be handled in a variety of ways thanks largely to that quintessential primate adaptation—the hand. We have argued that primates have also evolved cognitive adaptations for dealing with objects—systems for representing objects as external, permanent entities that can be grasped and moved, hidden and found, retrieved and lost, and so forth. These systems for understanding objects are part of larger systems of practical intelligence capable of producing flexible adaptive behaviors of varying complexity. Some aspects of these systems of practical intelligence appear to be common to all species of primates (as far as we can tell from the few species studied so far); for example, object permanence with visible displacements. Other aspects vary among species: for example, invisible object permanence and tool-using behaviors. An integral part of this system of intelligence is the presence of investigative motives and curiosity that make primates explore objects with their hands outside problem-solving contexts. The result is a flexible system for action—the ability to generate new behaviors by combining a set of basic motor units in an intelligent way. And the key to the intelligence of the system is that it works with representations of objects and actions.

4

Understanding Relations between Objects: Causality

While representing the world in terms of objects and their uses is a fundamental ability of primates, the world is not made simply of individual objects. Objects and their substrates are organized in space and relate among themselves. One fundamental kind of object relationship is causality, or how physical objects can influence each other.

Causes and Actions

When one object makes another change in some way (or when we make an object change), this is because a relationship of causality is established between them. For example, if a stone hits the water, it creates ripples; if a monkey pulls a fruit, this may detach from a branch; if the same monkey bites the fruit, this will change in shape. Objects are placed in the world in an enormous variety of causal relations: not only *dynamic* causal relations, as the examples I have just described, bus also *static* causal relations, such as a rock supporting a fallen tree, or the stem that keeps a fruit hanging from the branch, or a table that keeps objects on its surface. Many of these static causal relations have the effect of *preventing* a change from happening, but they are as important as the dynamic relations that provoke changes.

Understanding objects and events in causal terms involves not only seeing something as producing something else, but also focusing upon the *links* that connect one event with another event and objects among themselves. Intelligence is usually expressed through our ability to manipulate these causal links: from the use of a humble stone to break a nut open to the sophisticated use of power tools or motor vehicles. Intelligence and cognition have much to do with the ability to represent objects and agents as causally connected to each other, either actually or potentially.

The ability to detect and represent two events as causally connected is not the same as the ability to detect an association between two events. For example, we don't think that the door bell *produces* the appearance of a person at the door, even if one thing is almost invariably followed by the other; but we do think that a ball's impact produces the movement of another ball on the pool table. We therefore perceive that some associated events are connected in a special way—through a causal link—and we understand this causal connection as different from an association.

This distinction can be illustrated with another domestic experiment by Piaget (1936), who attached a string from a cradle's mobile to his four-month-old son's leg. By trial and error, his son quickly detected the connection between moving his leg and the mobile's activation. When Piaget untied the string, the baby continued to move his leg, his attention exclusively focused on the mobile without noticing that his action could no longer be effective because the causal link that made the effect possible was no longer there. From around 10 months of age, however, babies can tell the difference between a connected and an unconnected string: when given a choice, they pull the string that is connected to a toy in order to retrieve it. In a similar vein, Tom Bower (1979) reported that whereas younger babies can learn very quickly to control a slide projector that is activated when the movement of their legs interrupts an invisible ray of light, older babies learn more slowly because they appear to be initially confused by the apparent lack of a link connecting their action with the effect. Older babies try to figure out the causal relations connecting their actions and the objects in the environment, and they find it difficult (at least initially) to deal with apparently arbitrary contingencies that are based upon invisible connections.

In exploring to what extent the primate mind, with its focus upon object manipulation, is also a causal mind, we will concentrate upon one of the more prototypically intelligent behaviors reported in primates—tool use. This is not to say that direct actions without tools do not involve causal understanding. Some scholars (Dickinson and Balleine, 2000) argue that even in simple cases of associative learning by rats primitive causal representations may be at work. For a closer look at the organism's understanding of causal links, however, we need to study more complex behaviors that involve the use and creation of explicit connections between actions and objects; and this is precisely what tool use can offer.*

Using Tools and Understanding Causes

Tool Use and Intelligence in Teneriffe

Tool use was the main subject of one of the most famous and influential studies of primate intelligence: Wolfgang Köhler's experiments testing the intelligence of chimpanzees, carried out between 1914 and 1916 in the Canary Island of Teneriffe (Köhler, 1927). Köhler reported that his captive chimpanzees were capable of solving practical problems by, among other things, using sticks or boxes to obtain food items that were out of their direct reach. For example, when Köhler left an orange and a stick in front of the bars of the cage where the chimps were housed, so that they could not reach the orange with their extended arm, a chimpanzee took

---

* Tool use has been observed in species other than primates, such as birds and insects. For example, some vultures use stones to break open eggs of other birds, and zebra finches use small twigs to dislodge insects from their hideouts in branches (Beck, 1980). Traditionally, these were thought to be "instinctive" cases of tool use, that is, species-specific, relatively fixed action patterns. In recent years more sophisticated cases of tool use have been reported in birds (Lefebvre et al., 2002), findings which raise the possibility of intelligent tool use and causal understanding in brains that are very distant phylogenetically from those of primates.

the stick, extended it toward the orange, and dragged it toward himself—a simple but perfect example of tool use. If a banana was hanging from the ceiling of a large enclosure, the chimpanzee also used a stick to hit it and make it fall down, or, more innovatively, used the stick as a spring pole to catch the food with his hands in a pole vaulting maneuver. Alternatively, he would drag a box underneath the banana, climb onto the box, and reach the food.

Some chimpanzees were able to go beyond these simple instances of tool use; for example, they would combine two hollow canes to construct a long stick when their target was especially far away and none of the available canes was long enough on its own. They were also able to stack boxes one on top of another to construct higher climbing towers, or otherwise modify their tools to render them more suitable for the tasks at hand. Although their performance was far from perfect and they failed to solve many of the more complex problems Köhler posed them, the chimpanzees acted as if they understood some of the causal possibilities of the tools that could provide access to the objects they wanted.

Köhler's interpretation was indeed that chimpanzee tool use was *intelligent* or, to use the term that his studies popularized, "insightful." What he meant was that the chimpanzees were not acting under simple stimulus-response associations or by blind trial and error, but with some kind of understanding or perception of the relations between the implements and the target objects—what Köhler called a naïve or practical physics. He was careful to point out that, according to his extensive observations, this naïve physics of apes was not necessarily like that of human beings, but "weaker" and less sophisticated. But his main conclusion was, nonetheless, that in their tool-using activities the chimpanzees were demonstrating behavior of the type we call "intelligent" in humans.

Associative Learning versus Intelligence / Insight

Köhler's primary aim was to demonstrate that chimpanzee behavior could not be explained by simple associative learning, in the sense of learning to use sticks and boxes by a slow, progressive process of repeating initially random movements that happened to be successful by pure chance. A few years earlier, the psychologist Edward Thorndike (1898) had published an influential series of experiments with cats in which he demonstrated that these animals learned to give the adequate response to escape puzzle boxes (always involving undoing a latch or pulling a lever) by pure trial and error. Some people had believed until then that the frequently reported anecdotes of cats and dogs being able to open door latches was evidence of their understanding of the workings of these mechanical devices. Thorndike's results, however, suggested that this was just the product of blind learning, without any insight into the mechanical devices themselves.

According to Köhler, when chimpanzees were confronted with simple tool-using problems, they did not show any of the symptoms of blind associative learning such as random actions (for example, moving the stick in all possible directions until, by chance, it happened to touch and displace the objective in the correct direction) or progressive approximations to the solution; rather the chimpanzees frequently displayed their solutions suddenly. For example, in the stick problem, the chimp might start trying to reach the objective directly with his hand, but then suddenly interrupt these attempts, take the stick, put its end in contact with the objective, and drag it toward himself. This was very different from the gradual sieving of useful and unuseful movements that Thorndike (1898) had described in his cats. Chimpanzees were acting with *insight* into the structure and the requirements of the problem. This term—insight—has frequently been misunderstood in psychology. Many authors thought that Köhler was proposing a cognitive process that would explain the behavior of the chimpanzees (see Birch, 1945; Harlow and Harlow, 1949). But he was merely using the word descriptively, as a synonym of intelligent behavior in its ordinary sense—the ability to produce solutions to problems on the basis of some understanding of the situation, rather than relying on blind trials and errors. In this sense, "insight" means the same as practical or sensorimotor intelligence.

Köhler's work was enormously influential for the psychology of his time, specially among developmental psychologists. Some accepted and extended the idea of practical intelligence. Thus Piaget (1936) described a period of practical or sensorimotor intelligence that laid the foundations for the more powerful forms of symbolic and operational intelligence that developed later in children. For Vygotsky (1930) infants' and young children's intelligence is initially very similar to that of chimpanzees, but it becomes radically transformed by language and the child's immersion into culture during the second and third years of life (see chapter 9). A famous developmental psychologist of the time, Karl Bühler (1918), even coined the expression the "ape age" to refer to the period when children display their first examples of tool use before the onset of language.

But other scholars did not easily accept the idea of chimpanzee intelligence, or "insight" as it came to be known in the partially misleading English translation. In the first half of the twentieth century there was an intense debate about the nature of chimpanzee "insightful behavior"—was it genuine intelligence or an especially complex instance of blind associative learning?

The Role of Experience in Chimpanzee Tool Use

Critics were especially worried by a potential problem with Köhler's observations: the chimpanzees he had been working with had been captured in the wild when they were at least 4 or 5 years of age or even older. Köhler therefore did not really know about their previous experience; so perhaps what appeared to be insightful or intelligent behaviors were actually instances of a transfer of skills that had been blindly learned, by simple trial and error, during their life in the wild. For example, Bühler (1918) reasoned that chimpanzees in the wild routinely perceived and handled fruits attached to branches; therefore it was only natural that they would seek to re-instate this basic association between wooden sticks and fruits in tests like those used by Köhler. A crucial experiment was clearly in order: testing chimpanzees born in captivity who had had no previous experience with sticks.

The psychologist Birch (1945) conducted such an experiment. He had access to a group of young chimpanzees born in captivity who were reared in an environment free of sticks, so that they could not develop any conditioned responses with them prior to their testing. When the time came, they were given a simple test similar to those of Köhler: a piece of fruit was out of their reach, and lying next to it was a rake that could be used to move the reward toward themselves. None of the chimps was able to solve the problem.

As a continuation of the experiment, the chimps were allowed to have some "previous experience" with sticks. For a few days, different kinds of natural sticks (but no rakes) that they could manipulate freely were scattered in their enclosure. Birch took careful notes of the sorts of manipulations the chimps spontaneously made: essentially, all of them ended up using the sticks as an extension of their hands to "touch" things or other chimpanzees. None of them, however, used the sticks to drag objects to themselves. After this period of familiarization with sticks, the chimpanzees were given the same test as before: a piece of fruit out of their reach and a rake—not a stick—lying nearby. This time the chimpanzees readily solved the problem: they took the rake, placed its end beyond the fruit and then performed the adequate pulling movement to obtain the reward.

The results of this experiment are puzzling. On the one hand, the chimpanzees clearly needed some experience with sticks in order to be able to solve the problem *à la* Köhler. However, this experience had not provided them with the correct response *à la* behaviorist—during their games with the sticks they had not learned to perform any raking movements to drag objects; all they did was to touch or stab targets (a movement that, if anything, is opposite to raking). Yet as soon as they were confronted with the rake problem, the chimpanzees right away produced the act of raking for the first time in their lives, without engaging in trial-and-error manipulations. Neither a behaviorist interpretation nor a "nativist" interpretation could explain how the chimpanzees had developed their raking behavior. Some intermediate explanation was needed.

Birch's results fit Köhler's original idea that chimps produce new actions under the guidance of their perception (or *understanding*) of the situation. But the experiment qualifies his idea by suggesting that this understanding cannot emerge automatically out of simple perception in the absence of any previous knowledge of sticks and what can be done with them. In fact, these results fit better with Piaget's notion of sensorimotor intelligence, according to which new actions grow out of existing actions by a process of organized transformation in which both previous experience and understanding play a crucial role, but through mechanisms very different from simple conditioning or the mere application of innate schemas.

Manipulative Instincts

Another study critical of a practical intelligence interpretation of tool use in chimpanzees was conducted by Paul Schiller (1952). He found that if chimpanzees were given sticks and boxes and allowed to play with them without any food rewards, they eventually produced a repertoire of actions (touching things with sticks, climbing on top of a box, placing a box on top of another) similar to that displayed by Köhler's apes in problem-solving situations. Schiller's chimps were not trying to reach an object: they were just playing with the objects at their disposal.

Schiller argued that chimpanzees' stick use and box stacking were *innate* or *instinctive* motor patterns performed automatically, without any intention to solve a problem. When the chimps faced a problem situation, it must be a matter of time before they eventually happened to display, by mere chance, the "correct" pattern— moving a box exactly under a hanging banana, for example. They can then climb onto the box and get their reward. If this happy accident occurs often enough, the chimpanzees will eventually acquire the conditioned association of placing the box under the banana, and will produce the misleading impression of acting with understanding, when in fact they are producing the correct actions by blind association.

A problem with Schiller's interpretation is how to explain that the chimpanzees developed their playful stick- and box-using behaviors in the first place. He suggested that it was just a matter of "instinct," something that chimpanzees are somehow programmed to do innately; but other researchers concluded that self-motivated manipulations in play or exploration, far from being instinctive or automatic responses, can be a hallmark of complex practical intelligence—perhaps even a sign of the emergence of more explicit and flexible representations of actions and their relations to objects (see Chapter 3). Furthermore, as later studies of wild and captive chimpanzees demonstrated, the variety and flexibility of object manipulation and tool use among them is such (and so different between different chimpanzee communities) that explaining it all by instinct can hardly work, unless by "instinct" we understand an innate ability to learn to use objects in a flexible, goal-directed way, which is not what Schiller had in mind.

The unlikelihood of explaining chimpanzee tool use as an associative habit is further emphasized by studies in which authors have tried to train primates who do not spontaneously acquire tool use.

Monkeys Learn to Use Tools

The understanding that a stick must touch the object you want to move, that this contact must be kept throughout, and that you must pull in the direction you want it to move may seem so basic that it does not deserve the label of causal understanding. Yet some species of primates find it difficult to deal with this, even if they are given special training. For example, rhesus and Japanese macaques, which do not spontaneously use tools in the wild or in captivity, can be trained to use a rake to obtain out-of-reach food (Shurcliff et al., 1971; Ishibashi et al., 2000). But the training process proceeds in a slow, step-by-step way that greatly resembles the blind trial-and-error mechanism proposed by behaviorists. Moreover, the performance of the trained monkeys suggests a limited understanding of the causal connections between the tool and the target. For example, after learning to rake in food placed between them and the implement, the rhesus macaques were given tests in which the rake was not placed immediately behind the target. The monkeys failed to adjust the position of the rake before pulling it in: they simply pulled it as if expecting that the food would move toward them. This betrays a lack of understanding of the basic relation between tool and target (Shurcliff et al., 1971).

Japanese macaques also learned to rake in food after several hundreds of "easy" trials in which the food was in the way of the rake at the beginning; likewise, when the rake's position was moved sideways, they simply pulled it in as before. It took them several additional sessions to learn to move the rake toward the target first, and then pull. And even so, they would still commit errors, like pulling as soon as the rake was close to, but not behind, the target. They did not understand that positioning the implement behind the target and, subsequently, bringing the rake and the target into contact were necessary for the tool to be effective. Their performance could be described as an almost prototypical case of associative learning, in which they learned that certain stimuli configurations (tool close to food) are likely to be followed by successful retrieval if a pulling action is applied (Ishibashi et al., 2000).

The process of development of tool use in these monkeys appears to be in sharp contrast with that described for chimpanzees, who learn spontaneously and display flexibility in their use of object relations (Birch, 1945). Nevertheless it is possible to find evidence of some causal understanding in other species of monkeys using a different paradigm in which they are given a choice among possible tools. For example, Hauser (1997) reported that tamarin monkeys learned relatively quickly (in about 120 trials for those completely naïve to means-ends tasks) to pull a hooked cane with a food pellet lying in the way and ignore a cane with the food pellet outside the hook (figure 4.1). However, none of the tamarins was able to maneuver the cane with the pellet outside into the correct position when he made the wrong choice: instead, the monkeys just pulled as they did with the cane turned the right way. This suggest a lack of understanding of the causal details of the task, and therefore some sort of blind learning similar to that reported for other monkeys.

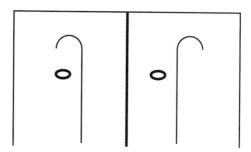

Figure 4.1. Which cane should you pull in to obtain the reward? Example of test given by Hauser (1997) to tamarin monkeys.

But when the experimenter offered a choice between new pairs of modified canes, the tamarins tended to choose in terms of functionality; that is, they ignored irrelevant changes such as color or texture, but avoided changes with functional consequences, such as shape. Moreover, when offered a choice among substantially different tools, some of which could be used exactly in the same manner as the canes (so that one pull was enough to obtain the reward) whereas others required a preliminary adjustment, the tamarins tended to choose the one-pull tools. Hauser interprets this as evidence that tamarins had learned to act on the basis of relevant abstract features of objects, rather than their superficial, irrelevant features. However, when the tamarins did choose the tools that required a preliminary adjustment, they were again completely unable to effect it—they just pulled these tools and therefore failed to gain the reward. Again, this might reflect an important limitation in their causal understanding that seems comparable to that found in rhesus and Japanese macaques. On the other hand, the ability of tamarins to recognize new tools that required a single pull shows some degree of understanding of the causally relevant properties of the potential tools. (Perhaps a similar understanding might be uncovered in other monkeys if tested with Hauser's procedure.) This recognition need not be based upon abstract representations, but it might indicate that the tamarins do not simply form associations with just *any* arbitrary features, but conduct a more sophisticated analysis of the perceptual properties of the situation, even if they cannot translate this analysis into intelligent adaptive action, as chimpanzees appear to be able to do. (This, by the way, is reminiscent of the perception/action gap found in human infants; see Chapter 3).

When the same experiment was conducted with tamarin infants of between 4 and 8 months of age who had been reared almost without any contact with objects, Hauser, Pierson and Selig (2002a) found that the infants reacted exactly like the adult tamarins: they significantly tended to choose the canes that would yield the reward with a single pull, and completely failed to correct the position of wrongly placed canes. The authors' interpretation is that the ability to perceive these causal features might be innate in tamarins. On the other hand, Hauser et al. (2002b) found that adult tamarins that were confronted with means-ends tasks for the first time were more prone to form the wrong association with the color of the tool than tamarins with more experience. This suggests that the supposedly innate ability to detect relevant causal connections is either fragile or easily overridden by later experience (or lack of it).

In sum, monkeys that are not spontaneous tool users can be trained to make some use of tools. Their performance appears to be devoid of causal understanding, however: they appear to be guided by associations between acts and outcomes. Upon closer inspection (Hauser's experiments), these associations may turn out to be not entirely blind; they may be accompanied by some ability to discriminate among configurations that are more or less likely to be successful. Yet whatever the nature of the representations supporting this discrimination ability, it appears that they cannot be used to generate intelligent actions to modify the relations between the tool and the target. These monkeys may perceive some causal texture, but not actively alter it.

Chimpanzee "Stupidity"

The performance of monkeys might appear to be in sharp contrast with that of chimpanzees in Köhler-like tasks. There is, however, one aspect of Köhler's studies with chimpanzees that has generally escaped the attention of the general public. His book is as much about chimpanzee "stupidity" as it is about chimpanzee intelligence. Many, if not most, of his observations are in fact about how chimpanzees failed to use tools successfully—careful qualitative descriptions of the errors the chimpanzees committed when trying to solve difficult problems. Although Köhler concluded that in general chimpanzees showed "intelligence of the same kind as humans" (Köhler, 1927), he added that apes clearly demonstrate important limitations and differences in their understanding when compared to adult humans. Many of his experiments were devoted to illustrate these differences and limitations.

Errors, Failures, and Mistakes

When some chimpanzees first faced the stick problem, they were able to solve it only if both the stick and the piece of fruit were in the same visual field, that is, if they could perceive both elements at the same time. As soon as the stick was placed, say, inside the cage, behind the chimpanzees, some of them were unable to use it, even if they could clearly see it or even walked on it as they paced during their attempts to solve the problem. If the stick was moved closer to the target, however, the same chimpanzee would immediately become capable of using it to reach the fruit. In the spirit of the nascent school of Gestalt psychology, of which he was a founding member, Köhler suggested that successful chimpanzees "saw" the solution once their perceptual field was restructured. This restructuring was easier if they could see the target and the instrument at the same time. Köhler was not very specific about what this perceptual restructuring consisted of, but he could have in mind some sort of cognitive process that would produce a new representation of the situation in the sense we discussed in the previous chapter.

Many of Köhler's experiments were devoted to exploring "causal understanding" in the sense we have discussed above, that is, of understanding how the tools produced their effects. His chimpanzees demonstrated a good understanding of some basic causal relations, such as the need to establish contact between the stick and the target object in a particular way (placing the end of the stick just beyond the target or pressing it) and that the stick had to be pulled in a particular direction. But he also found a surprising lack of understanding of other causal relations. For example, in one experiment the chimpanzees were confronted with a stick that hung on a nail by a ring. If one simply pulled at the stick, it stayed in place, but it was enough to move the ring up a little bit before pulling in order to free it from the nail. But the chimpanzees appeared to be unable to "see" this particular causal connection, and they kept pulling at the stick which stayed put because of the nail.

Most of the chimpanzees also failed to straighten a bent piece of wire to give it the correct shape and length to be used effectively for reaching a distant object (they tried to use the bent wire as it was). Likewise, when using sticks, they found it very difficult to move the target in directions other than those at angles of less than 90 degrees in relation to themselves, even if there were obstacles in the way and the only way to avoid them was to initially push the target away before pulling it in.

More famously, Köhler discovered that when chimps piled boxes in stacks they followed a peculiar sense of equilibrium: they sought the correct position almost exclusively by using proprioceptive feedback about whether the stacked box stayed or not in balance, ignoring the wealth of information about balance that can be obtained visually; by comparison, we humans can intuitively "see" whether a block placed on top of another will or will not fall when released. Chimpanzees did not appear to pay attention to how things stacked up, and as a consequence they attempted bizarre and highly unstable constructions that frequently collapsed or were kept in balance only because of the counterbalance effects their own bodies provided when they stood on the boxes. Remarkably, the chimpanzees did not appear to learn to pay attention to the visual cues during their prolonged exposure to boxes and their continuous attempts to solve these problems.

Paradoxically, their persistence in using this wrong strategy and their impermeability to experience can be taken as evidence that chimpanzees solve problems guided by their understanding of them, not by a simple associative computation of response/reward outcomes. The problem, Köhler suggested, is that the chimpanzees' naïve physics appears to be lacking in "statics," or, more interestingly, their sense of statics may be based upon a completely different kind of representation—proprioceptive information about the distribution of weight imbalances.

Errors as a Window to the Primate Mind

An original aspect of Köhler's approach to chimpanzee errors was his belief that it was precisely errors which demonstrated that the apes were acting with an understanding of the situation, even if it was a wrong understanding. For example, when a chimpanzee tried to reach a hanging fruit by pressing a box against a wall very hard while at the same time trying to climb on top of it, he was committing a stupid mistake, but at the same time he was revealing a good understanding of the basics of the problem. He understood the need for an intermediary step to reach the object and produced a solution that solved the problem of the distance between him and the target. Unfortunately for him, the only way to keep the box against the wall was by pressing it, and that was incompatible with climbing on top of it at the same time.

The chimpanzee was trying and erring, but his attempts were not blind. They were guided by a partial understanding of the situation. Köhler suggested that these funny errors, based upon strategies that could not possibly succeed, were the best proof that chimpanzees were not behaving by simple conditioned associations or by rote imitation of solutions they had seen in humans. These mistakes could only be an original, creative product of the ape mind.

This approach to unsuccessful performance as a window into the mind of subjects has been later rediscovered by developmental psychologists trying to understand the minds of young human primates.

Primate Causal Understandings and Misunderstandings

Although chimpanzees are the prototypical tool users among primates, and almost the only ones that systematically use tools in their life in the wild, the other great apes—gorillas, orangutans, and bonobos—routinely develop tool use in captivity, and they appear to do so *à la* chimpanzee rather than *à la* monkey (although detailed experimental information about this is not abundant). At least one species of monkey, however, spontaneously learns to use objects as tools—capuchin monkeys.* For example, they use sticks to reach for distant objects or to dislodge targets jammed inside a tube. Visalberghi, Fragaszy, and Savage-Rumbaugh (1995) carried out an experimental comparison of how chimpanzees and capuchins solve problems of the latter type. They discovered that both species solved with equal competence the simple problem of inserting a stick into a tube to force out a piece of food stuck inside. But capuchins were not so good in solving problems in which they had to modify their tools before using them. For example, when they were given a bunch of sticks tied together with a string, they tried to insert the whole bunch—an impossible action—whereas chimpanzees normally first untied the bundle and then used a single stick. Orangutans and bonobos behave like chimpanzees when confronted with this task (Visalberghi et al., 1995).

At the same time, Visalberghi and Limongelli (1996) pointed out that in every trial the capuchins, after their initial errors, engaged in a variety of seemingly aimless manipulations with the bundle which eventually resulted in the untying of the sticks, one of which they finally used to solve the problem. In fact, if the chimpanzees and the capuchins were compared only in terms of whether they eventually solved the task and how long it took them to do so, there were no important differences between them. Only the detailed analysis of the solving process revealed the difference between chimpanzees and capuchins, which the authors interpret as an indication that the capuchins were engaging in a process of blind trial and error in which they tried several manipulations until by chance they found one that worked.

This interpretation is supported by the fact that in the short term

* Baboons and lion-tailed macaques have also been described as developing some tool-using behaviors spontaneously (Beck, 1980; Westergaard, 1988, 1993).

capuchins did not appear to learn much from their success: when confronted repeatedly with the same problem, they always tried first to insert the bundle, and they had to rediscover the solution again and again. Only after many trials did they slowly learn to untie the bundle at the beginning of the trial—as predicted by blind trial and error.

In contrast, when chimpanzees confronted complex problems that they initially could not solve, they learned very quickly. For example, when given 3 sticks joined in an H shape that could not be inserted in the tube unless the transversal stick was first taken out, they initially committed the error of trying to insert the H-tool as a whole. But after a few trials they suppressed that error and always modified the tool in advance.

Visalberghi and Limongelli (1996) suggest that capuchins and chimpanzees represent causal relations in different ways. Chimpanzees might have a more detailed representation of the causal connections between their actions, the stick, the tube, and the food. It is not that capuchins completely lack any causal understanding of these. They clearly act in a goal-directed way and select some of the appropriate elements, though the precise connection between sticks and tube cavities does not seem to be part of their representation of the problem.

But as Köhler demonstrated in his pioneering studies, chimpanzees too may demonstrate failures of causal understanding if they are given the right (or perhaps we should say the wrong) tasks. Visalberghi and Limongelli (1996; Limongelli et al., 1995) found such a task—a version of the tube task in which a bigger tube, fixed to a standing structure, had a "trap hole" in the middle, such that if the food was pushed over it, it would fall down the trap and be lost (figure 4.2). To solve the problem, one had to insert the stick from the appropriate end, so that the food did not have to pass over the trap.

Three chimpanzees completely failed to solve this task; two eventually learned to avoid the trap (see figure 4.2B). The unsuccessful chimps did not improve their performance with experience: detecting the relevant causal connections was apparently beyond their understanding. The successful chimps, after their initial er-

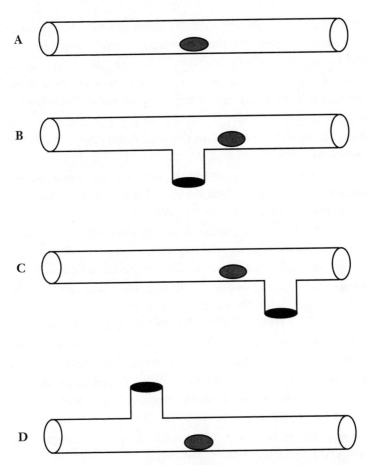

Figure 4.2. The tube and trap-tube problems. A: simple tube problem that can be solved by inserting the stick from either end. B: trap tube; the stick must be inserted from one end only or the reward gets lost in the trap. C: modified trap tube to check for simple association strategies (see text). D: rotated trap tube where the trap is innocuous. Adapted from Visalberghi and Limongelli (1996) and Povinelli (2000).

rors, may have learned a new representation of the task—one in which they made the crucial causal connection between trajectory of movement and falling into the trap.

Capuchin monkeys were also given this problem and all of them behaved at chance level. Eventually, after many more repetitions than the chimpanzees, one capuchin learned to solve the problem. The authors suggest that this individual may have learned the correct strategy for the B variant (always insert the stick from the end that is farther away from the reward) by blind association, without understanding why this strategy was successful. Indeed, when in a new experiment (the C variant) the position of the trap was changed, so that it was now in the way of the reward if this was pushed from the farther end, the capuchin did not change her behavior: she continued to push in the same way and, consequently, lost the reward. And this time she didn't learn a more flexible strategy after repeated exposure to this problem.

In contrast, the two successful chimpanzees, when confronted with this altered trap tube, did change their strategy almost immediately, after a few initial errors. They appeared to be taking into account the relative positions of the trap and the reward, and the authors suggest that this demonstrates they genuinely learned to understand the relevant causal relations between the objects.

Visalberghi and Limongelli's conclusion was that capuchins understand only very basic causal connections and, therefore, can solve only those tube problems in which blind associations are easy to form. In contrast, some chimpanzees, although initially challenged by the difficult tube problems, soon develop appropriate causal representations which lead them to success. Not everyone agrees with this interpretation, however.

Chimpanzee Failures in Causal Understanding

To probe chimpanzees' understanding of causality further, Daniel Povinelli (2000) introduced a variation in the original tube experiment. After some of his chimpanzees, like those of Visalberghi and Limongelli, had learned to systematically avoid the trap by inserting the stick while taking into account the relative positions of the trap and the reward, he rotated the tube 180 degrees, so that the trap was now on the top of the tube and was therefore harmless (figure 4.2D). Povinelli's rationale was that if the chimpanzees had really gained a causal understanding of the situation, they should realize that now there was no need to avoid the trap. Nevertheless his chimps continued systematically to insert the stick from the end that allowed them to avoid the now innocuous trap. According to him, this suggests that the chimps had merely acquired an association—more complex and detailed than that of capuchin monkeys—in which the relative position of the trap and the reward acted as a complex discriminative stimulus, but they had no real understanding of *why* one behavior led to obtaining the reward and the other to losing it.

This result by itself does not necessarily warrant this conclusion, as there was actually nothing wrong in the chimpanzees' "overzealous" responses. However, Povinelli used this experiment as the starting point of an extensive series of studies in which he tried to replicate and extend Köhler's descriptions of chimpanzee limitations in problem-solving situations. His hypothesis is that, all in all, chimpanzees lack *any* proper causal understanding of the world, which he takes to consist of explicit representations of unobservable entities such as force or gravity. He suggests that chimpanzees' actions with objects are guided by relatively complex associations between superficial features of objects and their typical reactions. For example, a chimpanzee using a rake might give the impression of understanding the connection between the transverse end of the rake and the effect of dragging the target—how that end "catches" the target and transmits to it the force that moves it. To test it he gave his chimps the choice of two rakes (one appropriate, the other faulty) and found that their choices were not often guided by a deep understanding of the conditions that would or would not allow the rake to catch the target. Thus when they had to choose between the specially designed rakes shown in figure 4.3 (a standing toothless rake [A] or a toothless rake turned upside down [B]) they did not show any understanding of the lack of functionality of the former in their first choices. They did understand, however, other contrasts; for example, they rarely chose a broken rake (C) over an intact one.

In another experiment, the chimpanzees had to retrieve an apple from a special apparatus—a sort of transparent vending machine—

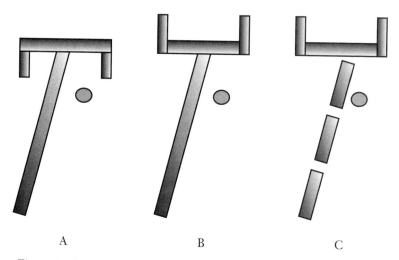

A   B   C

Figure 4.3. Types of rakes used to test chimpanzees' understanding of causality. Which rake will the subjects choose to pull first? (Adapted from Povinelli, 2000).

by inserting a stick through a circular hole to hit the apple and make it roll out of the apparatus (Povinelli, 2000). Chimps had no problem mastering this basic scenario. But when they were given a choice between different stick-like tools, some of which would not fit through the circular hole, they committed many errors and tried to use tools that could not possibly be inserted through the hole. Of special interest was one element of the test: when the chimpanzees were given tools that had one straight end, easily insertable through the hole, and a more convoluted end, very difficult, although not impossible, to fit, they tended to try to insert the difficult end and use the straight end as a handle. With time they learned to use the difficult end more efficiently to dislodge the apple, but did not realize how easy it would be to use the straight end, even though they did occasionally use the straight end and on these occasions solved the problem twice as frequently! This differential reinforcement, though, did not affect their behavior.

This result is specially interesting because it shows that, contrary to the blind trial-and-error hypothesis, when chimpanzees are confronted with a problem that they misunderstand, they may persist with their wrong strategy and fail to learn the correct superficial associations by associative learning. Their behavior is guided by their (mis)understanding, not by blind associations.

In developmental psychology, this insensitivity to superficial contingencies is taken as evidence that children's behavior is primarily guided by representations, not by empirical associations (Karmiloff-Smith, 1992). If we were to apply the same logic to chimpanzees, we might conclude that they too primarily act according to their causal representation of the problem even when this happens to be incorrect—a tendency so powerful that would override the more efficient strategy of acting according to superficial contingencies.

Povinelli (2000) presents many other experiments in which his chimpanzees fail to display a full understanding of the causal structure of many problems, which leads them to carry out "stupid" actions: trying to use inadequate flimsy rakes; not distinguishing between physically binding connections (a knot) and loose ones (a rope lying on a banana), and so on. He replicates and extends Köhler's pioneering descriptions of chimpanzees' remarkable combination of understanding and lack of understanding in their tool-using activities. But, in contrast to Köhler, he thinks that the chimpanzee failures demonstrate a fundamental divide between the human and the anthropoid mind: apes and nonhuman primates in general lack a true or "deep" understanding of causal relations, whereas humans, not only adults but also children from as early as 2 years of age, approach tool use armed with a qualitatively new type of concepts—explicit representations of unobservable principles and forces.

Causal Misunderstandings in Human Children

The above conclusions carry a double assumption: first, that human children confronted with Povinelli-like tasks would succeed; second, that success in such tasks requires explicit representations of invisible entities. Yet neither assumption might be justified. In relation to the first issue, a number of empirical studies with children suggest that misunderstandings of the causal properties of tools may happen until relatively late in development. Take, for example, the ability to understand the correct causal connection between a tool and an object. Pierre Mounoud (1970) conducted a series of studies involving the use of tools with children of different ages. In one test children had to "fish" for a toy which had a ring attached and was inside a bottle. They were offered a variety of implements, among them a simple straight wire rod and a rod with a hook at the end. Surprisingly, most children between 4 and 5 years of age, when asked to select the more appropriate tool, preferred the straight wire instead of the causally more appropriate hooked wire, and, when they chose the latter, they didn't try to hook the ring, but just used the tool to drag the object out by pressing it against the walls of the jar! They had a remarkable lack of understanding of this particular causal connection. After 5 years of age, children tended to choose and use the hooked wire correctly, but then most of the time they failed to construct the adequate tool when provided with a straight, bendable wire. This failure becomes all the more remarkable in view of the recent finding that a captive crow spontaneously developed the strategy of bending a wire into the appropriate shape to solve a problem (Weir, Chapell and Kacelnik, 2002), a move that suggests sophisticated causal understanding of the requirements of the task.

In a different study, Karmiloff-Smith and Inhelder (1975) asked children to balance blocks of wood one on top of another. They found that at 3 and 3.5 years they placed the blocks in all sorts of inappropriate positions, sometimes trying to compensate for the lack of balance by pressing down on the top block so that it stayed in place—a remarkable approximation to a typical chimpanzee error in the larger-scale scenario of box stacking. At around 4 years of age children became able to systematically find a stable position when asked to balance the top block across a beam, but they did not do so by choosing a visually stable configuration from the beginning, but moved the block around in search of proprioceptive stability—another resemblance with the behavior of chimpanzees stacking boxes. At 6 years children were capable of solving the balancing problem straight away by systematically placing symmetrical blocks exactly on their middle point from the beginning. They were using visual representations to find the balance position. But when the same children were given patently asymmetrical blocks (a block with an extra wooden piece glued to one end) or special "tricky" blocks with a weight invisibly concealed in one end, they persistently tried to balance these blocks on their geometrical center despite their continuous failure to achieve success. And here is something striking: the younger four-year-olds children, when given exactly the same asymmetrical blocks, had no problem balancing them with their procedure of proprioceptive groping. The use of visual representations is inappropriate for the asymmetrical blocks, but, as Karmiloff-Smith and Inhelder (1975) point out, these very errors demonstrate that the six-year-olds are following some sort of "theory in action" (in this case, the theory that all blocks must balance on their geometrical center). The fact that they do not learn from their experience of seeing the asymmetrical blocks fall again and again, further reinforces the interpretation that they are guided by an elaborate, albeit insufficient, representation of the causal structure of the problem, one in which visual information has taken control over their action at the expense of proprioceptive information.

Only later, at around 8 years of age, children show a complete mastery of the problem: they balance normal symmetrical blocks on their center and have no problem correcting the balance position of the asymmetrical ones and the blocks with hidden weights; they even verbally explain what they are doing and comment about how there must be something hidden in the tricky blocks, thereby demonstrating a deep, explicit causal understanding of the task. However, this happens only after a long period of development during which they showed less explicit, partial causal understanding.

The trap tube test used by Visalberghi and Limongelli (1996) with capuchins and chimpanzees has been given to human children as well. Although they can show an understanding of the basic mechanics of the task (the stick must be inserted in the tube) by 2.5

years of age after being shown a model, Want and Harris (2001) argue that their understanding is not truly causal until at least 3.5 years, when for the first time some children are able to correctly choose the appropriate end from which the stick must be inserted. But these children do not show spontaneous mastery of the problem: their success crucially depends upon being taught by an adult not only what to do (a demonstration of success by inserting the stick from the right end), but also what not to do (a demonstration of failure following insertion from the wrong end). Children who witnessed only successful demonstrations did not learn the right strategy.

In summary, tool use by human children is plagued by a variety of errors that denote inadequate understanding of some causal relations even at relatively advanced ages. This, however, does not mean that they wholly lack causal understanding until 7 to 8 years of age. At earlier ages, they demonstrate partial understanding based upon less sophisticated representations of causal relations. Something similar might be happening with apes and monkeys. Their errors might not denote a complete lack of causal understanding, but a partial—both in the sense of incomplete and biased toward particular aspects of the problem—causal representation. The partial understandings of apes and children may be biased toward different aspects of the problems (this remains an empirical question to be investigated), rather than denote a radical divide between human and other primates' understanding of causality.

Deep and Shallow Understanding

A second issue raised by Povinelli's experiments on tool use is to what extent are these practical tasks adequate to assess deep explicit causal understanding. Is success in such tasks really based upon an explicit or high-level representation of unobservable causal forces? For example, in both the rake and the apple-dislodging problems, the relevant properties of the instrument and the obstacle that need to be coordinated are fully visible—they are simply particular shapes. Success in such practical problems may not require any ability explicitly to represent deep unobservable variables. Some more basic, practical misunderstanding of visible variables may account for the failures of apes and children.

The debaters about whether nonhuman primates have causal understanding frequently fail to consider one of the main contributions of Köhler's early work—the notion of *naïve physics* as practical intelligence. Intelligence and understanding were once identified with conscious, verbally formulated thought. But Köhler and developmental psychologists like Piaget and Vygotsky firmly established that there is a preverbal, nonreflexive intelligence both in young human babies and in monkeys and apes. Köhler coined his term "naïve physics" to refer to *implicit* or *practical* ways of understanding physical principles. For example, commenting upon some observations of chimpanzees using sticks as levers, Köhler states that neither apes nor ordinary humans using a lever need know anything about the notions of Force, Direction, Work that form part of the physical concept of lever. They are using "some sort of practical or concrete 'understanding' of such instruments" based upon a "naïve optics and a naïve motorics" out of which the adaptive use of the instrument emerges (Köhler, 1927, pp. 53–4 of the German edition).

When Povinelli (2000) claims that apes lack a causal understanding of tools, he means that they lack higher-level explicit representations of causal principles. This in itself is not very controversial; few people if any have ever claimed the opposite. What is controversial is the implication that causal understanding can only occur with explicit representations of that kind. Other researchers who believe that explicit representations may be uniquely human (Karmiloff-Smith, 1992) still accept that there is developmental continuity between implicit and explicit levels of knowledge. Moreover, developmental data suggest that children present different levels of representational explicitness (Karmiloff-Smith, 1992). Perhaps not all levels of explicitness are exclusively human, and perhaps there are also different levels of implicitness, and the divide between implicit and explicit representations may not be clearcut, but fuzzy.

Observed Causal Relations

Can primates understand causal relations of which they are mere spectators? For example, do chimpanzees understand how a fellow chimpanzee manages to get food with a stick? And can primates *infer* unseen causes when they come across their effects or predict effects when they see that a cause has occurred?

Inferring Causes and Effects

David Premack (1976) investigated these questions with an ingenious task. Some of his chimpanzees, who had been trained with an artificial language of plastic chips (see chapter 10), were used to "answer questions" which the researcher made up using a sequence of "words" (plastic chips of different colors and shapes) with a gap or with a special chip (intended to function as a sort of question mark) at some point in the sequence. To respond, the chimpanzees had to choose an appropriate chip or object among several offered to them, and place it in the gap. Taking advantage of their facility to answer questions in this way, Premack gave them a series of tests in which, instead of plastic chips, he showed them real objects depicting a simple causal event that they knew well because they were used to performing it themselves. For example, they were shown an intact apple, a gap (with the plastic question mark), and an apple cut into two halves. Then they were given a choice among three items: a bowl with water, a pencil, or a knife. The chimpanzees consistently chose the knife. They also chose the appropriate instrument in other examples, like water for a sequence "dry sponge—gap—wet sponge," or a pencil for the sequence "blank paper-gap-marked paper." According to Premack, the chimpanzees were demonstrating their understanding of causal relations: they were able to infer in their minds the correct instrument that must have caused the change.

One might be tempted to explain away the chimpanzees' performance as based upon a mere association between knives and cut apples, water and wet sponges, and pencils and marked papers. After all, the chimpanzees had personal experience doing each of these things and the appropriate choice may have come to their minds by sheer, automatic association. Then Premack gave them the same test with the same objects but with completely new and rather bizarre causal events (which they had never experienced in their lives), such as "sponge—halved sponge," or "apple—scribbled apple." The chimpanzees did not hesitate to choose the instrument that would cause the funny transformation. Moreover, in another test in which they were shown the intact object and one instrument, they were able to choose the appropriate effect.

This suggests that the chimpanzees were not responding on the basis of superficial associations. If we still wanted to call "associations" the representations they were using, these must consist of a relatively abstract schema of the instruments and their "associated" effects, such that knives produce cuts and pencils markings, regardless of what is cut or marked. And this is what one would expect of a basic representation of a causal relation.

Premack's chimpanzees, therefore, appeared to have relatively abstract representations of events structured in causal terms, so the mere sight of an effect activated in their minds the correct "explanation"—the cause that had brought about such an effect.

When this experiment was repeated with chimpanzees who had had no "linguistic" training but had similar experience of the critical events, they were unable to make the correct choice. This could mean that the ability to infer causes might depend upon the possession of more explicit representations of the critical events, which could have been provided by the repeated training in the use of plastic chips to refer to objects and actions; or perhaps, more simply, success in this task depends upon a better established training of the testing format.

Understanding What Others Do with Objects

The causal schemes investigated in the above experiments corresponded to the kinds of actions that the chimpanzees themselves habitually performed. In a separate experiment (Premack and

Woodruff, 1978a and b; Premack and Premack, 1983), one of the linguistically trained chimpanzees, Sarah, gave evidence of having good representations of actions she had never done herself, but had watched others doing; for example, lighting a gas heater or plugging in a phonograph. She was shown videotapes on a television screen of a person shivering by an unlighted heater or a person trying to play an unplugged phonograph, and then she was asked to choose among several photographs depicting appropriate or inappropriate remedial actions. She consistently chose the appropriate solution—a photo of a match or of a plugged-in electric plug, thereby demonstrating not only a good representation of familiar events but an ability to select the causally relevant segment.

In a final experimental twist designed to revisit Köhler's studies on tool use from the chimpanzee's perspective, Premack showed Sarah a videotape of her favorite keeper vainly trying to reach a bunch of bananas hanging too high from the ceiling. Sarah did not hesitate to choose the photo of the keeper climbing onto a box as the correct choice for this video.

Sarah's choices did seem to have an extraneous dimension. When the person in the video was someone whom she disliked, she did not choose for her/him a solution to the problem, but a disaster; for example, the person falling down. Was Sarah merely choosing good outcomes for favorite people and bad outcomes for unpopular persons without taking into account what she had just seen in the video? According to Premack this was not the case, because her disaster choices were still connected to the problem, demonstrating that she had recognized the point of the situation depicted. For example, in dealing with the bananas hanging out of reach, she chose a photo of the disliked person falling through a flimsy chair seat, rather than of his sliding down on the floor.

This result suggests that the chimpanzee knows not only how to solve a problem at a procedural level, but also has some ability to access this knowledge off-line and use it to guide her choices in tests like this. This ability can be very useful for making sense of the actions of other chimpanzees or humans.

Conclusion: Causal Minds

Causal cognition in primates is currently a hotly debated area (Povinelli, 2000; Visalberghi and Tomasello 1998; Hauser, 2001), with little agreement about how much and what kinds of causal understanding, if any, primates other than humans have. Here I have argued that consistent evidence indicates a high degree of flexibility in the abilities of some primates to detect and use causal relations. Chimpanzees, and maybe other apes, may develop better and more detailed causal representations than the monkey species studied so far, but more studies are needed to test this hypothesis. To be sure, human children eventually excel in their ability to perceive and represent the world of objects in causal terms, becoming "little scientists" who not only make use of the causal texture of the world, but also reason about it, seek explanations, and construct their own explicit theories about why things happen (Piaget and Inhelder, 1966; Karmiloff-Smith, 1992; Gopnik and Meltzoff, 1997). But this is only after a long developmental process starting with humbler beginnings and plagued with partial understandings and misunderstandings. Nonhuman primates may help us understand the origin of causal intelligence—its foundation on implicit representations of mechanical relations among objects—and perhaps the origin of more explicit ways of recalling and using this knowledge in wider contexts.

The issue of how explicit is nonhuman understanding of causality remains unresolved. Some authors vehemently claim that explicit representations of causality are exclusively human (Povinelli, 2000), but evidence suggests that apes may handle some explicit representations of events structured in a causal way. This need not be the same as having explicit representations of causal concepts, like the notion of Force or the very notion of Cause, but it may be a more important core component of what it is like to have a causal view of the world. One increasingly clear conclusion from the available evidence is that a sharp distinction between explicit and implicit cognition may not fit the reality of primate minds.

5

The Logic of Object Relations

Having explored primates' understanding of causal relations, I will now address a different type of relations between objects—logical relations, or how primates understand the similarities and differences between objects, and how they organize and classify them in their minds.

Same and Different: Classifying the World of Objects

Most animals are capable of detecting similarities and differences among objects and adjust their behavior accordingly in what is known as discrimination learning (Pearce, 1997). Does this mean that in their minds they represent things in terms of *category* or *class*, that is, some abstract concept of what is an apple, an orange, a fruit, a tree? Can they distinguish between particular apples and the category "apple"?

Probably all nonhuman primates, and many other animals, are able to discriminate between stimuli from very early in their lives (for example, they are more or less attentive to a visual stimulus depending upon whether they have seen it before or not). But this can be done without using a representation that corresponds to the category "apple," "triangle" or whatever object is being shown to the infant. Young monkey and human babies may simply recognize a particular physical pattern, but not recognize it as belonging to a particular kind. In fact, an influential idea in psychology has been the proposal that categorical cognition might be linked to language—the ability to use explicit labels to organize objects into classes (Quinn, 2002). Indeed, humans have a complex hierarchical system of categories with which they organize the world into classes of objects that are identified with explicit linguistic labels ("apple," "orange," "fruit," "food," and so on). Obviously, if categorization depends upon language, it should exist neither in young babies nor in other living creatures.

Therefore the discovery by Herrnstein et al. (1976) that pigeons appeared to be able to respond to discrimination problems on the basis of categories like "people," "tree," or "water" came as a surprise. After very extensive training sessions in which pigeons were differentially reinforced exclusively for pecking slides which depicted a person, they were capable of responding correctly to completely new slides depicting people versus slides without people. Had the pigeons developed a representational category of "people" that controlled their behavior, instead of just remembering the particular instances of people they were shown on the slides?

Much controversy persists about the cognitive mechanisms behind the performance of pigeons and other animals in this type of tasks. Some researchers (D'Amato and Sant, 1988) suggest that animals may not really develop an abstract notion of "people" (or "tree" or "water"), but rather, in the course of their very extensive training, they learn to identify particular features that happened to be present in most instances of the slides with people or trees (for example, red spots in people photographs; patches of green in photos of trees). Far from learning an abstract category, they develop an ultra-concrete strategy for focusing upon very particular details of the stimuli and ignoring the rest. Other authors (Pearce, 1997) suggest that in well-controlled experiments animals might be learning genuine categories at least at the perceptual level.

Be it as it may, the techniques for nonverbal testing of category formation have been imported into primate psychology, and the results suggest that primates readily learn to respond to stimuli in categorical terms.

Roberts and Mazmanian (1988) trained both human adults and squirrel monkeys to choose images belonging to three possible categories of different level of abstractness: photos of kingfishers or other birds; birds or other animals; and slides showing animals or slides without animals. Humans learned quickly to give the correct response to the three kinds of categories; if anything, they found the more concrete level more difficult (distinguishing kingfishers from other birds). In contrast, the monkeys took much longer to learn the three categories, but found the more concrete level easier, the intermediate level harder (birds or other animals), and the higher level most difficult (animals or other entities). When humans and monkeys were given trials with completely new photographs after the training phase, the humans did well in all categories, whereas the monkeys only performed well at the lower-level category—kingfishers or other bird species. Only after much further training did the monkeys show some evidence of learning the superordinate category (animals or other entities), but their performance remained at chance level with the intermediate category (birds or other animals).

This study suggested that monkeys have some categorization ability, but it might be initially limited to dividing the world of objects into very basic, concrete types. They might be lacking the ability to organize their categories into a more complex hierarchical network of superordinate categories of increasing abstraction.

From another perspective, Fabre-Thorpe, Delorne, and Richard (1999) have recently claimed that this conclusion could be premature. They compared the performance of rhesus monkeys and human adults with exactly the same series of slides, but training the monkeys (and the humans) with a more extensive set of instances from the superordinate categories they were trying to induce—"food" or "not-food"; "animal" or "not-animal"—and constantly introducing new items during the training phase. This training procedure produced an excellent level of performance in the rhesus monkeys with both types of stimuli. When tested with completely new stimuli, they identified the category correctly in more than 80 percent of the samples, practically the same level as humans. Moreover, monkeys and humans tended to commit errors with the same "difficult-to-categorize" items.

When the monkey and human subjects were tested with black and white photographs (instead of the color photos used for training), their performance did not essentially change. This is important because in previous studies it was found that "pseudo-categorization" effects (selecting the right photos on the basis of superficial features) could be due to the systematic presence of certain colors in all the instances of the category (for example, red in all the photos of humans, or the particular colors of the kingfisher). The present results therefore appear to dispose of this criticism.

In a similar vein, Vonk and MacDonald (2002) have reported that one gorilla could deal not only with categories to distinguish at the species level (gorillas or humans), but also with higher-order, abstract categories differentiating between animals and other entities. The gorilla did have difficulty dealing with intermediate categories (primates or nonprimates). The researchers have reported similar results for orangutans (Vonk and MacDonald, in press).

Studies with human infants suggest that they can form some categorical representations from as early as 4 to 5 months of age if they are tested with procedures based upon measures of spontaneous attention. In one test, they are repeatedly shown pairs of pictures of one category (pieces of furniture), and then, once their level of attention has decreased, they are suddenly shown a pair of pictures consisting of a new piece of furniture and an object from a different category (a car). They tend to look for longer at the object that belongs to the new category, as if their repeated exposure to pieces of furniture had created in them some abstract representation of "pieces of furniture." Human infants are good at forming these primitive categorical representations at any level of abstraction, although they are particularly good at the intermediate level: "dogs" or "birds" or "cats" (Quinn, 2002).

These experiments indicate an interesting difference between nonhuman and human primates—humans have a tendency to categorize the world of objects starting at the level of so-called basic or intermediate level categories ("dogs," "cats," "birds"), whereas monkeys and apes appear to focus on concrete ("rhesus," "gorilla," "kingfisher") and superordinate ("animals," "food") categories. One speculation is that this might be linked to the effects of language upon cognition, specifically the effects of early naming when the first words are acquired by children (Tomasello and Call, 1997). But the discovery that young prelinguistic babies already show that bias toward intermediate categories would suggest that the way first words are learned is dependent upon this bias rather than the other way around. A definitive conclusion must wait until techniques of spontaneous attention are used to evaluate nonhuman primates.

In sum, although more research with primates is needed, it seems that some ability to group objects into categories beyond their physical similarity is part of the primate mind, and not a recent product of the linguistic mind of humans. In fact, it might be shared with animals other than primates. Perhaps language favors the use of this ability at more explicit and complex hierarchical levels of abstraction, rather than create the possibility of having such categories.

Doing Things with "Sameness"

A way of testing how complex are the representations of an organism is to ask it to do something with them. For example, we can make a monkey take decisions on the basis of whether one stimulus is the same as another. A way of doing this is the task known as "matching to sample," in which you show something to your subject—say, a green square—and then you give him a choice between an identical object and a different one (another green square and a red circle). If he chooses the same object, he will get a reward (usually a piece of food hidden under the correct object). This task was invented early in the twentieth century by the Russian primatologist Nadia Kohts (1923), and has become ever since a standard procedure for primate testing. Alternative versions are non-match-to-sample and oddity learning, in which the subject is reinforced for choosing the object that is *different* from the sample or the *odd* object in a group of otherwise identical items. In these tasks it is not enough to notice the similarity or difference of the objects: the subject also has to use this piece of information to guide his behavior.

As we have seen, a preference for looking at novel objects is consistently seen at 4 months of age in human babies and at around 1 month of age in pigtailed and rhesus macaques. However, the ability to carry out a required action (touching the new or the old object) in order to obtain a reward appears much later: human babies can learn to do this at one year of age but only after a prolonged and difficult training. They cannot learn it easily (at the same rate as adults) until around 4 years of age. Rhesus macaques can learn at 3 months after prolonged training, and do not reach adult levels until 2 years of age (Pascalis and Bachevalier, 1999; Bachevalier, 2001)

Detecting similarity is thus different from using this detected similarity to control more explicit, instrumental behavior. Interestingly, if one reduces the instrumental demands of the task by using the objects themselves as rewards (to play with, for instance) instead of hiding rewards under the objects, the experimenter may find some preference for getting hold of the new object in six-month-old human babies (Diamond, 1995).

An even greater developmental delay in using the ability to detect similarities and differences is found in the task known as oddity learning—one of the most difficult primate tests. In this task, the subjects are presented with 3 objects at the same time: two of them identical, the third different. The correct response is to choose the odd item. In every trial, a set of 3 new objects is used. It is not clear why this test is so challenging, but Harlow (1959) found that normal rhesus monkeys were not able to learn oddity problems until they were 3 or 4 years of age, in contrast with other difficult tasks like "learning set" which they mastered at 2 years of age.

When Overman and Bachevalier (2001) applied this test to human children of different ages (from 1.5 to 8.5 years) following exactly the same procedure as with monkeys—without any verbal instructions or any other indication of what was expected from them apart from differential reinforcement—they found that it was extremely difficult for all children under 7 years. They needed an average of 76 sessions of training in order to learn to systematically choose the odd item, and many of the younger children never did so even after 100 sessions of training. This parallels the findings with monkeys.

But here is the especially interesting part. When the children were told that the aim of the game was to choose the object that did not belong, they showed an instant mastery of the problem, as if their difficulty was not with the cognitive processes necessary to compare and distinguish objects, but just with discovering what the experimenter required from them—the rules of the game.

This finding is important in several respects. First, it is a good demonstration of the power of language and social interaction in regulating attention and cognition (as developmentalists like Lev Vygotsky claim). Secondly, it suggests that what the children are learning in those prolonged nonverbal trials is not the concepts of "similar" and "different" but the arbitrary rule of the game for selecting one or the other. Oddity tests do not directly assess the capacity of an organism to discriminate and categorize objects as same or different, but rather the capacity of the organism to infer the hidden rule of a game in which it has to use its categorization abilities.

An interesting question is what would happen if we were able to direct the attention of nonhuman primates toward the relevant parts of the task with some nonverbal method—would they achieve this sort of instant mastery? Or can this management of attention be carried out only through language and is therefore, again as Vygotsky pointed out (1930), a distinctive characteristic of human cognition, augmented through linguistic mediation?

A finding relevant to this question was reported by Davenport and Menzel (1960) in chimpanzees. They found that although adult chimpanzees needed a lot of time to learn to choose the odd of three objects in a standard task in which they obtained rewards, when offered exactly the same objects outside a learning context, just for the pleasure of handling them, they tended to select the odd object first to initiate their exploration. This parallels the finding with six-month-old human babies when objects themselves are the reward. It is as if the spontaneous visual attention to novel objects is easily prolonged into spontaneous manual exploration of novel objects, but it takes longer to use this representation of novelty as a tool to solve matching and not-matching problems. Perhaps the role of language in humans is to facilitate the conversion of those implicit representations of novelty or identity into more explicit representations that can be recruited for problem solving.

It appears therefore that one and the same representation—a record of objects as similar or different—may or not be available to primates depending upon how complex are the tasks they have to perform, especially depending upon how explicitly they have to handle that representation.

Concepts of Sameness

Monkeys, apes, human children (especially if tested without explicit verbal instructions) and other animals, like pigeons, usually need quite a lot of training the first time they are confronted with a typical matching-to-sample task until they learn to choose consistently the object that is the same as the sample (Thompson and Oden, 2000). Once they have learned their first matching task, an interesting difference emerges between these species. When given a new problem with completely new objects, pigeons have to start learning again from scratch. They have not learned that the rule of the game is to choose always "the same object"; rather, they have made some sort of elaborate association between the physical attributes of the particular objects used in their previous training. They are not focusing on the *relationship* of similarity or dissimilarity between objects. In contrast, primates do get this idea. Typically, monkeys, after being trained in a number of matching problems, can solve correctly from the very beginning any novel problem involving new objects, as if they have finally realized that the rule is to choose the object that is the *same*. Apes and children do even more impressively: it may be enough for them to learn to solve one single matching problem to become capable of correctly solving any new problem. As with monkeys, it can take them a very long time to learn the first problem, but once they have done so, their representation of the task dramatically changes—they understand that the rule is to choose the *same* object, whatever the actual objects are (Thompson and Oden, 2000).

It has been argued that this instant of comprehension can occur only if one has the capacity to attend to and represent the abstract relation of *sameness* between *any* objects, as opposed to detecting the similarity between particular objects (Thompson and Oden, 2000). Pigeons would be capable only of the latter (or perhaps of something even more primitive); in contrast, apes would be capable of generating and using an abstract category of sameness. A point of contention is whether monkeys who eventually learn to solve matching tasks with new objects do acquire that notion of sameness, or do they rather engage in some intermediate computation. After all, monkeys need to be trained with a lot of different objects until they achieve a good performance, whereas apes and human children show that striking ability to learn after solving a single problem.

Thompson and Oden (1996, 2000) and Oden et al. (1988, 1990, 2001) argue that there is something fundamentally different between the minds of monkeys and the minds of apes, not just a quicker learning ability. According to them, ape minds are not only prepared to perceive similarities and differences between objects, but also to categorize and represent the world in terms of these relations. Apes would be able not only to keep in mind the perceived similarity between two objects, but also to understand the concept of similarity itself.

To back their claims these authors conducted a study of learning to match with infant chimpanzees of about one year of age. First, they confirmed that the chimps could perceive similarities and differences by showing them one object and then recording their amount of visual attention to an identical or a different object. The infant chimpanzees consistently looked longer at the new objects (as human and monkey infants do very early in their lives).

After that, the infant chimps were presented with pairs of objects: sometimes identical, other times different. In this phase of the experiment, they were allowed not only to look at but also to touch and handle the two objects if they wished. In a given trial, after showing them two identical objects (A + A), they would be given a pair of new objects: sometimes a pair of new *identical* objects (B + B), other times a pair of new *different* objects (B + C). For example, if they were shown two identical cups in the first part of the trial, in the second part they were shown either two identical squares, or a square and a triangle. The objects are always new, but not their *relationship*. The point of this study was the following: if infant chimpanzees spontaneously look at the world in terms of relationships between objects, not only in terms of the objects themselves, then at some level they should be representing what they see not only as "two cups," but also as "two identical items." If this were the case, then a display of two new, dissimilar objects should be "more different" than a display of two new, identical objects, and therefore the chimps should pay more attention to the display that is more innovative: the one that not only contains new objects but also a new object *relationship*. This is exactly what the authors found: the young chimpanzees devoted more time to examining the pairs of objects that instantiated a new relationship.

In another experiment, these researchers demonstrated that their infant chimps were capable of mastering a traditional matching task (choosing from two objects the one that is identical to a previous sample) with a single training problem. They take this as evidence that the young chimpanzees indeed do spontaneously possess a notion of *sameness* and are able to use it to control their own behavior, whereas monkeys need to be taught this relationship or, perhaps, learn some functional equivalent thereof.

When the same chimpanzees were confronted with a "relationships" version of the matching task, the results were very different. As a sample, they were shown two identical objects; then they were offered a choice between a pair of new identical objects, and a pair of new different objects. The correct response is to choose the pair of identical objects, because it instantiates the same relationship as the sample. The infant chimps were completely unable to master this task, even if they received extensive cueing during the training (the experimenters not only reinforced them when they gave the correct response, but also tried to guide them towards the correct choice by gesturing).

The failure in this task may seem to contradict their good performance in the previous test: the one in which they paid more attention to the pair of objects that instantiated a new relationship. However, in the attentional test chimpanzees showed an *implicit* ability to take into account relationships between objects, whereas in the match-to-sample task with object pairs they had to make the comparison *explicit* and use it to guide an instrumental response. And here—in the explicitness of the representation required—is where the crux of the matter may lie. The chimpanzees may lack the ability to produce an explicit representation of the relationship of sameness which, however, we know they can detect.

Concepts and the Languages of the Mind

The inability of the infant chimps to match relationships in the explicit task came as no surprise to the authors. Several years earlier, David Premack (1976) had found that even older chimpanzees were completely unable to master this highly abstract task. Only one very special chimpanzee was able to master the relationships-matching task—Sarah, a female who had been subject to an extensive "linguistic" training that included learning to use plastic chips as a symbol to respond to a particular kind of match-to-sample task that Premack had invented for her—in which, instead of getting a sample and two objects, she was given the comparison objects directly and asked to place a particular chip between them if they were the same and a different one if the objects were different. To what extent these chips became for Sarah "words" that meant "same" and "different" as in a human language is something we will discuss in Chapter 10. What matters here is that this chimpanzee had been taught to make use of a concrete, explicit object (the plastic chip) when perceiving sameness, and another one when perceiving difference. She had been taught, at the very least, an explicit way of reacting to sameness and difference. It is tempting to conclude that Sarah had been provided not only with a physical tool—the plastic chip—but also, and more importantly, with a mental tool—an explicit way of representing the relationships of sameness and difference and, therefore, a symbol that she could use to increase her computational power. Lev Vygotsky would have enjoyed this experiment, had he been alive and known of it.

The issue remains of whether Sarah's mind had been globally upgraded by her learning of a symbolic system for thought (apart from "same" and "different" chips she was taught many other symbolic relations [Premack, 1976]), or whether the effects in the matching task were specific to the learning of symbols for those particular notions.

An experiment by Thompson, Oden, and Boysen (1997) addressed this issue. They taught chimpanzees always to select a particular token when confronted with two identical objects and use a different one when confronted with two different objects; it was "linguistic" training *à la* Sarah but strictly restricted to these two would-be symbols. After these chimps mastered the task, they were given the "relation between relations" task—and they passed.

A massive linguistic training that globally upgrades the chimpanzee's mind as a whole is not necessary to represent relations between relations. The localized learning of an explicit response with an object and its associated representations is enough to allow chimpanzees to go beyond their natural capabilities of representing sameness with their "chimp language of mind" into representing sameness with a different format, one that can be, first, manipulated with their hands, and later, apparently, manipulated in their minds. They may have been given a new *microlanguage* of mind.

It is, of course, possible to suggest other, more conservative interpretations, such as that the plastic chips are not symbols in the proper sense of the word, but just automatic associations. Perhaps the chimpanzees cannot avoid thinking of the chip (or of the action of selecting the chip) when seeing a "same" relationship (as they cannot avoid seeing the relationships themselves) and their hands are automatically primed to select the object pair that evokes the same unavoidable mental presentation of the same chip. They would be responding to their mental images of the chips as objects, not as representations of the sameness relationship. Hence Sarah and the similarly trained chimps would not be displaying abstract thought about relationships, but just a good imaging ability that has nothing to do with understanding analogies. Or does it?

Perhaps this parsimonious explanation is not so different from the first one. Such an automatic production of a mind image or action (especially if the image or the action is associated with the perception of sameness) might be a model of the sort of mechanism that evolution might have produced in human ancestors to start computing object relationships in more explicit formats, even if eventually more elaborate and efficient mechanisms for dealing with this task—those of modern human minds—emerged.

Monkey Logic and Ape Logic

Thompson and Oden's (2000) contention is that the ability to represent sameness is an innate property of the chimpanzee mind, but not of the monkey mind. When rhesus monkeys (who are capable of eventually learning match-to-sample) were tested with the novelty preference paradigm, in which same object pairs are contrasted with different object pairs, they showed no inclination to pay attention and touch the object pairs that showed a different relationship to the sample. The authors' hypothesis is that these tasks may be tapping a fundamental difference between the nonprimate and the primate mind, on the one hand, but also between ape (at least chimpanzee) minds and monkey (at least rhesus) minds in their ability and readiness to represent the world in relational terms. It is tempting to relate this purported cognitive difference with the findings (in Chapter 2) about the different propensities to perceive stimuli globally or locally, suggesting that chimpanzees, unlike baboons and rhesus monkeys, show more propensity to analyze displays globally.

Recently, Wasserman and colleagues (2001) have found that it is possible to train a monkey species—baboons—to succeed in a version of the relationship match-to-sample test. Instead of pairs of objects, they used computer matrices made of 16 small one-centimeter square designs symmetrically distributed in a larger square. The designs could be the same or different in each display. It took the baboons between 4,000 and 7,000 trials to learn to choose matrices with the same relationship with an 80 percent accuracy; and, as soon as the number of designs in the display was reduced to below 8, the baboons completely failed the task and had to be retrained to achieve some level of accuracy. This suggests that they were using a different processing strategy to deal with the experimenters' requirements. Possibly, as Thomson and Oden (2000) suggested, the minds of monkeys are not prepared to represent the relationship that the experimenters tried to elicit.

In sum, although pigeons, monkeys, and apes alike share an ability to detect similarities and differences, it is likely that the primate mind is better attuned spontaneously to represent the world in these terms; moreover, apes may have an ability to attend more explicitly to the relations of objects, although they cannot always make explicit use of this knowledge.

Understanding Complex Logical Relations: Conservations

There are more complex cases of "sameness" relations than the ones we have discussed so far. Some of the more interesting ones correspond to what Piaget called quantity and number *conservation*, a set of notions that are fully acquired by human children only at 6 to 7 years of age. The conservation of quantity and number is the ability to understand that the amount of a substance or the number of items in a set remain the *same* when they are subject to superficial transformations, such as changing their shape (squashing a piece of fruit) or spatial distribution (mixing up a collection of fruits). Quantity and number only change when quantity-relevant operations are carried out: taking away or adding a piece of the fruit or, in the case of number, adding or subtracting items in the set.

Piaget and his close collaborator, Bärbel Inhelder, created a set of simple tasks to analyze the understanding of conservation in children (Piaget and Inhelder, 1966). In the realm of liquid quantities, the experimenter shows the child two identical glasses containing the same quantity of juice. After the child agrees that there is the same amount of juice in both, the experimenter takes one of the glasses and, in full view of the child, pours its contents into a differently shaped glass—for example, one that is narrower but taller than the original glasses. Of course, now the level of liquid reaches much higher than in the first glass. Then the experimenter asks the child again, is there the same amount of liquid in both glasses? Piaget discovered that children under 6 to 7 years of age typically fail to realize that there *must* be still the same amount. They consistently claim that now the taller glass has more juice than the other, justifying their claim with the obvious fact that the level of liquid is higher in the new glass—therefore there *must* be more. When they are confronted with the logical inconsistency of their claim (the experimenter tells the child that other children say that although the new glass is taller, it is also narrower) they appear to be unable to appreciate it and stay with their interpretation. Children at that age appear to be genuinely convinced that quantity is a property that changes with shape and is linked to single dimensions, such as height.

At around 6 to 7 years of age, however, children not only consistently give the correct answer, but also provide an explanation of why there *must* be the same amount. If nothing has been taken or added, they argue, there must be the same amount because it is the same juice as before, and if the liquid is returned to the first glass we will have the same level again. Many go as far as to explain how the taller dimension is compensated by the narrower width, and appear to be stunned that someone may think that the amount is not the same! The logic of children appears to have radically changed (from a preoperational to concrete operational logic in Piaget's technical terminology).

Piaget and Inhelder (1966) carried out similar tests of conservation with solid substances and with other object properties, such as number, weight, and volume. They found that prior to 6 to 7 years of age, children are unable to conserve, whereas between 7 and 12 years they progressively acquire all those conservations as part of a radical change in the underlying logic of their minds.

How would a nonhuman primate react to a conservation test? Could they appreciate this highly abstract relationship of "sameness" across transformations? The obstacle to testing nonhumans with a complex task based upon a prolonged dialogue is of course their lack of language. It was therefore unsurprising that Woodruff, Premack, and Kennel (1978) took advantage of the "linguistic" skills of their chimpanzee Sarah to give her a simplified version of liquid and solid conservation. As the reader will remember, Sarah was able to tell if two things were equal or different by selecting plastic chips that were glossed as meaning "same" and "different." In the first part of the conservation test, Sarah was shown two identical containers with the same amount of liquid and the option of choosing the chips for "same" or "different": she readily selected the chip for "same". When she was shown identical containers with different amounts, she selected the chip for "different."

Next, she was confronted with containers of different shapes, which sometimes had the same amount, but other times had different amounts of liquid. Since the containers were of different shape, it was very difficult to tell if they had or not the same amount of liquid. And indeed Sarah was unable to choose consistently the correct answer from the available visual information. She was now ready for the critical conservation test.

Sarah was first shown the amounts of liquid in identical containers (as in the first part of the study) and then, in full view, one of the amounts was transferred to a differently shaped container exactly as in the Piagetian tests with children. She was, therefore, confronted with the same information as in the second part of the study—two differently shaped containers with amounts of liquid that might or might not be the same—but now she had the benefit of having just seen those amounts in identical containers before being transferred. When Sarah was given the plastic chips to respond, she made the correct judgment: regardless of the current levels of liquid, she chose "same" if the amounts were originally identical, and "different" if they were originally different. She was capable of overcoming the current perceptual information from the shape of the containers and guiding her response in accordance with what she had seen before. The researchers concluded that they had demonstrated conservation of liquid quantity in a chimpanzee.

They also found the same positive results when they tested Sarah with solid quantities—pieces of modeling clay that started with the same shape (two identical balls) but then one of them was given a different shape (a "sausage") always in full view of Sarah. They concluded that Sarah also had conservation of solid quantities.

Was the mind of the chimpanzee Sarah, therefore, similar to the mind of a six to seven-year-old human child? Of course, this need not be the case. For one thing, strictly speaking, Piagetian conservation does not only consist of giving the correct answer (believing that the quantity of liquid has not changed), but also of understanding why the amount of liquid *must* logically be the same. Piagetian tests of conservation require not only correct responses, but also correct explanations, that is, they require a very explicit understanding of the logical relations that make of conservation a logical necessity.

In fact, when children have been tested with nonverbal tasks that do not require a verbal explanation, they give conservation answers earlier than at 6 years. For example, Mehler and Bever (1967) claimed that very young children (2 to 3-year-olds) were capable of number conservation, another mental operation that Piaget found in children at around the same time as quantity conservation. The standard Piagetian test of number conservation consists of first asking children if two rows with the same number of objects symmetrically disposed have the same number of things, and then, once they have agreed to that, moving the objects of one row closer to each other so that now one row is longer than the other, and the perceptual correspondence is gone. Children under 6 to 7 tested with this explicit verbal procedure typically fail to realize that there must still be the same number of objects. But when Mehler and Bever simply asked children of 2 to 3 years of age which of two (uneven) rows of highly desirable sweets they wanted to keep for themselves, the younger kids didn't hesitate: they always selected the row with more sweets whether it had become shorter after a transformation or not.

Piaget himself (Piaget, 1968)) protested that this might not be a real test of conservation measuring the same thing as his original tests. For one thing, Mehler and Bever's was a test of "conservation of inequality" (the quantities to be compared were different from the beginning), and children were not probed to ascertain if they understood the logical basis of their choice. Piaget suggested that Mehler and Bever were just tapping some primitive component or precursor of conservation that did not require the same level of logical understanding. In fact, when the same test is given to older children (4 to 5), they fail to choose the larger quantity after the transformation. Although Mehler and Bever (1968) justified this interim failure as a "performance" problem masking a genuine underlying ability to conserve, a more convincing interpretation could be that these older children are developing a more explicit and systematic understanding of the logic of transformations, which is as yet unable to account for all the factors at work in the task. At this explicit representational level of understanding, children may genuinely believe that the quantities change with external appearance (see Karmiloff-Smith [1992] for more on how the development of more complex representations may produce transitory worse performances).

This argument could be applied to the case of Sarah: probably her understanding of quantity conservation is less explicit and less systematic than that of older human children, and therefore not entirely comparable to the sophisticated logical reasoning of a seven-year-old child. Still, it remains an impressive example of the ability to perceive the world beyond the information given—with the help of mental representations that can compensate for misleading perceptual information.

Was Sarah unique in her conservation abilities, perhaps owing to her extensive linguistic training? Muncer (1983) adapted Mehler and Bever's test for use with some chimpanzees who had received a much more restricted program of symbolic training. With one of his subjects he essentially replicated Woodruff and Premack's findings, and he even found number conservation, an ability that Premack and Woodruff could not fully test with Sarah because of her inability to complete some of the preliminary steps of testing.

In more recent experiments, Call and Rochat (1996, 1997) gave "conservation of inequality" tests *à la* Mehler and Bever to orangutans. Although their subjects proved very good at choosing the larger quantities of juice after the transformations, the authors concluded that the orangs were not engaging in true conservation, because actually many of them were able to choose the bigger amount even when the unequal containers (cups versus tubes) were offered directly, without showing the amounts in identical containers before the transformation. Their suggestion is that the orangs may be good at estimating quantities from containers of different shapes. Therefore what these tests would be measuring is not conservation, but the ability to make quantity estimates irrespective of superficial appearances.

But a careful consideration of their results shows that when highly contrasting shapes were used as containers, most of their subjects were misled by the appearances and failed to choose the one with more juice. More importantly, at least two of their subjects were able to overcome the misleading shape cues if first they were shown the quantities in identical cups and then saw the transformation, as in the standard conservation tests.*

This performance appears to be comparable to that described for chimpanzees by Muncer and Premack and Woodruff. Both chimpanzees and orangutans appear to be able to alter their purely perceptual judgments on the basis of information that is no longer available perceptually: they are somehow combining what they have seen before the transformation with what they are seeing after it, and they give precedence to the information seen previously.

All the same, Call and Rochat are still reluctant to attribute what they call true conservation to their subjects, because they failed an-

---

* For this result, compare fig. 2 of 1996 paper with fig. 4 of 1997 paper.

other version of the task in which the larger quantity is poured not into a single container but into several smaller containers, all of which constituted a single option. But this particular version of conservation can be very difficult even for older children, as Call and Rochat discovered when they gave the task to eight-year-olds.

In sum, it is difficult to decide what the apes' performance in these conservation tasks means. It is very unlikely that they are going through the same thought processes as a seven-year-old child tested *à la* Piaget. Nevertheless they could be using at least some of the representational processes that younger children use when confronted with similar nonverbal versions of conservation. What the data strongly suggest is that apes demonstrate an ability to go beyond the information given at a particular time on the basis of information available earlier: hence judgments and decisions concerning objects are made through complex representational strategies that go beyond immediate responses to stimuli or mere memory of static representations.

The Logic of Spontaneous Object Manipulation

Most of the studies we have discussed so far were based on complex trainings in relatively artificial laboratory situations. Is it possible that the classificatory and categorizing talents uncovered in monkeys and apes are just an artificial product of those laboratory settings and have little significance for their spontaneous interests and behavior? A growing line of research, based upon the analysis of completely spontaneous object manipulations seems to indicate otherwise.

Outside problem-solving contexts, many primates simply like to investigate objects by manipulating them (see chapter 3). The neo-Piagetian psychologist Jonas Langer and his collaborators (Langer, 1998, 2000a and b) suggest that this tendency can be exploited to probe the underlying logic of primate minds—how they literally and spontaneously put things together or set them apart on the basis of their similarities and differences. Langer divides cognition into three core domains, physical, logical, and mathematical, and, like Piaget, he assumes that these domains of cognition are first realized in action—doing things with objects.

Sorting Objects

To investigate one aspect of logical cognition—object classification—Langer and his collaborators developed the method of offering their subjects a set of objects, some of which were identical (two yellow cylinders), others partially similar (a yellow and a green cylinder), and others completely different (for example, a red triangular block and a long yellow cylinder). Typically, when offered the whole set of objects, younger human and chimpanzee infants pick up *different* objects (for example, a yellow cylinder and a green triangular column). At this stage, they never pick identical or similar objects. In a second developmental step, they produce all possible combinations of object selection and grouping as if following no criteria in their choice. In a third stage, they pick up and put together *identical* objects, thereby producing what Langer calls single or first-order classifications of objects. The next developmental step is the production of groups of *similar* (not completely identical) objects (for example, a yellow cup and a green cup). This, according to him, represents a more flexible way of classification that takes into account global features that objects have in common, ignoring their differences. Finally, in a fifth stage, infants may construct parallel sets of identical objects; for example, they put together on a heap the four cylinders, and on a different heap the four square columns available in the set. Langer calls this "second-order classifying," because infants are no longer using a single category to guide their actions, but two categories at the same time. They are dealing with the proposed set of objects by keeping in mind two classificatory criteria simultaneously.

Children and chimpanzees follow exactly this same sequence of five steps in the development of their object-sorting behavior, but at a very different rate. For example, chimps put identical objects together (stage 3) only at 24 months, whereas human babies do so at 12 months. Chimpanzees reach second-order classification (stage 5) at 54 months, whereas children do so at 18 months. The monkey species tested so far (capuchins and macaques) never develop second-order classifications; they only engage in first-order classifications, and they do so at the relatively advanced age of 48 months. Moreover, at least one monkey species, capuchin monkeys, develops its sorting skills following a sequence that differs from that of humans and chimpanzees—they start by random selection (instead of selection by difference, as chimpanzee and human babies), then change into sorting different objects together, and only later they move into classifying by identities and similarities, which they do simultaneously, whereas humans and chimpanzees do identities before doing similarities.

Chimpanzee and human development of spontaneous sorting differs not only in developmental synchrony but also in the absolute frequency and the relative prevalence of each type of classification. For example, when chimps start doing second-order classifications at 54 months, these represent only a very small proportion of all their classifications, whereas they represent a substantial share of human object handling.

Another difference has to do with the number of objects that are included in a particular class. Monkeys remain constrained to 3 or 4 units at the most, but chimpanzees can sort up to 5 units by 5 years of age. It is not clear if they can progress beyond this at later ages. In contrast, human children at 30 months of age are already grouping up to 8 objects, and more than half of the groupings produced by human infants at 36 months comprise 3 or more sets of objects, whereas chimpanzees remain constrained to 2 sets of objects until 5 years of age, and their overall rate of production of classificatory manipulations remains relatively low (20 percent of all manipulations).

Langer (2000a) thinks that elementary two-category classifications could be the ceiling of chimpanzee "logical" development. In contrast, the ability of children to classify objects into three or more categories may have far-reaching consequences. According to him, handling three categories at the same time leads to the possibility of *hierarchical classifications*, namely, those in which an object may belong simultaneously to two categories. A red square belongs to the set of red objects and to that of square objects, but also to the lower-order category of red square objects. This also opens up the possibility of so-called recursive forms of cognition, as elementary classifications become the object of classification themselves, so that infants can now operate not only upon objects, but also upon relations between objects. Langer's suggestion that this level of logical cognition is not spontaneously used by chimpanzees partially coincides with the findings discussed in a previous section—chimpanzees' failure to do "relationships match-to-sample" between pairs of objects, unless they had been "linguistically" trained.

Heterochrony as the Engine of Cognitive Evolution

A remarkable aspect of Langer's findings is the fact that in object-sorting behaviors—which he identifies as corresponding to *logical* cognition—the direction of the disparity between monkey, ape, and human rates of development is exactly the opposite to that found in Piagetian sensorimotor notions like object permanence—which Langer identifies with *physical* cognition. As we saw in chapter 2, monkeys develop object permanence much quicker than apes, and these, in turn, slightly quicker than humans. In contrast, human infants develop object sorting much faster than apes, who in turn develop it faster than monkeys.

Langer's wider theoretical perspective is based upon the idea that the brains of all newborn primates contain some core physical, logical, and mathematical notions that are essentially the same across species, in their initial state. But different species develop these core notions at different rates and to different extents. The result is that very different minds emerge out of essentially the same "cognitive seeds" through the process of cognitive development. For Langer, the ontogenetic asymmetries or *heterochronies* between sensorimotor domains are the key evolutionary/developmental factor that explains the cognitive differences among primate species.

Heterochrony refers to changes in the timing of development (onset moment and speed) of different aspects of sensorimotor systems (for example, object permanence as an index of physical cognition as compared to object sorting as an index of logical cognition). Biologists proposed long ago that heterochrony plays an important role in morphological evolution: the different shapes of organs like hands or faces in different species may be explained by changes in the growth rates of their different components during embryonic development (McKinney, 1988).

Langer and other researchers (Parker and McKinney, 1999; Antinucci, 1990) propose that something similar may happen in the realm of cognition. Evolution may have acted by altering the timing and rate of development of different cognitive components, with dramatic effects on the final kind of intelligence achieved. As Piaget proposed for human babies, primates would construct their own cognitive development by actively manipulating the world around them. In Langer's words, "species-specific cognitive specializations are developmental products, not innate givens" (Langer, 2000a; p. 368). Subtle differences in developmental parameters such as the onset/offset time, speed, and rate of production of different domains would unavoidably constrain what each species can attain. Development itself is not free to create any mind: it must act within the constraints provided by the starting states of each species (which Langer, however, appears to consider essentially identical among primates) and the differential patterns of emergence of each developmental component.

In Langer's view, this heterochronic evolution has resulted in three different patterns of cognitive ontogeny that roughly correspond to three different kinds of primate minds: monkey minds, ape minds, and human minds. Monkey minds complete their development in the domain of physical cognition very quickly and *before* they start developing any logico-mathematical cognition (remember that Langer is speaking of cognition as reflected in the structure of actions); the timing of ape minds' developments in each area has changed, and they benefit from a partial overlap between the physical and logical domains of development (they start doing first-order classifications of objects when they have not yet completed the development of object permanence). The full long-term cognitive benefits of this phylogenetic operation of synchronization of physical and logico-mathematical aspects of cognition occurs in humans, whose developmental trajectories in each domain overlap perfectly.

This is an ambitious and bold theory—one that surely is in need of much more empirical research and conceptual refinement—but it has the merit of directly addressing the issue of the mechanisms of cognitive evolution, and proposing that changes in developmental patterns may be the key factor.

Primate Logic

In our discussion of selected aspects of logical cognition in primates we found that they are capable of classifying and categorizing objects in terms of their similarities and differences, although it is still unclear at what hierarchical levels of complexity. The old idea that perceiving in categories might be the product of language with its hierarchical system of labels appears to be incorrect. Forms of categorical perception are present in primates (and probably in other mammals and birds). This does not mean that language is not important as a tool that enhances categorical cognition in humans.

When tested with different tasks (match-to-sample), important differences emerge between primates and nonprimates, and among primate species themselves. Nonprimates appear to have to learn every new matching problem from scratch, whereas monkeys and apes seem to learn something about the very notion of "sameness." In fact chimpanzees appear to display a natural tendency to attend to relationships among objects and some aptitude for learning to respond to relationships of relationships—a complex logical achievement for which they need special symbolic training.

Further evidence of important spontaneous differences in the logical approach of monkeys and apes to the world of objects can be found with a much simpler method—observing their spontaneous manipulations of objects. When left to their own devices, without any training or reinforcement, primates tend to pick up and group objects following peculiar patterns that take into account similarity and difference. Nonprimates have not been tested with this simple procedure because it requires manipulation, and all primates tested so far were captive. Perhaps the very act of picking up and grouping objects that are the same, different, or similar marks an important difference in what primates do with their basic abilities to perceive similarities in comparison to other mammals and birds. Using these abilities to organize the way in which they approach objects, and moreover to produce actual physical groupings of similar or dissimilar objects, may have the effect of making categorical representations more explicitly available to the primate mind. One obvious next step should be studying to what extent some form of spontaneous sorting is part of their everyday behavior in the wild.

6

Objects in the World

Primate knowledge of objects is not just a laboratory curiosity. Representing the world in terms of objects, their kinds, similarities, transformations, and most importantly their uses, is fundamental for the primate way of life in the wild. So far we have discussed aspects of object knowledge on a small scale: how objects are found and handled, and how they are related in logical or physical-causal terms in what Call (2000) so aptly identifies as the "manipulative space." But primates also have to represent the wider picture of how objects are organized in the world they really inhabit. Primate environments can be very complex: they can consist of several hundred square meters (not to mention the cubic meters if we consider the vertical dimension for arboreal primates!) full of natural objects and substrates: trees, rivers, rocks, stones, slopes, a vast amount of plants and insects, and a variety of other animals including conspecifics and potential predators and preys. Primates spend much of their time moving around their home range in search of food—foraging—and other resources. One of the fundamental tasks that a successful primate mind must confront is to have an adequate representation of his home range and the kinds of objects that lay (or roam) around in it.

Mental Maps

Field students (Garber, 2000) are frequently impressed that primates move in their environment with a surprisingly detailed knowledge of where and how they are traveling. They move around as if they had detailed global representations of their surroundings that they use to mentally calculate their moves. During their daily foraging excursions they appear to have in mind spatial/object representations that go beyond the immediate here and now. For example, species as diverse as tamarins, capuchins, and chimpanzees will ignore a nearby small resource of food that is fully visible in order to go to a more distant, currently invisible, much richer resource they have found before (Garber, 2000). This may sound as only natural—going for food to where you know there is good, abundant food—but the ability to *know*, to have in mind a detailed and precise picture of the distribution of relevant objects in a complex environment, and use this knowledge to think ahead about where to go for foraging is far from trivial.

Some authors (Janson, 2000) propose that the reason that primates (and not other fruit-eating animals, like bats) had to develop a complex cognitive skill for spatial navigation in their feeding excursions is that apes and monkeys cannot go in straight line—flying—from one tree to another. Often they have to climb down the tree and walk to the next or follow some intricate roundabout route, and primate locomotion is more costly in energy terms than that of bats. Also, since most primates are social, not just any resource may be suitable for them: they need to be able to select resources big enough to accommodate the feeding needs of the group.

In an experiment with a group of captive baboons housed in a big nature enclosure, the primatologist Jacques Vauclair (1990) investigated how well they could remember the location of food hidden by experimenters. The enclosure contained 135 stones, all of which were possible hiding places. In their everyday life the baboons spontaneously inspected the stones from time to time, probably in search of insects hidden underneath (as wild baboons do in nature). In each trial, watching from a distance, the baboons saw a human leaving nuts under 4 of those stones. Less than one minute later, they were allowed into the enclosure. In these trials the baboons found 96 percent of the nuts (they only failed to find a couple of nuts in 20 trials), and they did so rather quickly, in an average of 47 seconds per trial. In contrast, when they were not allowed to see where the nuts were hidden, they only found 69 percent of them, and it took them an average of two minutes of search. Clearly, their habit of searching under the stones allows them a high rate of success in the absence of any information about the location of the food, but still their performance is significantly better—almost perfect and extremely quick—when allowed to watch the food hiding.

To solve this problem the baboons had to use many of the abilities we considered in the previous chapters: a notion of object permanence, an ability to individuate objects spatially and on the basis of their appearance, and the ability to organize a search behavior on the basis of such representations. Moreover, Vauclair's baboons were also displaying some ability to quantify food, as revealed by experiments in which pieces of food in different amounts were left in various areas, and the baboons usually went to the locations where more food had been hidden.

But apart from the integration of these aspects of object cognition, the baboons also needed some form of organization of these pieces of knowledge into a wider picture or spatial framework—some sort of *mental map* of their environment which depicts the relative positions of objects and landmarks. This has been one of the core questions of research on primate spatial cognition: do primates have mental maps of their environments, and if so, what do they consist of?

Spatial Cognition of Marmosets

Marmosets are small New World monkeys once thought to have retained many primitive primate characters and to be rather unsophisticated. In time this evaluation changed, and it is currently accepted that they appear to have developed a number of remarkably original adaptations for their unusual lifestyle. Unlike many other primates, marmosets organize their food search (or foraging behavior) by looking for fruits that grow in small quantities in a varied number of locations and ripen at different times even if they are on the same bush or tree. This means that a given location is not permanently exhausted of food, and that it pays to return to it in the near future. To exploit this foraging pattern optimally, marmosets should be able to generate complex representations of multiple small food locations situated at different points in space, and the times they have visited them. Alternatively, they could just follow some sort of random sampling technique, trusting that they will find enough food each day.

A series of fascinating studies by Menzel and his collaborators (Menzel and Menzel, 1979; Menzel and Juno, 1982) suggest that marmosets do use spatial and object representations to organize their foraging. In these experiments, as in the baboon study above, the marmosets were tested as a group in an attempt to respect their natural behavior: in the wild marmosets search for food as a team, usually the young following the older, and they call out when they detect appropriate items.

A captive group of marmosets was allowed to forage in a room in which different objects (some with food, others without) were progressively accumulated from trial to trial, up to a total of 30 objects. The marmosets systematically approached any new object the first day it was introduced. If it contained food, they returned to it the following day; if it had no food, they ignored it the next day. As a group, they had an extraordinary ability to identify the new objects and to remember which ones were baited (even toward the end of the experiment, with 30 objects to inspect). In fact, their performance could be described as learning in a single trial a discrimination task (one of the traditional laboratory tests used with primates in which they have to learn to associate one particular object with the presence of food). The paradox is that marmosets tested individually, in a typical laboratory test in which they have to remember which of two objects contains food, take several hundred trials until they learn that the rule of the game is to select again the same object that was baited before. Menzel and Juno (1982) point out that in one laboratory study marmosets needed 1,000 problems to reach a 75 percent of accuracy, whereas in their own study, tested as a group, they went to the previously baited object in 75 percent of the occasions after only one trial.

Moreover, the marmosets not only recognized the previously

baited object, but they also remembered its position. If the original baited object was moved to a new location in the next trial, marmosets went to the empty area where the object used to be; sometimes they even looked around and made food calls. This demonstrates an ability to code object location, but it also suggests that their search is guided by some representation of what they are looking for—the food.

In other trials, after the previously baited object was moved to a new location, its place was taken by one of the other known objects in which the marmosets had never found food. In 75 percent of these trials the marmosets preferred to go to the food-associated object in its new location, rather than to the object without food that was usurping the location of the former. This shows the flexibility of the marmosets' representations: they can remember both the place and the identity of the object with food, and they give precedence to one or the other depending upon the context.

In further trials conducted when the collection of 30 objects was already in place, Menzel introduced changes in their distribution; for example, he swapped the location of two objects, or withdrew one and replaced it with another object identical to one of the remaining 29. In these cases the marmosets appeared to spot the change, as they approached the changed objects or the new exemplars of known objects. This suggests that they not only comprehend different object appearances, but also the identity of individual objects of the same kind (compare Hauser and Carey's studies in chapter 2).

Marmosets, therefore, appear to be able to build very detailed representations of their foraging environments, both in terms of spatial locations and of the individual objects situated in different locations. This ability, although documented only in laboratory experiments, appears to fit well what is known about the marmosets natural foraging behavior. Menzel's findings suggest that in the wild marmosets might well be using detailed spatial representations of their natural environments, rather than make random foraging excursions.

Spatial Cognition of Chimpanzees

The above experiments with marmosets were partly modeled after an earlier series of studies carried out by Emil Menzel with a group of chimpanzees in a big outdoor enclosure of 4,000 square meters (Menzel 1971, 1973b, 1974). Initially, Menzel did not use food as an incentive, but counted on the natural curiosity of chimpanzees toward objects. During 10 days the chimps found the same 20 objects scattered around the enclosure, always in the same position. The chimps explored the objects until they became habituated and stopped paying attention to them. On the eleventh day of testing, a new object was randomly placed in the enclosure (in such a position that it was visible from the point where the chimpanzees were released), and another on each successive day until 30 objects were present. After the chimps were released in groups of 3, it never took more than 15 seconds for them to spot the new objects and go to explore them.

In some trials, old objects were moved to a new position, replaced with a new object, or simply withdrawn from the enclosure. Chimps were not especially interested in the relocated objects they already knew, although they did increase exploration of them. They did carefully inspect any new object that appeared in the place of an old one. (But no special behavior was recorded around the empty area where a missing object used to be.) Chimpanzees therefore easily detected novel objects and changes in object location, even in the absence of food incentives. This suggests some knowledge of the items in their environment and their distribution.

To test the complexity of the chimpanzees' spatial representations, Menzel eventually introduced food as an incentive. He took one chimpanzee and showed him/her how 16 pieces of food were placed in 16 different hiding places in the enclosure. The chimp was then returned to the indoors cage and released after a variable amount of time. The response of the chimpanzee was to go immediately to the 16 baited places one after the other, and he followed *optimal* routes, namely, he chose the order of travel to each baited place as a function of the actual proximity among the places, which never coincided with the order in which they had been baited by the human. The chimpanzees, therefore, were not simply reproducing the path they had followed while witnessing the hiding events, but creating their own foraging route on the basis of some representation of the whereabouts of the 16 pieces of food.

Moreover, when the quality and quantity of the hidden food was varied, so that some hiding places contained more food or more appealing kinds of food, the chimps went first to the best places following the shortest routes. The chimpanzees, therefore, not only remembered the locations of the food, but they also integrated this knowledge into a coherent, spatially organized representation which, as Menzel suggested, could best be described as a "cognitive map"—some sort of detailed picture of the distribution of relevant objects in the space.

Menzel (1974) provides some interesting qualitative descriptions of the behavior of the apes during the baiting sequence that are suggestive of how they could be forming those mental maps. The chimps, observing always from the arms of a second experimenter, paid little attention to the food itself; they looked closely to the hiding place as the food concealment was completed (for example, by piling leaves on the food), and then struggled in the arms of the experimenter to orient visually to the nearest large vertical structure (for example, a prominent tree). When no such prominent structure was in the vicinity, they would simply orient to the field in general after focusing on the hiding area. The chimps appeared first to store the more local information of the whereabouts of the food in relation to the small objects and visual details of the hiding area, and then the larger-scale information of where the local area was in relation to the whole enclosure. To do so, they first searched for a landmark and, if none was available, then they took a general overview of the scenario.

According to Menzel, the searching behavior of the chimpanzees corroborated this impression: they usually raced in straight line toward the landmark closer to the food and, depending upon whether the food was hidden just there or over a wider area, they would go straight for it or slow down and look carefully around the local area as if in search of smaller, local cues. Their errors rarely consisted of choosing a wrong landmark. They tended to select the correct area where the food was hidden, though within this area they could occasionally commit the error of searching under a hiding place that was similar to the original one (the wrong pile of leaves).

Acquiring Cognitive Maps

How did chimpanzees acquire the complex representational background against which they coded the food position in each experiment? Before starting his experiment, Menzel conducted an observational study of how the chimpanzees explored their new home environment when they were first introduced into it. Adult chimpanzees engaged from the very beginning in wide, but relatively brief explorations that were aimed at large landmarks, such as tall trees, buildings, or the fence area. They did not move much, but devoted a lot of time to visual exploration.

In contrast, young chimpanzees (released in groups of three) acted more energetically, moving a lot, but concentrating on the exploration of smaller areas. They did not explore all the parts of the enclosure at once; they took several months, adding each day a little bit more of unexplored space until the complete enclosure was covered. Their movements were not random, but occurred as a function of the available landmarks. Every new day, they returned to an area already explored to launch from there new explorations of uncharted territory, always moving toward a new landmark object, such as a tree or a new part of the fence.

As the days passed, the young chimps moved more at ease and displayed more overt exploratory behavior, such as climbing on the trees or manipulating the objects. Their patterns of movement eventually (after 40 days!) started to resemble those of adult chimpanzees on their first hours of encounter with the new enclosure—few locomotor displacements, and much visual exploration.

Albeit performed with different styles and at different rates, for old and young chimpanzees alike the exploration of space arose out of the exploration of landmark objects. This could imply that chimpanzees build their spatial representations out of their object representations—as if space were something emanating from objects, or, to use the researcher's own words, "behavioral space was always structured in terms of objects" (Menzel, 1974, p. 94).

Prospective Object Permanence

In the experiments where food was hidden for later retrieval, Menzel used control trials in which the chimpanzees were not allowed to see the hiding of the targets. In this way he could determine the findability of the hidden pieces of food in the absence of previous information. Initially, the controls worked well: the uninformed chimpanzees took a lot of time to find any of the food, and they appeared to do so only by chance. Once the chimpanzees got to know what was going on, however (that in every trial some food was lying hidden somewhere), they demonstrated a remarkable ability to guess the hiding places from tell-tale signs. According to Menzel's qualitative descriptions, they inspected any known object that had experienced some change in location or orientation since the last time seen, or any new, unexpected accumulation of leaves or tree bark lying on the ground (specially if they were far away from any tree!). They appeared to be using some sort of object notion similar to that explored with Piagetian invisible displacement tasks, in which object locations are inferred, not remembered—a *prospective* object permanence.

Moreover, chimps were quick to spot any patterns in the hiding of the food. For example, in a variation of his experiments, Menzel allowed one chimpanzee to see the hiding event, but then released the whole group and compared the behavior of the informed and the uninformed chimpanzees. If one piece of food had been hidden by each fencing post following a regular pattern, after the informed animal had uncovered three sites in succession, the others raced ahead of him and started searching around the next posts. This ability to spot and use distributional *patterns* was specially impressive in a series of experiments in which only two piles of food were hidden, one in each half of the enclosure, in such a way that they occupied contralateral angles in relation to the release point. After a few repetitions of this test (each time using different locations and angles), the uninformed animals started to go to the contralateral place as soon as they discovered the first pile. They acted with a surprising degree of precision: they searched in the contralateral half within 4.5 m of the correct location!

All in all, Menzel's studies with chimpanzees suggest that they possess detailed and flexible representations of their everyday environment. As was true for marmosets, this would fit chimpanzees' natural foraging and ranging behavior consisting of daily travel throughout a relatively huge territory. To what extent these representations are really best described as "cognitive maps" is an issue of contention, to which we will return later.

Patterns of Object Search

One of the most remarkable findings by Menzel was what we have called "prospective object permanence," that is, the ability to infer the location of hidden food from tell-tale cues. Hemmi and C. Menzel (1995) and C. Menzel (1996) have further explored this ability with a monkey species—long-tailed macaques studied in captivity. Menzel (1996) gave them different kinds of foraging arrangements: in one, food was hidden in their enclosure at intervals along a visible edge (such as a cement wall or a grass border); in another arrangement, food was hidden next to similar objects, for example, a piece of food was buried by each crate present in the enclosure; the crates were randomly scattered. In other conditions, the food was hidden on the ground at 1 or 3 meter intervals following an invisible straight line that did not coincide with any visible structure in the enclosure (if anything, it cut across them). To give them a start-up cue in these conditions the three first food items of the pattern were visible.

The macaques were capable of using the visible structures and the visual similarity of the landmark objects from the very beginning: they found all the hidden food in the first experiments and subsequently kept a very high level of performance. Their performance in the invisible line conditions was initially much worse (although not random), but they showed signs of improvement in this condition after only a few trials.

The most effective searchers were adult animals. Young one-year-olds showed some sensitivity to the visible line condition only (searching for food along landmark borders). The ability to benefit from the visible pattern did not depend upon having found the initial food personally. As in the case of chimpanzees, macaque onlookers were also able to engage in a patterned search.

Finally, in a control run after completing the previous trials, only one piece of visible food was placed by one of the visible longitudinal landmarks; no other food was hidden. The macaques unsuccessfully searched along the wall border where the food had appeared. This proves that they were not detecting the hidden food by any other means (olfaction), but were genuinely inferring its existence.

This study suggests that the long-tailed macaque possesses a complex representational ability for objects in space similar to that found in chimpanzees—a *prospective object concept* that is combined with an ability to perceive visible structures (or object similarities) in the environment to produce organized food searches without having to depend upon slow associative learning of the kind typically found in laboratory learning tests. More surprising was that the macaques appeared to be capable of using some entirely subjective structures when the straight line formed by the three visible pieces of food did not coincide with any existing visible structure. Interestingly, in these cases they acted after consuming the visible food items, that is, after the elements suggesting the straight line were no longer visible. Hemmi and Menzel (1995) point out that a simple continuation of an initiated movement is an unlikely explanation because the macaques did not move right away, but took their time to eat the food already found and even looked around before continuing. Thus at the very least they displayed an ability to keep in mind their planned direction of movement.

Akebi Fruit and Cognitive Maps in the Wild

C. R. Menzel (1991) conducted an interesting field experiment to investigate cognitive maps in wild Japanese macaques. He placed in their way either a piece of chocolate (a relatively infrequent, but preferred food item for them) or an akebi fruit, one of their favorite natural foods, which was then out of season. Upon finding the chocolate, the macaques ate it and then manually searched around the area where the piece was found as if in search of more; they also returned frequently to the area and searched it during the next 20 minutes and even on the next day. Sometimes they also searched the ground surface of areas similar in appearance to that in which the chocolate finding had occurred.

In contrast, upon finding the akebi fruit, their typical reaction was to look up at the branches above them or up the slope of an adjacent hill, sometimes engaging in what appeared to be an elaborate distal visual inspection (akebi vines tend to occur on trees and at relatively high altitudes). Moreover, when they finally abandoned the area where they found the piece of fruit, they went on to visit trees with akebi vines (sometimes sharply deviating from the route they had been following before the finding): they looked at their branches, touched and inspected them, and even tasted some unripe fruits.

Upon finding the akebi fruit out of season and out of context, the monkeys recognize this kind of fruit, and their knowledge of it is activated: first, they try to locate a vine from which the fruit may have come and then, under the guidance of some notion that the akebi vines may have come into fruit, they start a search for more fruits by traveling to the distant trees they know have akebi vines and searching them. This example demonstrates how knowledge undoubtedly acquired by repeated experience (which trees have akebi) is not synonymous with blind stimulus-response associations, but rather may consist of internal representations that guide the behavior of the monkeys when the proper context is activated. It is this kind of representations of objects in the world that lead many scientists to speak of *mental or cognitive maps*.

Maps in the Mind?

It is not always clear what researchers mean by "mental or cognitive map." One possibility is that a mental map is precisely an equivalent of a physical map, that is, some sort of iconic global representation of the relative spatial position and distances of relevant objects and landmarks that can be mentally consulted to take decisions about directions and routes of movement. Another possibility is that effective spatial cognition is achieved with other kinds of representations, or even more interestingly, with a combination of different kinds of representations. These may not necessarily consist of global images or layouts of a whole territory, but rather comprise a mixture of iconic views of particular landmark places and motor images of the displacements one has to carry out in order to move from there to a different place (the path that leads to the big tree with akebi vines; the rocks behind the pool, and so on). These local representations may not be articulated into a global map. Primates may have some sort of unfolding representation of spaces—something like a folded map that cannot be fully spread out and has to be consulted by parts, each part activated by actually performed (or in the case of humans, imagined) goal-oriented movements. Physical maps are a new kind of tool that humans use in combination with the set of mental skills with which primates in general find their way in the world; but maps may not be direct reflections of the kinds of natural spatial representations primates use in their everyday lives. These are likely to be more dynamic and object-dependent than the static, aerial-view images we think of as a map.

Some current hypotheses about spatial knowledge in primates do indeed emphasize its heterogeneous and hierarchical nature. For example, Poucet (1993) has proposed that primates represent space using a mixed system: on the one hand, detailed Euclidean representations for small portions of space; and, on the other, rough topological representations (in which only some relative positions of significant objects in relation to certain landmarks are recorded) for larger-scale spaces. In the wild, monkeys would have detailed representations of a number of focal areas, but only a general, approximate idea of the wider space in which these focal areas are situated.

Monkeys would know a few, relatively fixed routes to travel from one focal area to another, but within those focal areas they would be capable of moving around in flexible and precise ways.

Garber (2000) tried to test this hypothesis by studying the daily movements of a group of tamarin monkeys in the wild. He found evidence of focal areas of which the monkeys appeared to have a relatively detailed knowledge, as suggested from the great variety of routes they could follow to reach any of the large fruit trees that constitute their food source once they were within one of those local areas. The results were not so straightforward, however, for traveling between these areas. The monkeys would start traveling from one area in a straight line, but they did not follow fixed routes. Moreover, during their travel they frequently performed 90 degree turns at the beginning or at the end of these straight line moves. These turns were performed at particular areas of the forest range between the focal areas. One possible interpretation is that the monkeys use a variety of local landmarks to reorient themselves, so that they do not have to rely entirely on rote-learned routes.

Understanding Physical Maps

Having talked about whether primates use mental maps, we now turn to the intriguing question of whether they can learn to use physical maps. Physical maps make two main cognitive demands: one is obviously the ability to use symbols; but a second requisite ability that is easily overlooked is the ability to engage in "microspatial" cognition, meaning the ability to apply spatial representations that are usually used in relatively large spaces to small portions of space. This can be demanding in itself, as the following studies suggest.

Microspatial Cognition

In an experiment with human children, Lasky and colleagues (1980) taught them the following game: a toy was hidden in one of two identical boxes fixed on a board. The boxes could be differentiated only because they occupied different positions in relation to a face that was drawn on the board and could be used as a "landmark." The hiding of the toy was performed in full view, but then a screen was placed in front of the board, which was rotated out of sight of the children. The screen was removed and the children were then asked to find the hidden toy on this rotated "landscape." Three- and five-year-olds consistently failed to find the hidden toy in their first attempt, even when they were explicitly instructed to try to use the face as a guide. Only at 7 years of age children started to be able to solve the problem, and even then their performance was not perfect. If the rotations of the board were made in full view after hiding the toy, 7-year-olds solved the task perfectly, whereas 3 and 5-year-olds performed better than with invisible rotations but still committed frequent errors.

Branch (1986) gave exactly the same test to chimpanzees of different ages, except that the landmark was a solid object (a clicker) mounted on a red square on a board, and the chimps were required to press the clicker before the trials proceeded as a way of calling their attention to the landmark. Chimps (including the younger 3-year-olds) had no problems retrieving the hidden food when the rotations were made in full view. But as soon as a screen was interposed during the rotation, all chimps, including the adults, failed the test. Branch managed to train them to solve the invisible rotation task after a prolonged period of painstaking trial and error learning. Nonetheless there is every indication that their eventual success was not due to the use of a spatial representational strategy to calculate the position of the target. Both in the original study with children and in this study with chimpanzees, the authors took measurements of the reaction times of their subjects. Reaction time can be used as an indication of the amount of thinking one needs to do before giving a response. In the initial study of Lasky and colleagues (1980), the children and the adults who managed to solve the invisible rotation problems had longer reaction times in these than in the visible rotation trials, meaning they had to think to decide which was the correct location. In contrast, the extensively trained chimpanzees had exactly the same reaction time when solving the visible and the invisible rotations. They were not using the landmark to infer the location of the target; they probably had just learned to give direct responses to each possible combination of initial and final configurations.

Chimpanzees and children under 7 years, therefore, had difficulties dealing with this microspatial task. Children eventually compensated for the rotations, not so the chimpanzees; but, on the other hand, the chimpanzees, even at 3 years, were capable of solving correctly the visible rotation problems that children of 3 and 5 years of age found very difficult. Difficulty in this area contrasts with the impressive performances of chimpanzees (and other primates) in large-scale spaces. Remember that in Menzel's studies the chimps were capable of retrieving 16 different pieces of food scattered around the enclosure even after they had been withdrawn from it and came back later. The actual pathways they followed (and, therefore, the viewpoints from which they could see the landmarks) were of no consequence for their success.

One possible explanation for the extraordinary difficulty of the rotating board task is that this microspace with its landmark is inserted into a wider space frame with its own landmarks (the experimental room), whereas in Menzel's studies there is a single, well-known space whose major landmarks are always preserved. Similar difficulties dealing with object locations in microspaces have been reported in chimpanzees in a variety of other tasks: for example, they can commit serious errors in tasks in which a reward is hidden in one of two different objects, and then, while they cannot see it being done, the object positions are swapped. Frequently the chimps commit the error of going to the wrong object, as if they were confusing positions and object identities (Fobes and King, 1982). This sort of error appears to be rare in bigger settings like those used by Menzel.

Using Three-Dimensional Maps

Given their difficulties with microspaces, chimpanzees would not be expected to be able to use a map, because this requires not only that they perceive and understand a microspace, but also that they subsequently act upon a physically different space. Premack and Premack (1983) carried out a number of ingenious experiments trying to induce physical map use in young chimpanzees. The basic procedure involved using a miniature model of a room (with miniature pieces of furniture) as a source of information about the location of hidden food in the real room: they showed the chimpanzees how a miniature banana was hidden in a miniature box, and then they took the chimps to the normal-sized room where a real banana was hidden in the corresponding box. The task of the chimps was to find the banana with the help of the information acquired in the miniature room. But the chimps were unable to recognize the map value of the miniature room—they searched randomly in the real room. They were given an extensive step-by-step training, starting with the use of two identical normal rooms (food was hidden in a particular part of one room, and then the chimps were allowed to search in the other, identical room). The chimps managed to solve this problem. Then, little by little, the first room was made smaller until they were able to use a small model of the large room as a guide to find the food. Their performance was fragile, however, and success was crucially dependent upon the model room being shown in exactly the same orientation as the real room. As soon as any rotation was introduced in the model, their performance dropped to chance levels. As we saw, chimpanzees have problems even with rotations of the same space if these are performed out of their sight. It was not clear whether the chimpanzees had developed a fragile understanding of the model as a "map" of the room or were dealing with the problem in some other way.

This paradigm was successfully imported into child psychology by Judy DeLoache (1995). She showed children a rectangular large-size room with 4 objects or pieces of furniture in the corners, and an exact miniature replica of the room with 4 corresponding miniature objects. The children's attention was drawn to the exact parallelism between the rooms, and then they were asked to participate in a game: a miniature toy (a small duck) was hidden in one of the objects in the miniature room; their task was to find a larger duck that was hidden in the same place but in the large room. Young human children can solve this model task as early as at 3 years of age, but not at 2.5 years. Crucially, the 2.5-year-olds who fail to find the object in the large room do still remember very well where the miniature object is in the model, and they can find it after failing to find the big object in the large room. Moreover, some of these 2.5-year-olds can be induced to find the target object in the real room if, instead of presenting the task as involving a small and a big room, they are told that there is just one room that is shrunken or enlarged using a magic machine. This implies that the difficulty has to do with understanding the *mapping* relationship between the two spaces, not with any inherent difficulty in recognizing the similarity between the rooms owing to the different sizes. Indeed, DeLoache (1995) suggested that this task could be used to measure the achievement of some sort of "representational insight" into the nature of symbol-referent relations, or an ability for "dual coding" of objects (treating the scale model both as an object on its own and as a symbol of the real room).

Recently, Boysen and Kuhlmeier (2002) have brought the scale model paradigm back into primatology, testing a number of chimpanzees with experience in laboratory tasks that had received some linguistic training. In a first study, closely following the standard procedure used with human children, two chimpanzees were shown a real room with 4 objects and, outside this, a corresponding miniature model with its corresponding miniature objects. The target object was a soda can, a miniature replica of which was hidden in the model. The chimps, after contemplating the hiding event in the model, were encouraged to search in the real room. One of the chimpanzees, a female called Sheba, went straight to the correct hiding location in 7 out of the 8 trials, whereas the other chimpanzee only succeeded in one trial. In a second experiment, the authors tested 7 chimpanzees, this time using a model of their outdoor enclosure in which 4 possible hiding locations had been planted. Three of the chimpanzees were able to make use of the model. One of them was again Sheba, this time with only 55 percent of correct responses; another successful chimp was that well-known character in primate research—Sarah, the former subject of Premack—who at the advanced, for a chimp, age of 38 years, outperformed her younger partners getting the correct result 65 percent of the trials. Four chimpanzees paid no attention to the information provided by the model. When allowed into the outdoor enclosure, they searched all four locations systematically (starting always with the same object) until they found the target.

The successful chimpanzees were clearly able to extract some information from the model and use it to guide their search in the large space. But were they really understanding the model as a *map* of the other space, or were they using some other strategy? Since the four objects used as hiding locations were different in shape and color, perhaps the chimpanzees were simply matching the properties of the relevant individual items without appreciating the mapping relationship of the whole model. For example, they could see that the miniature target was placed in the miniature black rubber tire, and then, when allowed into the enclosure, they could simply go to the black object, or a similarly shaped object, or both.

To test this possibility, the authors created new versions of the scale model problem in which they controlled for the possibility of using an individual object-matching strategy. Instead of using different objects, they used four identical objects as possible hiding places, ensuring that each object occupied exactly the same relative position in the model and the outdoor enclosure. The chimpanzees' search could only be guided by information about the relative spatial position of the objects in the model, and therefore could only be based upon some global understanding of the relationship between the small and the large space. None of the chimpanzees was able to find the target above chance in this condition; three of them showed some tendency to do slightly better than one would expect by pure chance (around 50 percent of success, instead of 25 percent), but still their performance was far from impressive. Yet when the performance of all subjects is put together, statistical tests suggest that they were finding the target in their first attempt slightly more frequently than one would expect by chance. This could be interpreted as evidence that the three chimps who were 50 percent correct may be after all sensitive to *some* of the spatial information provided by the model: perhaps rather than obtain a clear picture of which object they must search by way of a global understanding of the whole model, they just derive some vaguer information, like going to the left or to the right of the enclosure.

In another condition, the individual identity of the objects was preserved but their relative positions in the enclosure and the model differed (there were the same 4 different objects in both spaces, but they occupied different relative positions). The chimpanzees did much better as a group at this trial, although still their performance was worse than in the standard test in which they had both object identity and spatial information.

If instead of preserving a perfect parallelism between the real objects and the miniatures, only individual features are preserved (for example, in the model there is a black rubber tire miniature, but in the real space there is only a black box (color preserved) or a red tire (shape preserved), the chimpanzees' performance is much worse. This suggests that they are not relying upon simple color or shape associations to solve the problem, but at the very least are doing a global matching between the miniature and its real-size counterpart, that is, they are competent in recognizing the correspondence between objects that vary greatly in size, which, like understanding microspaces, could be considered to be a prerequisite for understanding maps.

Similar experiments have been carried out with human children using the scale model task. The results are very similar: when completely identical objects are used, children have more problems solving the task; they appear to have difficulty in using spatial information only. When the objects' differential identity is preserved but their spatial location is changed, they do almost as well as in the standard task, but their performance decreases a little (Solomon, 2001). This appears to indicate that human children, in normal circumstances, use both types of information simultaneously—they attend both to where the object is and which object it is—and the removal of any of these cues makes the task more difficult. The fact that chimpanzees react in a similar manner suggests that the way in which apes and humans represent the place of objects in space may share this feature of combining spatial and identity information. This similarity could exist independently of whether the chimpanzees understand the symbolic mapping of the spaces. In fact, it is unclear if young children, when they first pass this test, are really using the models as maps through some "representational insight," or relying upon some other strategy such as object matching (Perner, 1991).

Overall, the results obtained by Kuhlmeier and Boysen suggest that the chimpanzees were to some extent able "to use the model as a source of information" to guide their searches, but this ability does not necessarily consist of "recognizing the correspondence between the model and the corresponding full-size enclosure" as adult humans do when using a map.

Primates' Representation of Objects in Space

Primates in the wild have been frequently reported to act as if they possessed precise mental maps of their home ranges, which they use to plan their daily movements in search of food, water, or any other resources in an intelligent way. Experiments in captivity, and even some field experiments, confirm that primates appear to be able to use elaborate and detailed representations of their environments. They can recognize changes in landmarks or relevant objects, remember the location of food, and organize their searches in optimal ways. It is not clear, though, that the representations they use are literally "cognitive maps" in the sense of global descriptions of the whole space with an accurate distribution of landmarks and objects. Rather, from the qualitative descriptions of studies like those of Menzel with chimpanzees, it appears that these may be *practical* maps—representations of how to get to a place from another and what to expect to find there. These practical representations may incorporate spatial knowledge, but probably not in an abstract, outlined, objective way. More likely, primates use spatial pictures acquired when they move around their environment—a collection of navigational clips that they may never be able to contemplate together.

This may also be true of the everyday navigation behavior of humans. Although we may have the illusion that we use mental maps when taking navigational decisions, it is possible that in fact our primary orientation procedures are more like fragmentary practical sketches that are put together during actual movement.

Conclusion: Primates and the World of Objects

Thus far we have described how primates learn to do intelligent things with objects. Their anatomical adaptations—especially hands and eyes—are complemented by a complex set of cognitive tools that control what they see and touch, and what they do. These comprise abilities to identify and individuate objects, to situate them in space and time, to detect and use some of their physical and logical relations, and most importantly, abilities that allow them to generate and execute plans for searching, finding, and manipulating the objects of which their world is composed. This set of cognitive skills, working in coordination, is capable of producing *representations* of that world of objects. These representations are not ready-made adaptations, like the hands or the eyes themselves, but a product of one of the most powerful tools of evolution—*development*. Primates are motivated and partially prewired to look at, touch, and handle objects, and to put together all this information in cross-sensory representations.

This development is at once the product of evolution and the open achievement of individual learning. To use an expression coined by the zoologist Peter Marler (1991), primates have evolved "instincts to learn," and a fundamental thing they learn under the guidance of those instincts is to represent the world as a network of objects in space.

Primate brains construct representations of objects as individual units, of their position in space, of the variety of ways in which they are interrelated (being the same or different, together or separate, inside or next to, causally connected or not, and so forth). More importantly, primates can use all this cognitive material to construct complex representations for action with the help of a set of cognitive tools—working memory, inhibitory control, intentionality—whose nature and variety we are only now starting to understand.

Of course, the world of objects is only half of the environment. The other half—primates themselves as objects of knowledge for the primate mind—will be our next subject.

7

Faces, Gestures, and Calls

Complex social groups are one of the key features of primate life. Hence we need to analyze some of the sociocognitive skills of primates, that is, the cognitive adaptations they possess to deal with themselves as key elements of their environment. To begin with, let us look at communicative signals.

When a primate wants to do something with an object (for example, eat a fruit) he has to touch the object and mechanically act upon it (grasp it, take it to the mouth, chew it, and so on). But when a primate wants to do something with another primate, to play, for example, he has to act very differently—he has to produce *communicative* signals such as play faces, postures, and vocalizations. Communicative signals are patterns that have been evolutionarily selected for their ability to make other animals do (or refrain from doing) things through their mere perception. Communicative signals rely upon a kind of causal connection that is very different from the mechanical connections with and between objects. Communication is the transmission of information rather than the transmission of mechanical forces.

Primates have an extraordinarily rich repertoire of communicative signals: they usually have a collection of distinctive calls associated with different kinds of behaviors and the different kinds of relations in which they can enter among themselves (play, courtship, mating, threat, aggression, appeasement, external predator threats, food search and find). Characteristically, they also have collections of facial expressions, which they frequently use in conjunction with their vocalizations. Moreover, they also possess repertoires of postures and gestures that are frequently combined with calls and faces. Some species have also evolved distinctive colors or appearance that may serve communicative functions. The complex social life of primates is supported by complex, multisensory systems of communication (Snowdon et al., 1982; Seyfarth, 1987; Hauser, 1996, 2000).

In the past it was generally thought that primate facial and vocal communication did not require complex cognitive abilities. People tended to think of these signals as stereotyped, essentially instinctive behavior patterns that operated automatically to express emotions (Seyfarth, 1987). This view appeared to be confirmed by experiments with monkeys showing that their calls were under the control of "primitive" parts of the brain and therefore were not amenable to voluntary, representational control (Myers, 1978).

This is why it was all the more surprising that one primate species—humans—besides having calls, facial expressions, and postures, had come up with what appears to be a radically new and smashingly effective means of communication: speech. Speech is the most quintessentially human and quintessentially cognitive of all mental abilities: how can such a sophisticated ability have evolved out of those cognitively unsophisticated forms of communication? Is language truly unique to humans, as appearances suggest, or is it possible to find in primate communication traces of what in humans has become linguistic communication?

Various people have tried different strategies to answer this question. One of the most radical approaches has consisted of directly trying to teach linguistic skills to captive apes subject to strict educational regimes. We have already encountered some of these linguistically trained primates earlier in the book and will return to them later. Here we will concentrate on the analysis of the spontaneous communication of monkeys and apes in natural or captive conditions from the point of view of how similar and different they are from human language and other sophisticated forms of human communication.

Vervet Words and Worlds

The calls, facial expressions and gestural displays of primates, like those of other animals, were thought to be instinctive forms of communication under the direct control of emotions. For example, in response to the presence of a predator, the primate experienced an automatic emotional reaction (fear) and this triggered an emotional expression (a call and a facial expression of fear) and probably some sort of action to avoid the danger. This chain of reactions was supposed to be under the control of subcortical brain structures and thus to be completely involuntary. Other primates present in the area would hear the call (if sufficiently close to the caller, they would also see his facial and postural expressions) and this would automatically provoke a corresponding emotion of fear or alarm that would allow them to react in an appropriate, adaptive way (Seyfarth, 1987; Cheney and Seyfarth, 1990). Other calls and expressions would have been selected for other purposes: for signaling playful or affiliative moods, anxiety (in young primates separated from their mothers), or perhaps simply as a way of keeping in touch with one another when feeding in a dense forest. The underlying assumption was that no sophisticated cognitive mechanisms need to operate in any of these communicative events. Animal calls and displays would be a very old invention of evolution entirely based upon primitive brain networks that do not need complex cognitive representations. Unlike human words, these calls and responses evoke and are evoked by emotional states, not by representations of the world. Human words may also be connected to emotions (for example, through intonation), but they primarily transmit *referential* information, meaning information about things and events in the world, in such a way that people may get to know things and events that they have not experienced in person. Nothing could be more cognitive than this.

All these assumptions about the nature of natural primate communication were shattered by a series of field experiments carried out on an African monkey species—vervets—in the 1980s by the psychologists Cheney and Seyfarth (1990). Vervet monkeys, a distant relative of humans from which we are separated by about 20 million years of evolution, possess a repertoire of vocalizations that are used in different situations and were thought to be just emotional signals without any referential content.

In this spirit, the first people who systematically studied vervets did not make much of the fact that when these monkeys are frightened by the appearance of a predator, they use different vocalizations depending upon the kind of predator. The world of vervets is a specially dangerous one: Hauser (2001) estimates that 70 percent of young vervets die before maturity, most of them killed by predators. These unfortunate monkeys are a favorite target of many different predators: several species of eagles, leopards, several species of snakes, not to mention humans, and, occasionally, even baboons. Alert vocalizations are therefore specially important for them. It makes good evolutionary sense that these monkeys have evolved cries that they use upon discovering a predator, so that all members of the group, including their relatives, have a better chance to escape.

The traditional idea was that when a monkey sees a predator, he gets scared and cries out in fear; the cry is heard by other members of the group who, in turn, become frightened, interrupt their activities, look around, discover the predator, and escape from it, perhaps following the lead of the monkey who gave the alarm. What is communicated by the alarm call is an emotion of fear.

Cheney and Seyfarth (1990), however, were impressed that not only did vervets consistently use a special vocalization for each kind of predator (one for snakes, another for leopards, another for eagles, and perhaps another for humans), but they also acted in a completely different way depending upon the predator's identity. If the predator is an eagle, the best way to escape is to run under a bush. If it is a leopard, running to a bush is a dreadful idea: that is just where leopards hide to stalk their prey; moreover, a vervet could run into a python that might be sheltered in the bush. The safest way to escape a leopard is to climb up a tree, but this, in turn, is a very dangerous place if you are the target of an eagle, which can easily snatch a monkey from a branch. Finally, when the predator is a snake, typically vervets stand on their legs and keep an eye on the animal and perhaps engage in some mobbing against it. The only way to explain the accurate correspondence between type of predator and type of behavior of the monkeys was to assume that, upon hearing the alarm call, the monkeys, apart from becoming scared, looked to the caller and followed his escape behavior or perhaps very quickly spotted the predator and reacted to its sight.

Cheney and Seyfarth wondered why vervets should have acoustically distinct alarm calls if they were only signaling fear of predators. Was it not possible that actually the calls were transmitting some *referential* information, something about the identity of the predator that provoked the fear? Cheney and Seyfarth came up with an ingenious way of testing this idea: after recording examples of natural alarms produced by the monkeys in real situations, they manipulated the recorded alarms with a computer, eliminating other sounds and making them equivalent in terms of duration and intensity. And then, using a hidden loudspeaker, they started to conduct field experiments in which they reproduced particular alarm calls *in the absence* of any real predator. Their hypothesis was very simple: if the alarms only communicate some *unspecific* state of fear, the monkeys should be upset, interrupt their activities, look at the loudspeaker (well-hidden among vegetation), and produce escape responses in an indiscriminate way; they would not produce the adequate escape response for the predator that originally provoked the recorded alarm.

In effect the monkeys responded in an exquisitely attuned way to the kind of predator the alarm corresponded to. When they heard a leopard call, they ran to the trees; when it was an eagle call, they ran under a bush and scanned the sky; when a snake alarm, they stood on two legs and scanned the ground. The monkeys were reacting appropriately to each type of alarm call. It could be objected that the monkeys might have different types of fear paired with different kinds of instinctive escape reactions without the call actually evoking the identity of the predator. Against this interpretation

A. Vervet Monkeys' System of Alarm Calls

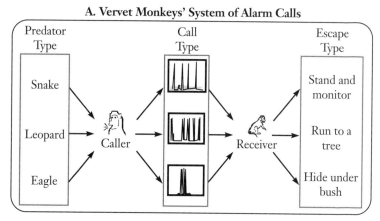

B. Experiment to demonstrate the semanticity of calls

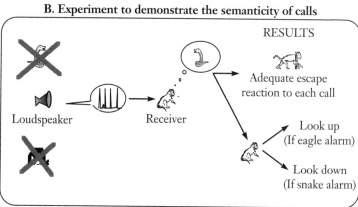

Figure 7.1. A. Alarm calls used by vervet monkeys; each type of predator evokes an acoustically different kind of alarm and a behaviorally different type of escape response. B. Field experiment demonstrating that the alarms themselves, in the absence of a real predator and a model of the escape behavior, can evoke the appropriate response in the listeners.

stand the reactions of scanning the sky or the ground as if in search of the predator: it seemed that the call activated some sort of *representation* of the appropriate predator, and the monkeys acted on the basis of that representation, actively looking for the *referent* of the call, namely the predator that should have provoked the alarm of their fellow monkey. The vervet monkeys appeared to be engaging in a rudimentary form of referential communication with primitive "words."

Further studies with vervets showed that referentiality was present also in other kinds of calls. For example, the monkeys use specific calls when they detect another group of vervets and either move toward the other group or away from it. The hypothesis that the calls activate representations of targets in the monkey mind was further supported by a number of studies in which monkeys were repeatedly exposed to a certain call (for example, one of the calls used when they spot another monkey group) until they "habituated" and ceased to react by looking to the horizon or in the direction of the loudspeaker. At that point, a completely new call was played; this call was acoustically very different from the habituated one, but it is used by monkeys in exactly the same context—spotting a foreign group—so it appears to have the same basic referent as the previous call. The monkeys did not show any reaction to the new call. But if a new call, associated with a completely different meaning (moving away from the group), was played, the monkeys did look in the appropriate direction, even if acoustically this call was similar to the first one. Interestingly, the monkeys could also discriminate the identity of the caller: if the same call recorded from a different monkey was played back, the monkey listeners would also show interest, as if the change in the identity of the "speaker" made the message worth attending to again. These studies appear to confirm that vervet monkeys attend to the *meaning* of the call, rather than to its physical structure, and that, apart from the generic referents associated with each call, they could be representing a much wider picture in which the author of the call plays an important role. This fits well what we know about social relations in monkeys, in which individual identities are crucial for interactions (Smuts et al., 1987).

Learning Vervet "Words"

What is the origin of the singular system of communication of vervet monkeys? Seyfarth and Cheney (1980) discovered that the alarm vocalizations of vervets are subject to an interesting developmental process. There is no doubt that the form of the calls is innate: any vervet, even if reared in a zoo without contact with others, is capable of producing each call. When they first produce their calls, however, the young vervets don't appear to know their meaning. Or at least, not all of their meaning, because they do have a spontaneous tendency to use the eagle alarm calls for birds or objects moving in the air, but in an indiscriminate way. They give the eagle call to any bird passing by, sometimes even to an innocent leaf falling in the air. They learn to restrict their calls to the appropriate birds only progressively, probably under the influence of the reactions of the other members of the group. As mentioned before, vervets can recognize the "voices" of individuals, so that they know who is giving the call they hear. They can therefore tell if the alarm call is produced by an adult or by an infant. When it is produced by infants, they tend to check if there really is a predator before engaging in any escape action or before echoing the call (repeating the alarm call is part of the normal reaction of a vervet monkey upon hearing one). Thus if the adults discover a harmless bird in the sky, they will refrain from escaping and alarm-calling. But if they discover a dangerous eagle, they will echo the infant's call and escape. In this way infants get differential feedback depending upon the appropriateness of their calls, and may eventually learn to restrict them to the appropriate referents.

This phenomenon of initial "overgeneralization" in the use of the call is similar to what human children experience when they learn their first words: they go through a period during which they may use, for example, the word "dog" to refer to any furry animal and learn only progressively to restrict the referential field of the word (Karmiloff and Karmiloff-Smith, 2001). An important difference between vervets and human children learning words is that the initial extended meaning appears to be innately given to vervet babies, whereas humans develop it after an initial phase of over-restricted use (so babies start using the word "dog" to refer only to one particular dog or one particular furry toy and later give the semantic leap of overextending it). This hints at the possibility that the cognitive system vervets and humans use to learn calls and words respectively is different.

Diana Monkeys

Referential calls similar to those of vervets have been described in
other monkeys in recent years. For example, Klaus Zuberbühler
(2000a, b and c) has identified referential calls for aerial (eagles)
and ground (leopards) predators in diana and campbell monkeys.
These two monkey species live in the same areas of the Taï Forest
in the Ivory Coast. In fact they spend a lot of time together, feeding
in mixed groups of dianas and campbells. Another thing they share
is their predators: both are the victims of eagles and leopards, and
each group has developed its own distinct vocalizations to refer
to them. Diana calls for eagles and leopards are acoustically very
different from the campbell calls for the same predators. Yet in
what one is tempted to identify as a case of nonhuman primate bi-
lingualism, each monkey species appears to understand very well
the meaning of the other species' calls. Zuberbühler has found that
they react to playbacks of their own calls as well as to playbacks of
the other species' calls.

He took advantage of this fact to test the "semanticity" of the diana calls (the extent to which they evoke the representation of a
referent in the minds of the monkeys, and the extent to which the
reaction of the monkeys is controlled by such representation). He
observed that if dianas are played the shriek of an eagle once, they
react by giving the eagle alarm call, just as if they had seen a real eagle. During the next minutes, they keep giving occasional calls, but
not as often, and after 5 minutes they stop altogether. If then the
same shriek of the eagle is played again, they don't pay any attention and produce no further calls.

Taking advantage of this interesting pattern of reactions,
Zuberbühler conducted the following experiment. He played one
diana eagle alarm call, and 5 minutes later an eagle shriek, and
found that the monkeys reacted in exactly the same way as with
the two eagle shrieks: they produced many eagle alarms upon hearing the first call, fewer and fewer during the next 5 minutes, and
when they heard the played back eagle shriek (acoustically very
different from the diana's call), they ignored it. The same happened

when they were first played a campbell's monkey eagle alarm and then an eagle shriek. But when a leopard alarm call was played first (whether dianas' or campbells'), and an eagle's shriek 5 minutes later, the monkeys reacted by producing eagle alarm calls. Zuberbühler's conclusion is that the monkeys were representing and reacting to the *meaning* of the calls.

In the Taï Forest chimpanzees inhabit areas that may overlap with the home range of the diana monkeys. Chimpanzees are dangerous for dianas, because they occasionally hunt them. Upon detecting a chimpanzee group, dianas keep silent and go away. They don't have a chimpanzee alarm call (and perhaps that is just as well, because chimpanzees can hunt very effectively in groups, pursuing a prey until it is cornered in a tree; the calls of an individual monkey could give away his position and route of escape). If dianas hear chimpanzee vocalizations, they react similarly: they refrain from making any call themselves and quietly move away from the chimpanzees. There is one particular chimpanzee vocalization, though, to which some diana groups (those that share a part of their territory with a group of chimpanzees) react in a different way—the chimps' alarm scream. In the Taï Forest, where Zuberbühler has carried out his studies, chimps make that sound almost exclusively when they detect a leopard—a potential predator for chimpanzees and dianas alike. When the diana monkeys hear it, they react by making their own leopard alarm vocalizations. It seems therefore that they can identify the referent of the chimpanzee vocalization and vocalize in their turn accordingly, but they only do so if they have had enough experience to learn the meaning of the chimpanzee call.

Monkey Blunders

Monkeys are not always as clever communicators as the examples we have discussed so far suggest. Thus vervets appear to be unable to infer the presence of a snake from the (for experienced humans) unmistakable track snakes leave on the ground when moving around. Vervets do not give the snake alarm call when confronted with such a print leading to a bush; even worse, they do not refrain from approaching the bush, as if they really could not infer the potential presence of a snake from the tell-tale track. They similarly ignore a fresh carcass on a tree—another unmistakable sign (for a human mind) of the presence of a leopard nearby. And they do not appear to control their referential vocalizations when their audience already knows about the presence of a potential danger (Cheney and Seyfarth 1991). They do take into account whether they have an audience at all before giving alarm vocalizations: if they are alone, they don't call, just concentrate on escaping the danger (Cheney and Seyfarth, 1990).

Notwithstanding the possible inferential shortcomings of monkey minds, it seems now clear that the assumption that primate vocalizations are exclusively emotional signals was unjustified. When properly analyzed, many of their calls appear to convey referential information about relevant environmental objects. Monkeys appear to be able to represent that referential information in their minds and act according to it even in the absence of the real referent.

The use of the term "referential" or "semantic" to describe these calls has not been without controversy. To avoid this, authors like Cheney and Seyfarth (1999) emphasize that what they are claiming for vervets and other monkeys is a "functional semantics," in the sense that their calls work *as if* they were referential. This does not mean that they are referential in the human sense; they may not be produced by the same cognitive mechanisms, and their "meaning" may be very different from what we humans understand as the meaning of a word (see also Hauser, 1996; Gómez, 1997). What are the representational mechanisms behind monkey calls remains an open question.

Referential Calls in Species Other than Primates

A natural question that comes to mind is whether similar referential vocal communication can be found in the closest relatives of humans, the anthropoid apes. Surprisingly, as far as we can tell from the available evidence, the great apes, including chimpanzees, seem to have no system of referential calls comparable to that of vervets or dianas. Chimpanzees do have calls, some of them for alarm and others that they give when they find food, but it is unclear if they work like vervet "words." A recent study (Crockford and Boesch, 2003) suggests that some calls of the Taï chimpanzees tend to be produced in very specific contexts and therefore have the potential of working as referential calls. But the relevant experiments about how chimpanzees would react to played-back calls in the absence of real referents have yet to be done.

"Semantic" calls, however, have definitely been found in species other than monkeys. Surprisingly, squirrels and domestic chickens (of all unlikely candidates for cognitive sophistication) have a system of alarm calls that differentiates between aerial and terrestrial predators (Macedonia and Evans, 1993). This may be interpreted as an indication that, rather than being related to intelligence or cognitive sophistication *à la* primate, semantic vocalizations depend crucially upon the kinds of ecological pressures sustained by vertebrate species. When a species has at least two different kinds of predators that require incompatible ways of escape (as is usually the case with aerial versus terrestrial predators), it is likely that the species will have evolved referential calls.

The possible absence of semantic calls in apes and their presence in other vertebrates might appear to make the monkey system of vocalizations less relevant for the origins of human language. Yet the fact that a typical response of vertebrate brains to certain ecological pressures is the evolution of functionally semantic calls may be far from irrelevant for the issue of the origins of human speech. Our hominid ancestors may have evolved some such primitive set of referential calls as a first step in what much later, in an unprecedented combination with other cognitive systems, would become speech.

Reference without Symbols

If apes really lacked referential calls like those of vervets, would that then mean that they are incapable of referential communication, so they cannot communicate about external targets in their environment? Evidence suggests that, far from this being the case, apes might not only be capable of referential communication, but also of a specially effective kind of referential communication that, in some respects, bears more resemblance to human communication than the semantic vocalizations of monkeys.

So far we have been using the terms "semantic" and "referential" interchangeably, but they can be distinguished. "Semantics" stands for the meanings that words or symbols contain or have specifically attached to them ("snake" has a meaning which is different from "leopard" or "eagle"). Because words carry their own meaning, they can *refer* to objects (or actions, events, imaginary entities) even if these things are not present at the moment. The essence of reference, however, is the ability to direct someone's attention to a particular target. And reference in this more basic sense can be achieved without words. My gesture of pointing at a snake purposefully *refers* your attention to the snake, even though nothing in my pointing gesture contains the meaning "snake." My pointing could have referred to any other object—a tree, an apple, a flower.

This is an extremely useful feature of the pointing gesture—it can be used to refer (direct the attention of others) to a huge variety of things, whereas individual words have a much more restricted meaning. Of course, the advantage of using words, especially when they are combined into sentences, is that I can refer to many more things than I can do with pointing gestures, and with complete independence of the here and now. In this sense, the semantic way of reference has definite advantages over the nonsymbolic one. But although a symbolic language is ideally suited for performing virtuoso acts of reference, the basic referential act of directing another person's attention to an environmental target can be achieved without words or any other symbols.*

Referential communication of this presymbolic type appears in children's development before linguistic communication. Most

---

* The term "reference" is used by most linguists and philosophers in a more complex way (taking for granted symbolism and language) than I am doing here. I believe that it is more useful here to return to the original, functional sense of this word as the act of directing someone's attention to a target.

children can communicate with gestures before they can use even single words, and their first steps in word development often occur with the support of referential gestures (simultaneously pointing to and naming an object [Bruner, 1975]).

Prelinguistic Communication in the Young Human

Bates, Camaioni, and Volterra (1975; Bates, 1979) provided a careful description of the development of the first referential gestures in human infants. Sometime toward 9 to 12 months of age babies start communicating about external targets in their environment. They may request a favorite toy by extending their arm with the hand open, perhaps making beckoning movements, toward the object (what the researchers called "protoimperative" gestures). Or they can point with their extended finger to a light or another event that excites their attention (a "protodeclarative" gesture). Importantly, these gestures are frequently accompanied by the baby's alternating her gaze between the object and the person to whom the gesture is addressed. In fact, we know that the gesture is addressed to that person because of the gaze alternation. Bates and colleagues (1975) suggested that this criterion—looking at the object and at the human, and even more specifically, looking at the eyes of the human, engaging in what is known as "eye contact"—was fundamental to identify early intentional communication. The child seems to check the success of the gesture in directing the attention of the adult to the correct target, and at the same time uses his own gaze as an additional gesture to clarify the focus of their joint reference.*

"Prelinguistic" Communication in Young Gorillas

In the 1980s I conducted a longitudinal study specifically aimed at determining if young gorillas engage in gestural communication

---

* Human babies usually accompany their early gestures with nonlinguistic vocalizations. The richness of prelinguistic vocal behavior in humans has been somewhat obscured by the conspicuousness of their gestures, but early vocalizations may play an important role in the functions of *attention direction* and what we will call later *attention contact*.

similar to that described in preverbal human infants (Gómez, 1990, 1991, 1992). The subjects were young wild-born orphan gorillas (from around 8 to 10 month of age) who were being hand-reared by humans in a zoo nursery. They had access to a variety of objects and toys and engaged in considerable interaction with their human caretakers, for example, bottle feeding, nappy change, bath time, walks around an outdoors area, and some intelligence testing. This hand-rearing environment is similar to that used in some language training experiments (see chapter 10), but we refrained from teaching any artificial signs—we wanted to see if the gorillas would spontaneously develop their own ways of communication with humans.*

We found that they did. Initially, they developed gestures in face to face interactions without external targets, such as extending their arms to a caretaker as a way of requesting being taken in arms. Human infants do something similar, although the form of the gesture may differ in some respects (Lock, 1978). But a request to be picked up is not referential in the sense we have discussed above: it does not involve the redirection of the human's attention upon an environmental target distinct from the gorilla herself.

Human infants start engaging in referential gestures at around 9 to 12 months of age. Our gorillas took a little longer to show referential gestures: only at around 18 to 20 months of age they started to do things like handing us objects they wanted to have manipulated (a mechanical toy in need of rewinding), extending their hand toward objects they wanted, leading people to places by the hand, or, more idiosyncratically, taking the hand of the person to the target they wanted (see figure 7.2 for some examples).

Interestingly, the gorillas combined their gestures with the sort of joint-attention behaviors described for human babies: they looked at the eyes of the addressee at different moments during their gesturing and sometimes alternated their gaze between the

* Later in this longitudinal study we did try to teach the gorillas a few manual signs and a few plastic-chip "words." The training was limited, however, and they never appeared to learn to use either the signs or the chips in a symbolic way comparable to that of "linguistic" apes; see Chapter 10.

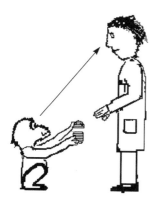 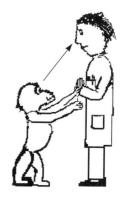

Request to recompose a toy
(toy is offered to human)

Request of object
(hand of human taken to his pocket)

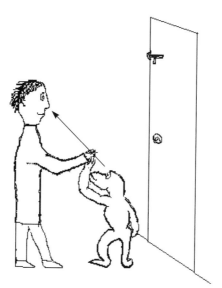

Request to open a door
(hand of human taken towards latch)

Figure 7.2. Some examples of referential gestures used by hand-reared gorillas to interact with humans.

eyes of the person and the target of their interest. In contrast to human babies, though, the gorillas never developed pointing gestures (with the index finger extended), and they showed little interest in showing things to the humans by other means (for example, they could have held an object in front of the caretaker) unless they were trying to make the human do something with the target object (Gómez, Sarriá, and Tamarit, 1993).

The spontaneous communication of gorillas is, therefore, both similar and different from that of human babies. It is similar in some basic gestures, like offering objects or extending the arm to request things, and in coordinating the gestures with joint-attention patterns like looking at each other's eyes; but it is different because it is apparently limited to requests or "protoimperative" functions, whereas human babies also use their gestures for showing things for their own sake—the so-called "protodeclarative" function (Gómez et al., 1993). Moreover, human babies appear to have a specialized gesture for referential communication—pointing with the extended finger. In some situations where human babies would typically use a pointing gesture, gorillas used more bizarre "contact gestures." For example, to request a piece of food in the pocket of a caretaker, they would take the hand of the person and direct it towards the pocket (figure 7.2). They also frequently requested to go to various places by taking the caretaker by the hand or wrist. Although the hand-taking gestures are rare among typically developing children, they are more frequent among children with learning difficulties, especially among some children with autism. However, children with autism who use hand-taking gestures do not usually look into the eyes of the other person (Phillips et al., 1995), whereas our gorilla did look into the eyes of the person whose hand she took.

The joint-attention component of communication is relatively elusive. Babies in free interaction often use gestures without checking the attention of the other person. Typically, though, they will make such a check at some point in the interaction, especially if something unexpected happens, such as the adult's failure to respond or an unusual reaction from him (Bates et al., 1975). For example, two-year-old children look immediately at the eyes of a person if she, instead of finishing the action of handing them an object, unexpectedly withdraws it at the last moment. This has been interpreted as an indication that children are trying to find out about the intentions of the person (Phillips et al, 1992). Children with autism, in contrast, rarely look at the eyes of the person in a situation like that: they concentrate their attention on the object. Chimpanzees react like typical children: they make instant eye contact upon being teased with the unexpected withdrawal of food (Gómez, Texidor, and Laá; unpublished data).

Why is eye contact behavior apparently so important among young children and apes starting their communicative careers? It will aid our discussion to take a closer look at how one referential gesture developed in one of our gorillas (Gómez, 1990, 1991; Gómez et al., 1993).

The Development Of Requests in Gorillas

A frequent problem for one of our subjects—Muni—was locked doors. The latches that kept the doors shut in the indoors area where she was reared were set up higher than she could reach without climbing on boxes or broomsticks. We then took advantage of her interest in entering locked rooms to study her problem-solving skills. At the age of 10 months she started to show some ability to use tools to solve the problem of the closed door: she would move a box under the door and climb it to reach the latch. In the course of one of our experiments Muni surprised us with a new solution: instead of going in search of a box, as we expected, she turned to one of the experimenters who was taking notes, pulled at his lab coat, and then pushed him with all her force in the direction of the door. The experimenter decided to move in that direction in response to each push or pull. Muni only stopped when the experimenter was by the door. Once there, she started literally to climb up the experimenter, with her attention divided between the latch she was trying to reach and the body of the person she was trying to climb. Not a single look was directed at any point to the experimenter's eyes. She finally reached the latch and opened the door.

During that period, whenever she tried to use people in relation to an external target, she treated them as objects. On another occasion she was trying to reach a windowsill under which a caretaker was lying on a bed. She took up one of his legs lifted it against the wall, trying to climb on it.

These actions cannot be described as referential communication. It is true that the gorilla has a target and produces a goal-directed action, but the action is not designed to be communicative; rather, the young gorilla acts with people in the same way that she handles physical objects, and her visual checking is not directed at the eyes of the human.

The contrast is all the more surprising because at this age Muni did engage in communicative interactions with humans when these did not involve external targets. For example, she was already capable of using a gesture to request being taken in arms, which was accompanied by eye contact. Muni's approach changed when she had to communicate about an external target: when she wanted the other person to move in a particular direction or perform a particular action. Then, she was unable to recruit her communicative schemes and had to rely upon her object-using schemes.

This is interesting because it means that the communication problem for the gorilla does not arise out of the need to coordinate two action sequences. She can do that, as when she moves a box under the door to reach the latch. Her problem is specifically one of combining persons and objects. Exactly the same problem has been described in human infants under 8 months of age; they are able to engage in face to face communicative interactions, in which they make extensive use of eye contact, facial expressions, and vocalizations. At the same time, they are able to manipulate a variety of objects. But they cannot yet combine these "intersubjective" acts with their practical acts with objects: it is as if the world of objects and the world of people are still divided in their minds (Hubley and Trevarthen, 1979). In human infants, the emergence of the ability to combine people and objects roughly coincides with the emergence of the ability to use tools (end of the first year of life). This led some authors to propose that early referential communication could be based upon the same ability as tool use. After all, communication could be defined as using someone as a tool to achieve one's own goals (Harding, 1982). The findings from our gorilla study suggest, however, that the ability to use objects as tools to manipulate other objects is not sufficient for referential communication. Muni was able to use tools at a time when she was unable to direct another person's attention to an object. In fact, she literally treated others like tools, and the results were far from referential communication. When detailed studies of the actual correlation between communicative and other cognitive skills have been carried out in children, the correlation between intentional communication and tool-use has been found to be low (Bates, 1979; Sarriá and Riviere, 1991).

Treating Others as Agents

A few months after her first attempts at using people's bodies as supports, Muni started to modify her strategy. In the door situation, now she approached the human, pulled him gently (usually from the hand or wrist, instead of grabbing anywhere, as previously), as if expecting the human to move by himself, and then, upon reaching the door, she sometimes requested being taken in arms, and then operated the latch from the human's arms, or waited for the human to operate the latch. In the latter case, no eye contact was made with the human: Muni was just waiting for him to act (if anything, she would look at the hand of the human—the part that was expected to act upon the target—not at his eyes). That Muni was waiting for the human to act suggests that she perceived humans in relation to external targets in a new way, perhaps as some sort of "goal-directable agent" capable of acting on his own in relation to the object. In a sense, she was already "referring" the person to the target. Still, she was only directing the *action* of the human to the object, not his attention. In this sense, this is a very weak case of reference, one that can hardly be considered to be communicative.

Treating Others as Subjects

The other person's attention did not enter into the picture until a few months later. At the approximate age of a year and a half, when Muni wanted to get the door opened she approached the person, made eye contact with her, took her hand, and gently led her to the door, occasionally looking again at her eyes. At around two years of age, she did that and, once at the door, she also lifted the person's hand toward the latch while making eye contact or alternating her gaze between the person's eyes and the latch. Now, apart from directing the *action* of the person to an environmental target, Muni was checking his *attention* before and during the requesting gesture. Whereas in the previous months her attention was drawn to the latch and the hands of the person, now she appears to consider that the eyes of the other are also a relevant component of the whole procedure. Since the eyes, in contrast with the hands, are never part of the actions of the person, the inference is that the gorilla must now be representing the person as something more than an animate agent. One possible interpretation is that this search for eye contact by the gorillas is a search for *attention contact*, which in social interaction is the relevant causal link that connects one subject with another (whereas in object manipulation it is physical contact that constitutes the crucial causal link). The gorilla appeared to understand that recruiting and keeping the attention of the agent was a crucial part of a request.

From this period onward, Muni was capable of integrating external targets and face to face behaviors like eye contact. In fact, "attention contact" became so important that she (and the other gorillas studied) developed a whole set of gestures whose aim was to call the attention of the person before engaging in a request. For example, they pulled the clothes of the person until she looked at them, and only after making eye contact, they proceeded to take her hand toward the desired target or offer her an object. Other times, they moved the face of the person toward them, or pulled her hand, or made a gorilla vocalization (the so-called pig grunt; Fossey, 1983) until the person looked at them.

Referential Gestures in Apes

Our description of the communicative abilities of Muni appears to be representative of many great apes interacting with humans, with or without extensive hand-rearing. Recently, Leavens and Hopkins (1998) have conducted a series of studies about the abilities of captive chimpanzees to engage in intentional communication using criteria similar to the ones we have described. They found that caged chimpanzees routinely combine their reaching gestures with glances at the eyes of the human (and, interestingly, with vocalizations) when they are trying to induce a human to give them some food.

But is the strategic use of eye contact really so important as to suggest that it indicates a change in the way apes represent their interactions with other people? Perhaps there is a simpler explanation. For example, Povinelli and Eddy (1996b) have proposed that apes may simply like making eye contact with people. Since people may also like having apes look them in the eye, perhaps gorillas and chimpanzees by pure chance discover that they are more likely to receive what they want if they look at the eyes of the person. This would be simple associative learning, not an understanding of the function of attention in referential communication.

Associative Learning

Our longitudinal study of the gorilla Muni seems to be a good case to test this hypothesis. As we saw, she went through 3 phases in the development of her referential actions: first, she produced just instrumental manipulations of people as objects; then, she produced schematic actions akin to gestures but without eye contact; and finally, she produced gestures with eye contact. Were these changes, especially the addition of eye contact, accompanied by an increase in the probability of getting rewards (having her requests granted)? Surprisingly, the answer is a definite no: the proportion of requests granted did not change with the strategy Muni used; she was given what she wanted (food, a toy, an open door, a change of place) in less than 50 percent of the occasions independently of how often eye contact accompanied the request (Gómez, 1992). The final outcome of a request was controlled by factors extraneous to eye contact. Most of the refusals were because the thing requested was inconvenient or the person was engaged in something else or was not in the mood of obliging the gorilla's demands.

A simple conditioning model is unable to explain the passage from gestures without joint attention to gestures with joint attention, because the addition of eye contact was accompanied by no change whatsoever in the probability of obtaining the reward. Why then did the gorilla incorporate joint attention into her requesting procedures? The new approach did have a consequence upon the reactions of the humans. When requests made with joint attention were refused, it was done in a different way. Instead of simply not responding to the request, the person would *say* "no" and give explanations ("you cannot get out"). Although the gorilla probably understood nothing of the contents of these explanations, these were usually accompanied by more joint attention and emotional expressions. For one thing, the gorilla understood that the failure of her request was not due to a *lack of attention* contact with the human, but to a *refusal* (in whatever way gorillas can represent this difference).

The data are not consistent, therefore, with a simple conditioning explanation. They rather fit an explanation in terms of joint attention and exchanges of socioemotional information, of patterns of interaction in which the actions of the other are not computed in terms of "reward" against "no reward," but in more complex sociocognitive categories, like "attending," "aggressive," "friendly," "oriented to object," "acting on object," and so forth. The issue of how much of the sociocognitive domain monkeys and apes can understand is addressed in the next chapter.

The Anthropoid Way of Reference

The referential gestures of apes and human infants contain both similarities and differences. Are the differences just superficial variants or are they indicative of some deep disparity in the underlying cognitive processes? Take, for example, the case of contact gestures like taking the hand to an object. One possibility is that contact gestures are just a relatively clumsy solution to the problem of directing other people's attention to an object in the absence of a better adapted gesture like human pointing. But why wouldn't the ape use the extended arm gesture, which many captive apes use to request objects and which, in other contexts, appears to come so naturally to them? In fact, some linguistically trained apes with extensive human rearing have used such gestures to direct people to places. For example, C. R. Menzel (1999) found that one "linguistic" ape—the chimpanzee Panzee—was able to participate in a "hide and show" game with humans. In full view of Panzee, a human hid an object in an outside enclosure; then Panzee was allowed to direct another human (completely ignorant of the nature and whereabouts of the object) toward the target. The chimpanzee would, first, point with her extended arm in the direction of the outdoor enclosure, and then if the human responded to his initial indications, she specified the location of the object by pointing with her extended index finger through a wire mesh, sometimes accompanying this pointing with vocalizations. The humans searched guided by this information, as well as by Panzee's direction of gaze. (Going beyond these basic referential gestures, Panzee also ventured into what we have called "semantic" communication by using symbols of the artificial language she had been taught to identify the object for the naïve human; see Chapter 10.)

Perhaps this style of referential communication is just superficially different from that demonstrated by our gorillas, but it is also possible that there is a deeper difference in the way this "linguistic," domesticated ape and his less domesticated cousins represent referential communication. One hypothesis is that Muni and the other gorillas organize their referential communication around the core notion of the action they are trying to trigger in the human (making him go to the door and open the latch). Yet during the execution of her contact gestures the gorilla looks into the human's eyes, as if action is not everything she is trying to manipulate. She is directing the action—not the attention—of the person to the target, but at the same time she is checking his attention. Why? One possibility is that the gorilla is looking at the eyes of the person not to check that he is attending to the right target, but to check that the person is attending *to her* and her request.

It is possible to distinguish two distinct joint-attention components in referential communication. One is the ability to follow or direct the attention of another upon a target; the second is the ability to recruit the attention of someone upon oneself and establish what we have called "attention contact" (Gómez, in press). Following the path of someone's attention can occur without communication: I may simply follow your gaze to the object you are looking at without your even noticing that I am watching you. Attention contact, however, is intrinsically communicative: if I call your attention, it must be to tell you something (Sperber and Wilson, 1986; Gómez, 1994). Attention contact is what confirms that a given behavior is *intended* as a communicative gesture.

Perhaps apes using contact gestures are engaging in a rudimentary type of referential communication in which they combine attention contact with action direction, instead of the more common human version of attention contact plus attention direction (Gómez, in press). This would make these apes' referential communication all the more interesting, because it would offer a genuine "co-cursor" (an evolutionary variant) of the sort of reference characteristic of human children.

In summary, when apes are placed in interaction with humans, they develop referential communication gestures with them in the sense we discussed before, namely, gestures by means of which they direct other people to targets in the environment, usually with the aim of making them do something in relation to that target. The manipulation of the attention of others does not appear to be accidental (a by-product of the attempt to direct the action of the other toward the object): apes specifically seek and monitor the attention of others, not only their actions. But because the studies we have reviewed so far are of apes interacting with humans, the question is: are referential gestures used only by apes interacting with humans?

Referential Gestures among Chimpanzees

Very few referential gestures are reported in descriptions of communicative behaviors in the wild or in captivity among apes. The only consistent report is that of begging gestures to request food, in the context of food sharing among wild and captive chimpanzees (Goodall, 1986). Plooij (1978, 1979) found that from 9 months of age (roughly the same age as human babies) the chimpanzees would show some gaze alternation when begging food from their mothers with arm-extended gestures. Tomasello and his associates (1985, 1989, 1997) analyzed the gestures that captive chimpanzees use among themselves and found gaze alternation and a tendency to produce visual gestures (such as extending the hand) when the recipient was visually oriented, whereas touch-appealing gestures (such as pulling) were unrelated to the visual orientation of the recipient. But apart from food begging, most of the gestures described among chimpanzees are not referential—they are not used to direct the recipient to an external target.

There is, however, a singular series of studies in which the spontaneous appearance of more complex chimp-to-chimp referential behaviors has been reported. These are the studies of Emil Menzel (1973b) with a group of young chimpanzees. To remind the reader, Menzel's chimpanzees were housed in a big outdoor enclosure with trees, grass, plants, and a variety of objects and structures. There was also a smaller indoors area where the chimps were usually kept overnight or when the experimental program so required. In the present series of studies, Menzel took a single chimpanzee to the outdoor area, while the rest were kept inside, unable to see what happened. This single chimpanzee was shown how food was hidden in one particular part of the enclosure, and he was then returned to the indoors area with the other chimps. After a time, the whole group of chimpanzees was released.

Menzel knew from his previous studies that the informed chimpanzee would have no problem remembering the location of the food. He also knew that these young primates were scared of traveling alone in the outside enclosure and would only go to the hiding place if the rest of the group (or at least a few) would accompany them. The question was: would the informed chimpanzee be able somehow to direct the others to the appropriate spot?

All the chimps were made to take the role of informed individual in turn, and all managed to make the others follow them by various means: some started walking in the appropriate direction, then stopped, turned, looked to the others, and waited until they started to follow them. If the others did not follow, a common procedure was to approach them and tug their arm or body, or pass the arm over the shoulders and then "lead" them toward the target. Menzel described a great variety of behaviors used by the chimps. None of them implied the use of a specialized, species-specific signal of "follow me" or "food over there," although eventually the procedures used to indicate the direction to go became more standardized. In the end, the chimps would essentially resort to their body orientation as a way of signaling the direction to follow. Menzel explicitly compares this "expanded" way of pointing with the whole body with the more condensed version of pointing with the hand used by humans (Menzel, 1973b).

The situation became more interesting when problems of dominance affected the access to the hidden food. One female, Belle, was low in the ranking. When she played the role of informed chimpanzee leading the others to the food, frequently she would find herself deprived of any food because the others, specially the dominant male Rock, would rush to the food and consume the lot. In this case, the ability to indicate the location of the food proved to be disadvantageous to Belle. In reaction to this state of affairs, Belle started to refrain from walking in the direction of the food. But the clever Rock would scrutinize her and discover the right direction from the direction of her gaze. Belle eventually learned not only to suppress the telltale gaze, but also to walk in the wrong direction, in what appears to be a case of literally misleading referential behavior.

In some special trials, Menzel showed the informed chimp that a snake, instead of food, was hidden in the enclosure. When the group was released, their attitude was—sometimes from the very beginning—very different from that of the food trials. They were excited and scared; the informed individual approached the target site cautiously; and the followers, once the site was identified, did not rush onto it, but rather threw stones or sticks at the place where the snake was hidden (but not visible to the chimps). Eventually, they approached the site and carefully uncovered the snake with a stick.

Remarkably, all these reactions by the chimpanzees occurred when the obnoxious stimulus was invisible: the chimps must have been reacting to a representation of the snake (or of something dangerous), much as vervet monkeys do in response to specific alarm calls, except that here there was no special vocalization, no special gesture that means "snake"—just a suite of referential behaviors accompanied by emotional displays and other contextual cues.

The parallel with the studies of vervet monkeys was even closer in some trials in which Menzel withdrew the hidden snake before releasing the group of animals, so that now the target place was actually empty. The chimps continued to react in the same aggressive and cautious way towards the critical spot, and appeared to look around as if in search of something dangerous.

Menzel's experiments suggest that nonsemantic referential communication is not limited to apes interacting with humans. A simulated environment with a certain set of constraints (the need to travel together plus an asymmetrical distribution of information) gives rise to the invention of a simple form of referential communication among young chimpanzees. The referential communication invented by captive apes is rudimentary and in many respects far from optimal (such as the hand-taking method of gorillas); this suggests that it is not based upon a set of ready-made adaptations, but rather upon some process of *exaptation* or re-adaptation of abilities that initially were selected for different purposes (see Chapter 11 for more on exaptation).

In their normal everyday interactions, wild chimpanzees and other apes are rarely seen engaging in productive referential gestures like those described by Menzel or like those seen in apes interacting with humans in captive settings. Yet chimpanzees and other apes may use "receptive" or "passive" referentiality as part of their everyday life. The behavior of other chimpanzees (and practically that of any animal) is always full of unintentional referential cues. For example, a chimpanzee looking at a piece of food is orienting himself toward a target. Even if this is not done for the benefit of an observer, a human watching this is able to infer that the chimpanzee is interested in the food. Chimpanzees may be capable of making similar inferences. They certainly are able to follow the focus of attention of other chimpanzees from cues such as gaze direction (Tomasello et al., 1999). Their receptive referentiality may present important limitations, however, at least when it is tested with humans who *intentionally* try to convey information about a hidden object with their gaze (Call and Tomasello, in press; see also next chapter). Paradoxically, chimpanzees may be better at snatching involuntary referential information from unsuspecting others than at picking up referential information that is intentionally given to them by humans.*

It is also possible that the natural referential abilities of chimpanzees and other apes are more sophisticated than we suspect. Most studies on referential communication in apes have been conducted in relation to the gestural modality; very few have attempted to address the issue of vocal referentiality in a way different from the "semantic referentiality" *à la* vervet. A largely unexplored possibil-

---

* Note that the meaning of "reference" is stretched here to include not only nonsymbolic, but also unintended reference. It is important to keep in mind that each type of reference may require different or additional cognitive mechanisms.

ity is that chimpanzee vocalizations do work referentially but not semantically, that is, that they function as some sort of vocal pointing, a way of communicating the presence of relevant targets but without vocally specifying the identity of these (beyond some basic valence like positive/negative, or a little more specifically, "food" versus "danger"). The precise identity of the targets would have to be discovered personally or inferred through the contextual knowledge of the protagonists.

In sum, the referential communication of apes might be different from that described in monkeys as functionally semantic. Ape referentiality may be based upon different cognitive processes, which may be closer to the nonlinguistic referential communication of humans. On the other hand, apes' referential gestures may have the peculiarity of being organized with the ultimate aim of directing the *action*, rather than the *attention*, of others to a target. This direction to action is accompanied by attention contact, that is, the apes appear to understand that in order to direct the action of others to a target, they first need to have their attention. They may even know that directing action is inevitably accompanied by directing attention, but their own attention appears to be geared primarily toward guiding the actions of others, and only secondarily to guiding their attention. This would explain why they do not engage in "protodeclarative" behaviors, whose primary aim is to direct the attention of others to objects.

What matters for the evolutionary cognitive scientist is that apes might possess the ability to invent forms of referential communication, based not upon an existing repertoire of semantic signals (signals with particular meanings), but upon a more general ability to direct and follow the attention (or the action) of others to targets.

Conclusion

The studies lead us to conclude that primate communication is cognitively more sophisticated than once thought. Many monkey calls are semantically referential, in the sense that monkeys activate with them representations of some relevant events of their environment, instead of merely activating stereotyped responses or emotional reactions. Although the temptation to consider them "words" or the evolutionary precursors of words is great, many researchers prefer to be conservative. The fact that similar semantic calls are found in animals as evolutionarily separate as chickens and squirrels, but so far not in any of the great apes, suggests that the cognitive mechanisms underlying these calls might be different from those evolved by humans. But we still know very little about these mechanisms in monkeys and apes.

Although apes apparently lack specific semantic calls, they are capable of another kind of referential communication—one that is more flexible and not based on "word-like" signals, but upon perception of the intentions of others and manipulation of their attention and actions. When compared with the nonlinguistic referential communication of humans (especially that of very young children), we are confronted with a complex landscape of similarities and differences. Humans possess a number of specific adaptations for this kind of referential communication, most notably the pointing gesture and the motivation for so-called protodeclarative gestures, whereas apes, when placed in a situation that demands referential communication, have to invent referential gestures (hand-taking) and remain mostly interested in requesting and directing functions. This invention of rudimentary forms of reference may be based upon a number of abilities, among them that of understanding others as subjects with intentions and attention.

8

Understanding Other Subjects

Just as objects are the fundamental units of the physical world of primates, *agents* or *subjects*—other primates—are the fundamental units of their social world. Subjects are physical objects too, but they have a number of properties that make them radically different from other physical objects, to the extent that many object notions are not applicable to them. Thus objects never (or very rarely) move on their own, whereas subjects do so most of the time. If you want to move an object, you normally have to touch it. This is not true of subjects, and the way a subject reacts to being touched or pushed is not at all the way objects do. Subjects, therefore, are not simply physical objects with new properties added to them. They are entities of a different nature—animate beings that move on their own, breathe, eat, drink, look, and engage in actions with objects or interactions with other subjects. Dealing with the behavior of other subjects is a cognitive challenge for which evolution has produced a number of specialized cognitive abilities in primates.

Understanding Minds and Behaviors

Humans represent the behavior of other people in a peculiar way. If, for example, we are asked to describe what is happening in a scene where a person is pulling at a drawer that does not open, and then searches around and tries different keys in the drawer's lock, we readily describe this by saying that the person *wants* to open the drawer but he does not *know* which is the right key. We have an irresistible tendency to translate behavior into mental states, to represent what people do in terms of what they want and what they know or don't know. This ability has come to be known in cognitive science as "theory of mind," because we cannot see what a person has in her mind when doing something (Premack and Woodruff, 1978b). In the above example we infer from the person's behavior that he *wants* to open the drawer and that he doesn't *know* which key, but we have no direct knowledge of either her wishes or her knowledge—these are inferences that we make thanks to our naïve theory that people's behavior is caused by internal mental states (Astington, 1994).

Do nonhuman primates represent other primates' behavior in a similar *mentalistic* way?

Sarah's Theory of Mind

Paradoxically, the very notion of theory of mind, which seems to fit so well the way humans think about each other, was created by primatologists. In an experiment by Premack and Woodruff (1978a and b) with their chimpanzee Sarah, they showed her videotapes of people trying to solve problems, like reaching a bunch of bananas hanging from the ceiling or turning on a heater. Sarah was able to select photographs that depicted solutions to the problems, thereby demonstrating an understanding of the relevant causal connections (see Chapter 4). But she may have been demonstrating something else. Consider the following alternative descriptions of a scene similar to those shown to Sarah:

A. Marc moves to the center of the room, he looks up, he stretches his hand up, then drops it while looking up, he jumps up while stretching his hand again; he repeats these movements several times; a bunch of bananas is hanging from the ceiling (just over the place where Marc is)

B. Marc wants the bananas and he is trying to reach them, but they are too high.

A is a mere description of a sequence of movements and objects without a connecting link between them, especially not between Marc and the bananas. In B there is a connection between Marc and the bananas: he *wants* the bananas and he is *trying* to reach them. His intention in relation to the bananas is what gives sense to the whole scene. In contrast to, for example, the physical relationship of distance between him and the fruit, Marc's intention to get the bananas is not visible on the video clip: we don't get to see him grabbing or eating the bananas at any point, yet, at least for us human beings, the *intentional* link between Marc and his goal is absolutely evident, and it is the factor that creates the problem for Marc. Do chimpanzees see things in the same way?

Premack and Woodruff (1978b) think that they do. Sarah's ability to select the correct photographs (Marc stepping on a box or the photo of the instrument Marc needs to reach high enough) would prove precisely this. Sarah appeared to be making an intentional reading of the video clips—going beyond the physical information given in the tapes and detecting the intention that gave sense to the actions. Thus she could be said to have a "theory of mind."

As Woodruff and Premack and other scientists participating in the ensuing debate soon realized, however, the issue of theory of mind is much more complex. Exactly what kind of theory of mind did Sarah need in order to choose the correct photographs? What sort of intentional description of the situation (among the many possible) was she generating? Was she perceiving "Marc *trying* to reach the bananas" or "Marc *wanting* the bananas"? In "Marc wanting," we attribute to Marc an intention that is *in his mind* and can be there independently of his actions (he could want the bananas even if he were not doing anything to get them); however, in "Marc trying to reach," the intention is a way of representing the action of reaching *as directed* to the bananas, and we don't need to think of this intention as being in the mind of Marc: it is a property of his action that puts him in an *intentional relationship* with the bananas.

Moreover, Sarah could be choosing the correct photographs without using any of the above mentalistic understandings; perhaps she simply has a good representation of different action sequences on the basis of which she is able to predict the more likely (or desirable) outcome. The video clips test, therefore, was an inconclusive way of examining theory of mind in primates.

Cognitive scientists came up with a solution: moving away from the problem of others' intentions and considering a different kind of mental state—*beliefs*, or what people know about the world. Imagine Marc: he is really hungry and wants some bananas. He sees through a window that Mike puts a bunch of bananas in a box; happy, Marc leaves the window, and goes to the door. But just as Marc is walking to the door and cannot see what happens in the room, a third character, Danny, enters and moves the bananas to a locker. A few seconds later, Marc enters the room in search of his bananas . . . where is Marc going to look for the bananas? Obviously, he will go to the box; he *believes* that the bananas are there because he saw that Mike put them there (and did not see that Danny removed them later). In this task you cannot predict the action of looking for the bananas by simply putting together an agent and a goal; you need to understand that what matters now is not where the goal actually is, but where it is *in the mind* of the agent. Predicting the behavior of someone with a mistaken belief is only possible if one can grasp the representations that others have of the world, and this is why it is an excellent indicator of having a theory of mind.

Human Children's Theories of Mind

By confronting children of different ages with a false-belief scenario like the above and asking them to predict where the main character would go in search of the object, developmental psychologists discovered that understanding false beliefs happens relatively late in the development of human children—toward 4 years of age. But developmental psychologists consider that understanding the notion of false belief is the crowning achievement of a long and many-sided developmental progression (Astington, 1994). For example, although children of three years do not understand false beliefs, they do understand whether someone knows or ignores something (for example, Marc who has looked inside a box, knows what is in it, but not Mike, who didn't look). Children of two years may not understand what it is to know or not know something, but they understand mental states like intentions, desires, or pretending (Astington, 1994). Finally, some authors propose that the very first manifestations of theory of mind occur at around one year of age, when children start using joint-attention behaviors (gaze following) and prelinguistic communicative gestures (Bretherton et al., 1981).

One interesting point of contention is whether all these manifestations of theory of mind share a common notion of mental states as unobservable, internal representations that reside in the mind of other subjects (like the notion of *belief*), or whether some of them are based upon a different notion of mental state, especially those that involve understanding attention and intention. For example, in the case of understanding the attention of others, do infants represent "noticing" as something that happens inside the head of the other person and that is different from his behavior of looking, or do they *see* "attending" or "noticing" as a property of the behaviors themselves, maybe as a relationship between subjects and objects (Gómez, 1991, in press)? Perhaps, after all, to represent Marc as *trying* to reach the banana is a way to understand the mental state of intention without detaching it from behavior.

This issue, as we shall see, is especially relevant for the question we are addressing in this chapter: which, if any, of the mentalistic skills that progressively unfold in humans during their first four years of life can be found in nonhuman primates? This question has proved hard to answer, partly because of methodological problems—we cannot use language to ask a chimpanzee what is her prediction in a false-belief test—but also because of the theoretical problem of what is a mental state and how it can be represented. No wonder then that the question of primate theories of mind is currently the subject of a hot debate (Heyes, 1998; Tomasello et al., 2003; Povinelli and Vonk, 2003).

Machiavellian Primates

While developmental psychologists invented the false-belief test and other tests to ask children about what they knew of the beliefs of other people, primatologists, unable to use language with their subjects, had to resort to other methods. One consisted of trying to analyze the spontaneous behavior of nonhuman primates to see if there was any evidence of their taking into account the beliefs and knowledge of others.

Andy Whiten and Dick Byrne (1988) came up with an interesting suggestion. During their work as field primatologists, they had frequently witnessed behaviors like the following: a female baboon is interested in a young male; however, the dominant male will promptly intervene if he sees them doing things like grooming each other—the sort of affiliative exchange that forges bonds among baboons and other primates. One day, the young male is sitting behind a rock, invisible to the dominant, and the female moves herself slowly but steadily toward the rock, apparently just paying attention to minute details in the grass and the ground. Eventually she moves behind the rock, but in such a way that the upper part of her body is still visible from the other side, whereas what she starts doing with her hands—grooming the completely hidden young male—remains invisible to the dominant male. The situation is perfect: the dominant cannot see the offending action, but he can see where the female is (dominant baboons will search for missing females of their groups) and the female can watch the movements of the dominant male.

So do the young male and female understand the cleverness of what they are doing? Are they acting according to a plan to conceal the offending action? Or, even more interesting, given that the female makes herself visible, is she somehow reckoning that the dominant will *mistakenly think* that she is alone behind the rock?

As Byrne and Whiten pointed out, the problem with a single spontaneous observation is that it could have happened by mere chance. Perhaps the female was just anxious to watch the dominant while engaging in the dangerous grooming, and by pure coincidence she happened to adopt the happy position without realizing it.

To overcome this problem, Whiten and Byrne (1988) conducted a survey among other field and laboratory primatologists to find out if apparently deceptive behaviors like the above had been observed by others. And they found that many other primatologists had witnessed cases of apparent deceit and "Machiavellian" behavior: subordinate monkeys may refrain from trying to get a piece of food they have discovered if a dominant individual is watching, and they most certainly will not try to have sexual intercourse with a female until the dominant is out of sight or looking away. And while they are covertly engaged in this activity, they suppress the vocalizations that they would otherwise produce. Chimpanzees had been observed not only refraining from going for food in the presence of a dominant individual, but also refraining from looking at the place where the food was hidden, as if they understood that their gaze could give away the location of the food.

Frans de Waal (1982) has described in detailed some of the more intriguing mentalistic scenes in the life of chimpanzees: for example, a subordinate chimpanzee took advantage of the fact that the dominant was having a nap to start flirting with a female. The dominant unexpectedly woke up and, noticing the other male and female together, started to approach them. The subordinate chimpanzee's problem was that he had a conspicuous penile erection that would leave the dominant in no doubt as to what he was trying to do with the female. The subordinate, however, instead of fleeing, stayed on the spot but carefully kept his back to the approaching dominant, while he anxiously looked in turn at the approaching dominant and his own erect penis; only when the erection had disappeared did he turn and greet the dominant.

An observation like this, especially when described with the mental-state words I have chosen, strongly suggests that chimpanzees understand what other chimpanzees can or cannot see and what are the subtle ways in which knowledge is acquired and intentions are detected.

It might therefore appear that nonhuman primates are capable of acting like natural-born Machiavellians, as Byrne and Whiten put it. But did these deceptive behaviors really involve a theory-of-mind ability in the full sense of the term—an understanding of the distinction between reality and the representations that others may have of it?

As Byrne and Whiten recognized, a problem with their compilation of natural observations is that frequently it was unknown how the relevant behavior first appeared; perhaps they were simple conditioned responses acquired by repeated experience without any understanding. Thus females that meet other males in secluded places and suppress their copulatory calls may do so not because they understand that the dominant will *hear* the call and then *know* that the female is engaging in illicit sex, but because in the past having sex in the presence of the dominant became very quickly associated with the pain of being punished, and emitting copulatory calls became associated with the dominant coming along and punishing them, whereas copulating in silence and when the dominant is not visible became associated with the pleasures of sex without retaliatory pain. Perhaps when a subordinate refrains from going for a piece of fruit while a dominant is present, she has simply learned that such an attempt is "fruitless" because he will always snatch it.

Observations of natural Machiavellian behavior were suggestive of theory-of-mind abilities in nonhuman primates, but the hypothesis was in need of more solid empirical ground—such as only experiments can provide. We will start with experiments on how primates understand states of attention.

Primates' Understanding of Attention

Recall that joint-attention behaviors have two components: attention following and attention contact. Although in referential communication both tend to occur together, attention following can occur without attention contact. If I see another person looking somewhere intently, I can look in the same direction without the other person noticing me at all. Also, I can engage your attention upon myself (for example, ask you what time is it) without having to follow your gaze. Ontogenetically, we know that in human babies the two patterns may appear at different times: first, attention contact (at 9 to 12 months), then attention following (11 to 14), and finally (at 13 to 15 months) the combination of the two (Carpenter et al., 1998).

Can Nonhuman Primates Follow the Attention of Others?

Several studies have now firmly established that monkeys and apes will spontaneously look in the same direction as a conspecific or a human, especially if the attention of the model is expressed with head and body orientation (Tomasello and Call, 1997; Call and Tomasello, in press). More "primitive" primates, for instance lemurs, may fail to do so (Anderson and Mitchell, 1999). Developmental data about the emergence of gaze following in macaques are contradictory. In pigtailed macaques Ferrari et al. (2000) found gaze following in response to head/eye movements only at 2 to 4 years of age, but only adults responded to eye direction without head movement. Moreover, the researchers found a steady correlation between age and the ability to follow gaze with any cue, which indicates that at least in these monkeys this was a progressively acquired skill. In contrast, Tomasello, Hare, and Fogleman (2001) found that 6-month-old rhesus macaques could reliably follow head movements. Apart from the species difference, the subjects of Tomasello and colleagues were housed in large social groups and in large enclosures, whereas the subjects of Ferrari and colleagues (2000) were laboratory primates reared in less complex social and physical environments. If gaze following is an acquired skill, then Tomasello and colleagues' subjects may have had more opportunity to develop it.

In the same study Tomasello et al. (2001) found that chimpanzees were slower in their development of gaze following: they responded reliably only at 3 to 4 years of age. Humans show an intermediate schedule, with infants following eye direction at 14 to 18 months, although earlier they readily follow gaze if expressed with movements of the head (Butterworth, 1991).

Although experience plays an important role in learning to follow gaze in all species studied so far, there are indications that it might be built upon some predispositions to attend to faces and to discriminate between direct and averted gaze; both abilities have been found in human and gibbon babies at one month or earlier (Farroni et al., 2002; Myowa-Yamakoshi and Tomonaga, 2001). Moreover, it has recently been discovered (Lorinctz, Perret and Gómez, in press) that adult rhesus monkeys look in the same direction as the subjects in photos of not only familiar species such as rhesus macaques and humans, but also of unknown species (lions, domestic cats, orangutans) which they had never before seen. This indicates that what monkeys learn about direction of attention is some abstract schema that is applicable across species with highly diverse face and head configurations. This would make evolutionary sense if one of the functions of detecting attention direction is to help avoid predators: monkeys would not need to have had previous experience with them.

This evidence about the spontaneous tendency of primates to follow the attention of other primates coexists with at best ambiguous results as to what primates can achieve with this ability. Take for example the following experiment: you hide a piece of food in one of two containers, then you place the containers in front of a monkey or an ape (who did not see the baiting); you look intently to the correct container and then allow them to choose one. Surprisingly, in many experiments like these, most monkeys and apes fail to use the attentional cue from the experimenter to choose the baited container, even if sometimes they appear initially to look at the correct container. Moreover, they may even fail to follow more explicit signals, like pointing to the correct container (Call and Tomasello, in press; Povinelli et al., 1997). Only if the attentional orientation is accompanied by appropriate vocalizations (food-barks in the case of chimpanzees) and foraging postures, some subjects show some degree of competence in finding the hidden food. The few subjects that succeed from the beginning have had an extensive hand-rearing experience with humans (Call and Tomasello, in press). It also contributes to their success if instead of closed containers, tubes or screens are used such that the human (but not the chimpanzee) can actually see the target he is trying to alert the ape about.

Is Gaze Following a Reflex?

These ambiguous results have led to questioning the real under-standing that monkeys and apes have of attention when they follow gaze. What sort of representations, if any, do primates use when following the attention of others? Povinelli and Eddy (1996a, 1997) suggest a radical hypothesis: no representation is necessary for fol-lowing attention, because attention following may be a quasi-reflex or mechanical action built into chimpanzees and other primates (a little like what happens when humans cannot prevent themselves from following someone else's gaze). In Povinelli and Eddy's view, gaze following would not amount to attention following because the chimps do not understand the *mental* connection between a person's gaze and the object she is looking at. Nonhuman primates are simply endowed with an automatic response that makes them look in the same direction as others and, therefore, they frequently end up looking at the same target, but without realizing that they are sharing their attention with others upon the same object; with-out realizing even that the others are looking at anything at all, and, of course, without realizing the intentions that may accom-pany the gaze of the other primate. This hypothesis could explain the paradox of gaze-following behavior coexisting with the inability to make good use of the information conveyed by gaze.

Nevertheless empirical evidence does not appear to fit this radi-cal proposal. Paradoxically, a study by Povinelli and Eddy them-selves (1997) provided the first experimental evidence against the reflex theory. A room was divided in two sides by a panel, one part of which was opaque, whereas the other was transparent. The chimpanzee was in one side, and a human in the other. When the human looked at a distant point through the transparent part, the chimpanzee would turn and look in his own side; but when the hu-man looked in the direction of the opaque part of the partition, the chimpanzee would try to look through the glass *into* the side of the panel inside the human quarters. The chimp was not automatically turning his eyes in the same direction as the human, but taking into account where the human could possibly be looking. Nothing beyond the opaque section of the partition could have been the target of the human gaze. The chimp behaved as if he understood that gaze is directed at targets and cannot be projected through opaque screens.

Building upon this study, Tomasello et al. (1999) replicated this finding. Moreover, they showed that, if allowed, the chimps would manually search the place where a human was looking intently if they were not able to visually inspect it. The chimps did this spontaneously, without any training. This suggests that the chimpanzees represent the human's attention as directed to a target, and that they can infer the existence of the target from the agent's gaze alone.

A further indicator that primates may be representing attention as a relationship between a subject and an object is their reaction when an experimenter looks at a place where there is nothing to be seen. Chimpanzees have been reported to check back by looking again at the eyes of the agent when nothing is found (Call and Tomasello, in press). Scerif, Gómez, and Byrne (2003) found something similar in captive diana monkeys. When exposed to photographs of conspecifics, dianas not only tended to look in the same direction as the animal in the photograph, but also, in the absence of a congruent target, they would look back more frequently to the photo of the conspecific than when there was an object to be seen.

These findings appear to disprove a simple reflex-like theory of gaze following, but on the other hand they deepen the mystery of why chimpanzees and other primates typically fail to use a human's gaze to find hidden food. We will return to this problem.

Understanding Attention Contact

So far we have been discussing the case of understanding the attention of someone looking at a target, but what happens when that target is oneself? In the discussion of the development of referential communication in prelinguistic children and apes, we mentioned that one of the key criteria to identify communicative intentionality was the behavior of looking at the eyes of the other person while gesturing. We suggested that eye contact was a way of establishing *attention* contact—the crucial causal link for social interaction.

One might think that attention contact can be explained by the same mechanisms as attention following; sometimes the focus of another's attention just happens to be oneself. Indeed, when a person is looking at my hands or my shoes, I may detect this by using the same gaze-following mechanism by means of which I can tell that you are looking at the TV set. But when the other person is looking at my eyes, subjectively I tend to experience this as something very different (Kendon, 1967), as if the other person were trying to engage me somehow. In part this may be because in eye contact we perceive the attention of the other not merely as directed to ourselves, but as directed to our own *attention;* we are literally placed in a situation of *attention contact*, and this opens the doors of mutual intentional communication (Gómez, 1994, in press).

This subjective impression of attention contact being different from attention following has started to be supported by empirical findings. For example, distinct patterns of brain activation have been detected in humans when confronted with faces looking directly at them versus faces looking elsewhere (Wicker, 2001). Perret (1999) found in rhesus monkeys neurons that fired exclusively to direct gaze stimuli. A pop-out effect (that is, a very quick detection) has been reported for faces looking forward versus faces looking sideways (von Grünau and Anston, 1995).

Evolutionarily, the distinct pattern of a pair of eyes fixed on oneself appears to have a long history as an especially relevant stimulus, one that might advertise that one is the target of attention of a predator. Many animals react with automatic alarm or escape responses. Other animals, like certain moths, have taken advantage of this by developing wings that simulate two big eyes, which may scare away some potential predators hastily reacting to what could be a bigger predator that has detected them (Baron-Cohen, 1995).

Among primates, monkeys are known to show a special sensitivity to another monkey or a human staring at them. Many species have been reported to react to a prolonged gaze at their eyes as a threat (Gómez, 1996b). Yet prolonged eye contact appears to have a different connotation in other species, like chimpanzees, who use it in a variety of contexts, among them reconciliation, the opposite to threat and aggression. Chimpanzees, after a fight, usually engage in affiliative behaviors in which they embrace and exchange other signs of positive bonding. A fundamental pattern that accompanies these reconciliatory exchanges is prolonged mutual eye gaze; so much so that an unwilling chimpanzee may refuse to reconcile by simply avoiding eye contact (De Waal, 1989). Finally, we recall that gorillas and chimpanzees check the attention of humans by making eye contact when they engage in rudimentary referential communication. What do primates really understand about attention contact and its role in social interaction?

Experiments On Mutual Attention of Primates

In line with their arguments about the lack of understanding of attention in gaze following, Povinelli and Eddy (1996a) suggest also that chimpanzees do not understand if someone is looking at them or not in communicative situations. They have good experimental reasons to believe this. In an extensive series of studies, they confronted a group of six young chimpanzees with two humans. One had his eyes open and looked to the plexiglas partition wall behind which the chimps were, and the other displayed some form of inability to see the chimpanzee (her eyes were closed or she looked to one side or was blindfolded). Prior to this, the chimpanzees had been extensively trained to put their arms through one of two holes in the transparent wall opposite one human experimenter, who rewarded the chimpanzee with a piece of food that lay visibly on a box by him.

In the experimental condition with the two humans, the chimpanzees had a choice: they could insert their arm either in the hole opposite the human who was oriented to the wall and with his eyes open, or through the hole opposite the human who was looking elsewhere or had her eyes covered. None of the chimpanzees was capable of systematically choosing the correct person, except in the most extreme case of lack of attention—when the inattentive human was sitting with her back to the chimp.

The conclusion of the authors was that the chimpanzees could not understand who was in a position of *seeing* or *attending* to them. When chimps are observed looking at the eyes or following the gaze of other people, they don't really understand the psychological counterpart of looking—the inner experience of seeing—nor they appear to understand the difference between someone attending or not attending to them.

These results may appear to contradict other findings. For example, chimpanzees tend to use visual gestures when their recipients are visually oriented to them, and gorillas go as far as to provoke eye contact with humans before making a request from them. But Povinelli's point is that, although apes do engage in mutual looking and gaze-following behaviors, they do not relate these behaviors to the mental states of seeing or attending; they do not understand the mental connection that is established between an agent and the targets he is looking at.

A recent experiment by Hare and colleagues (2000) seems to challenge this interpretation. A common feature of almost all experiments concerning nonhuman primates' theories of mind has been that the primates were usually confronted with humans as the actors whose minds they had to understand. This amounted to asking them to display a theory of the human mind, not a theory of their own species' mind (Gómez, 1996a)! To overcome this problem, Hare et al. (2000) confronted chimpanzees with other chimpanzees, not with human beings; and put them in a typical chimpanzee problem situation—competing for food—instead of a typical human situation—sharing food. They chose one subordinate and one

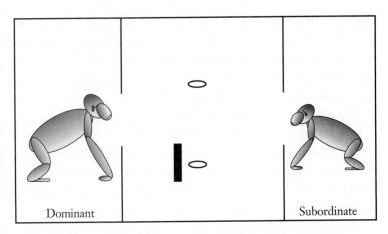

Figure 8.1. Testing chimpanzees' understanding of what their fellow chimps can see in a competitive situation (Hare et al., 2000). One piece of food is visible only to the subordinate chimpanzee. Will she specifically target this when she is allowed into the central room?

dominant individual and placed them in two separate rooms with a third room between them. In this middle room there were two pieces of food, sometimes placed in such a way that both were visible to both individuals; at other times only one food item was visible to the dominant chimpanzee (see figure 8.1). For example, one piece was on top of a tire, visible from both cages, whereas the other was just behind another tire, visible only to the subordinate. After allowing them to watch the scenario, both animals were released simultaneously into the enclosure. In normal circumstances, dominant individuals eat more food than subordinates (preferential access to food is one of the advantages and measures of dominance). Subordinates may not even bother to approach a piece of food when the dominant is present. In this experimental arrangement, though, subordinates showed a significant tendency to approach and consume the piece of food that was visible only to them.

To make sure that the subordinates were not simply responding to the initial movement of the dominant, who will naturally approach the visible piece of food, the subordinates were released slightly earlier than the dominants, so that they would have a head start. The result was that subordinates still preferred to approach the piece of food that was visible only to them. Finally, when instead of an opaque barrier, a transparent one was used, the subordinates' preference for the now exposed food disappeared.

When Hare et al. (2003) tried the same experiment with capuchin monkeys, these failed to take into account whether their rivals could or not see the available food. This suggests that, contrary to the conclusion of Povinelli and Eddy (1996a), chimpanzees (but not capuchins) do understand what other chimpanzees can or cannot see.*

A possible explanation for these contradictory results is that chimpanzees can only demonstrate their mentalistic understanding among other chimps. But Hare and colleagues (2000) point out another important difference with previous studies. The chimpanzees in this case were not requested to engage in a *cooperative* interaction—one in which the other party is expected to hand food to the subject—but in a *competitive* context—one in which the other party is expected to take the food for himself if he can. Perhaps the chimpanzees' theory of mind is a mechanism that has been selected for competition, not for cooperation (Hare, 2001). This means that chimps would be able to compute "who can see what" in order to decide whether they should approach a target or not, but they would be unable to make a similar computation with the aim of influencing or understanding the behavior of cooperative others. Thus, the chimp theory of mind would be a domain- or context-specific skill. (This could partly explain the puzzle of why chimpan-

* Karin-D'Arcy and Povinelli (2003) have recently repeated this experiment with other chimpanzees. They found too that subordinate chimpanzees get the partially hidden food more frequently than the fully visible one; but they report that, contrary to Hare and colleagues' results, their subordinates did not *try* to get the hidden food first. They conclude that their chimpanzees did not react to what the dominant could see, but to his behavior when approaching the fully visible food. Karin-D'Arcy and Povinelli may have changed a fundamental aspect of Hare and colleagues' design, however, because they did not release the dominant individual until the subordinate had made his choice with no competitor around (dominant chimpanzees don't usually try to grab food that is already in the hands of a subordinate).

zees, despite their gaze-following skills, are so bad at being able to use the gaze of cooperative humans to find hidden food [Call and Tomasello, in press].)

In fact, there is another important difference with Povinelli and Eddy's (1996a) study. Hare and colleagues' experiment is about the ability to detect gaze upon an external target (and as such has more to do with the understanding of gaze following), whereas Povinelli and Eddy's was about the ability to detect which person was attending to the chimpanzee himself—what we have called attention contact. Is it possible that chimpanzees can understand whether others can see a target, but not whether others can see them? Or to put it differently, perhaps chimpanzees can understand if someone is or is not looking at them in the same way as they understand if someone is or is not looking at an object, but they do not understand that underlying the gaze is the mental component of attention, and in the case of mutual gaze, the *attention-contact* component that is so fundamental for communication.

Understanding Human Attention in Cooperative Settings

The following experiment suggests that neither of these explanations is correct. Gómez, Teixidor, and Laá (1996) confronted chimpanzees with a single human who would routinely respond to any requests of food (figure 8.2). The chimps were in a standard zoo cage with bars and were free to request whenever they wanted and use any gesture from their own repertoire (they were not trained to use a particular gesture in a particular direction). The food was placed on a platform, out of reach of the chimpanzees, just next to the crouching human. Chimps needed no prompting to request food by extending their arms to the food or, in a few instances, taking the hand of the human toward the food. They were all capable of doing this from the very beginning. Interestingly, in this routine situation, they would look at the eyes of the human when performing their request only in about 50 percent of the trials.

Once we checked that the chimps were requesting in this situation, the real test started. From time to time (once every 3 or 4 nor-

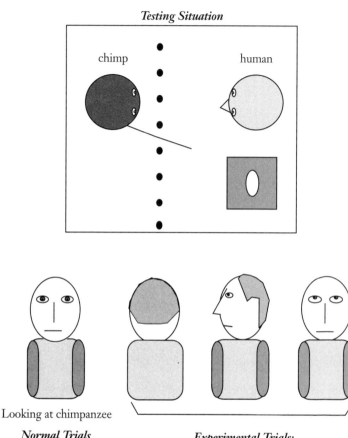

Testing Situation

chimp   human

Looking at chimpanzee

Normal Trials   *Experimental Trials:*
(immediate response)   *Displaying Inattention*
and Control Trials
(no response in 5 seconds)

Figure 8.2. Testing chimpanzees' understanding of attention contact in communication (Gómez, Teixidor and Laá, 1996). A human sits in front of a caged chimpanzee who requests a piece of food. In normal trials the human is looking at the chimpanzee and responds immediately to any requests. In experimental trials, the human is not attending to the chimpanzee. In control trials, the human is attending, but does not respond for 5 seconds. Will the chimpanzee call the attention of the human in the experimental trials?

mal trials) an experimental trial was carried out. In it, the person was not attending to the chimpanzee (she had her eyes closed or was looking elsewhere) and therefore could not respond to the request. Would the chimpanzees check the attention of the person and, upon discovering that she was not attending, try to engage her attention? To make sure that any attention-calling behavior was in reaction to the lack of attention and not to the lack of response by the inattentive human, we introduced a control condition—one in which the person was looking at the chimpanzee but did not respond for a few seconds.

In this experiment we used 6 chimpanzees: 3 of them had been individually hand-reared by humans for at least one year; the other three were used to contact with humans as a group but had never been individually hand-reared. The results of our study were different for each group of chimps. The three who had had individual experience with humans systematically looked at the face of the person when there was no response from her and, if (and only if) the person was not looking at them, they would touch or pull her, make eye contact, and then execute again a request; that is, they were *calling the attention* of the inattentive humans before making their requests. The 3 chimps with less experience with humans might look at the face of the person when no response was given, but they simply repeated their requests without first engaging the attention of the inattentive human.*

Clearly, the extent of experience with humans is a very important variable when one is trying to test nonhuman primates with human models—something that Tomasello and his collaborators (Tomasello, 1999) have emphasized repeatedly. Once the chimps have a minimum of human exposure, they do show an understanding of the role of attention and lack of attention from the addressee

---

* In a study based upon preliminary reports of our own (Gómez, 1995, 1996a), Theall and Povinelli (1999) found that during requests their chimpanzees always touched humans who remained unresponsive for 20 seconds, regardless of whether they were attending to them or not. This ceiling effect could be due to the unusually short distance separating humans and chimps—30 centimeters in contrast with the 150 centimeters of the standard request situation of Povinelli and Eddy (1996a).

in cooperative situations. Perhaps this is the factor that explains the difference with the chimpanzees studied by Povinelli and Eddy (1996a), who apparently did not have a history of individual hand-rearing with humans. But the disparate results may also be due to some interesting differences in the experimental designs.

Displaying Attention

For one thing, Povinelli and Eddy (1996a) did not record whether their chimps were looking at the face of the two humans before choosing one of them. In our experiment we discovered that chimps in such routine requesting situation looked only about 50 percent of the time. Perhaps some of Povinelli and Eddy's negative results are attributable to the chimps' responding without checking the attentional state of the humans. This possibility is underscored by the fact that, in the condition in which the humans were looking elsewhere, the chimpanzees showed gaze-following responses only in about 50 to 60 percent of the trials.

More important, the "attentive" humans were instructed to look fixedly either at a point on the plexiglas partition midway between the response holes, or (in later experiments) at their own response hole. Therefore, the supposedly attentive experimenters never looked at the chimpanzees themselves, let alone at their eyes. This means that the human that was supposed to be displaying attention was in fact not attending to the chimpanzees in any of the conditions. And only in about half of them were they looking at a point that was potentially relevant to the task—the hole. To succeed in the latter trials, the chimpanzee had first to look at the right person, then to follow his gaze to the hole, and then to infer that even if this person was not attending to the chimp, nonetheless he was in a position to see the extended hand, and that upon seeing the hand, this person would respond by handing over the food that was resting on a box next to him. This is very different from understanding attention to oneself in a communicative situation.

The chimpanzees might have been expected to have learned the importance of the experimenter's gaze to their hands during the extensive preliminary training phase. During all the training phase, however, the human was looking fixedly at an imaginary point on the plexiglas. Thus the chimpanzees may have learned that the response of the humans had nothing to do with the direction of their gaze. Povinelli and Eddy may have unwittingly trained their chimps to ignore the gaze of the humans as completely irrelevant to the task!

It appears therefore that Povinelli and Eddy's experiments were not really measuring chimpanzees understanding of attention, perhaps not even of seeing. Another study by the same authors (Povinelli and Eddy, 1996b) confirms this impression, and the sensitivity of chimpanzees to whether they are actually paid attention. Using the same basic setting as before, the authors confronted their chimpanzees with humans who were looking at the holes (as in the condition that counted as "attentive" in the previous series of experiments), and humans who were looking at the eyes of the chimps, trying to make eye contact with them. In this setting, the chimpanzees systematically chose to extend their hands to the human who was making eye contact with them. Only one condition was more powerful than eye contact in eliciting a chimpanzee request: one in which the persons were moving their heads mimicking what the authors identified as typical movements made by chimpanzees who are *attending* to something. These movements could be effective even if they were performed with the eyes closed. This finding highlights the importance of attention as a category of behavior that is not linked to a single signal like eye contact, but may encompass a variety of behaviors. And it also suggests that understanding attention may be independent of understanding "seeing."*

The available evidence suggests overall that chimps do discriminate between behaviors displaying attention contact and inattentive behaviors, and that they can even intervene when there is a condition of inattention by calling the attention of the person and

---

* An alternative interpretation is that chimpanzees may understand "seeing," but they don't understand the role of the eyes in this (Call and Tomasello, in press).

establishing attention contact before making a request. This understanding can be demonstrated even when tested with humans in cooperative tasks, provided the apes have enough experience with humans and are confronted with a genuine choice between attentive and inattentive conditions.

This, paired with the evidence that chimpanzees (and other primates) understand gaze as a target-directed behavior, suggests that apes have a relatively sophisticated understanding of attention.

A different problem is how apes represent attention. The current results fit especially well the idea advanced by Gómez (1990, 1991; see also Hobson, 1994, for a similar idea applied to human children) that apes' understanding of attention is based upon the representation of external expressions of this mental state, not necessarily upon the computation of internal, unobservable mental entities.

The mental state of attention has the peculiarity of being overt. A person attending to something physically turns her eyes, and usually also her head and body, in the direction of a particular target. Of course these overt movements are accompanied by events in the nervous system that are not directly observable, and by an internal, subjective experience of seeing, hearing, or feeling something. But the overt side of attention—in contrast with beliefs and knowledge which we can never see directly—offers the possibility of representing it by its visible counterparts only, without having to represent the invisible part of the process. From an evolutionary perspective, it is possible that mechanisms for representing the overt mind exist independently of mechanisms for understanding the covert mind.

Understanding Knowledge (and Ignorance)

Understanding what others know (and how they get to know it) and realizing that sometimes what someone knows might be wrong are more complex theory-of-mind abilities than understanding attention and seeing. Human children only develop an understanding of *epistemic* mental states well after having understood attention (at 3 to 4 years).

Although some of Whiten and Byrne's (1988) observations suggested that primates may sometimes understand what others know, even if these others misrepresent reality, the first experimental attempts at validating this impression failed. For example, Povinelli, Nelson and Boysen (1990) tried to make a systematic replication of a study originally conducted by Premack (Premack and Premack, 1983), in which an experimenter put food in one of two boxes placed in front of the chimpanzee's cage. A screen prevented the chimpanzee from seeing in which box the experimenter had placed the food. The screen was then withdrawn and a human who had seen the baiting from behind the screen (and therefore was in a position to know where the food was) pointed to the correct box. The catch of the experiment was that a second human, who was not present during the baiting, would simultaneously point to the wrong box. To which human would the chimpanzees pay attention? Would they understand that only the human who had been watching could know where the food was? Initially, the chimpanzees chose at random, but after several sessions of training, they learned to pay attention only to the knowledgeable human. Had they realized the importance of witnessing the hiding event for knowing the location of the food? To decide this, the authors gave them a transfer test in which both humans were present during the baiting, but one had his head covered with a paper bag, so that he could not see what was going on. The rationale of the experimenters was that a good performance in this transfer condition would be suggestive of understanding knowledge. And certainly the chimpanzees performed clearly above chance in the new trials. But when the authors reanalyzed their data following a suggestion by Heyes (1993), they discovered that although the chimps performed above chance in the whole series of new trials, they had performed at chance level during the first trials (Povinelli, 1994). They were not transferring a complex knowledge acquired during the previous phase, but quickly relearning to solve a new, but similar problem.

The negative results in this rather complex test appeared to be fully justified by the subsequent findings of Povinelli and Eddy (1996a) that suggested chimpanzees did not even understand attention and seeing. As we have seen, however, these findings are now into question, and it seems worth revisiting the problem of whether chimpanzees understand knowledge.

Hare, Call, and Tomasello (2001), again using a competition paradigm, have recently presented evidence that chimpanzees might have some notion of what others know about something. As in their previous study about chimpanzees understanding of seeing, they created a competitive context in which chimpanzees confronted one another. One subordinate chimpanzee, looking from his own cage, saw how a piece of food was hidden in a particular location in a central room. In a cage opposite the subordinate's, a dominant chimpanzee was also watching the food placement. In some trials, after the food was in place, the door of the dominant chimpanzee was shut and, while he was unable to see it, the food was changed to a new location (all in full view of the subordinate). After that, both chimpanzees were released into the central room and were free to go for the food. Would the subordinate chimpanzee realize that in the covert transfer trials the dominant did not know where the food was, and would he (the subordinate) therefore go for it more frequently than in the other trials? This is exactly what the authors found: the subordinate chimpanzees appeared to take into account whether the dominants knew or did not know the location of the food. Moreover, in trials where the position of the food was not covertly changed, if the identity of the dominant chimpanzee changed (one dominant was present during the baiting, but then a different one, not present during the baiting, was released), the subordinates also went for the hidden food more frequently. This indicates that chimpanzees might be able to keep track of who knows what.

Hare (2001) claims that the success they obtained with their intraspecific paradigms points to the possibility that theory-of-mind abilities in chimpanzees (and perhaps in apes in general) are specific adaptations for competition. Previous experiments had tested apes in contexts of cooperation, usually with humans as partners whose mental states had to be understood. Perhaps cooperative motives like those involved in communication are not common among primates other than humans; this would explain why chimpanzees failed to recruit their understanding of mental states to deal with the sort of problems they had received earlier.

Yet this conclusion does not fit well with the fact that apes, when confronted with humans, engage in requesting behaviors in which they do expect that the human will be cooperative. Moreover, when chimpanzees were properly tested with genuine states of attention and inattention, those that have had enough experience with humans do take into account whether they have established attentional contact. Could apes also take into account whether other primates know something in a situation of cooperation?

Relevance and Theory of Mind: A "Key" Experiment

A powerful variable that affects what we tell or point out to others is what we think they know or ignore. Typically, we tend to tell others (verbally or gesturally) things that they don't know and that we assume are of interest to them, or that it is in our interest that they know. Human communication is governed by this principle of "relevance," to use the expression of Sperber and Wilson (1986). For example, if my wife wants me to throw the trash bag into the garbage can, but she left the can in a unusual place, she will make sure not only to tell me to take the trash out, but also to inform me of where the can is now. As we recall, apes are able to ask people to do things for them: for example, to give them food that is lying outside their cage. But can they also point out relevant things to people, depending upon whether or not the apes think these people know about them? This is essentially asking whether they have a theory of mind that is transferable to communicative and cooperative situations.

Gómez and Teixidor (1992; Gómez, 1998) developed a task that assesses exactly this. Their subject was a female orangutan—Dona—housed in a zoo cage. Two boxes were placed in a room adjacent to the orang's cage. The boxes were locked with padlocks. One person—the baiter—entered the room, picked the keys for the padlocks from a small box hanging from a string, opened one of the big boxes, placed some food inside it, locked the box, and put the key back in its original location. She then left the room. A few moments later, another person—the giver—entered the room, and sitting in front of both boxes, addressed the orangutan. If Dona pointed with her arm toward one box, the giver went for the key, opened the box and gave her the contents. The giver then returned the key to its box and left. A few seconds later, the baiter would return and a new trial followed along the same lines.

The fact that Dona pointed to the hidden food is not enough evidence that she understood that the human did not know where the food was and therefore needed to be informed of its whereabouts. Like the chimpanzees of the experiments in the previous section, the orangutan requested food and objects that were in full view of the human. She might have been requesting the hidden food simply because she knew it is there, without considering whether the human knew this as well. We needed a different test to check Dona's ability to understand the knowledge of the other party. This consisted in the following.

Once every ten or more normal trials like the above (and only once in a given day), the baiter, after leaving the food in one box and after locking the box, did not return the keys to their usual location but *hid* them in a completely new place, and then left the room. Then the giver entered the room as usual. Now, if the orangutan wanted the giver to give her the food, she had to point not only to the food but also to the keys, which the person would otherwise be unable to find.

In six such experimental trials, carefully interspersed with normal trials, Dona did not point to the keys *before* the human tried to find them in the wrong place. In the very first trial, she simply pointed to the food, and when the human failed to find the keys in the usual location, she offered him no help. The giver had to leave the room without opening the box and giving the food to the orang. However, in the next 5 experimental trials, carried out over the next few days, *after* the giver tried to find the key in the usual place, the orang immediately pointed to the hidden location of the key (which was different in every experimental trial), so that in all these trials the giver was eventually able to find the key, open the box, and give her the food.

This is an intelligent reaction by the orang (one that demonstrates a good understanding of what the human has to do), but it does not demonstrate an ability to understand the state of ignorance of the giver. Pointing to the key is not a reaction to the wrong knowledge of the human, but to his wrong behavior—his failure to get the key. It therefore does not imply a theory-of-mind ability.

The Spur Of Deceit

We then decided to pass to phase two of the experiment, in which we would use a different context. Some studies of theory of mind with children have found that their performance can be enhanced by the way the task is explained to them. If instead of telling them that the change of location of the object happens by chance or inadvertently, you explain that the agent is trying to deceive or play a trick on the main character, typically more children are able to give the correct answer (Núñez and Rivière, in press). This is consistent with another finding in humans: certain complex logical tasks can become surprisingly easy if posed in the context of a story that involves the possibility of deception (Cosmides, 1989).

We decided to change the critical trials for Dona in a similar fashion. Instead of having the baiter leave the keys in a new unexpected place, a completely new character—a stranger—entered the room unexpectedly after the baiter left, went for the keys, and hid them in a new location, leaving the room before the giver entered. Dona reacted with alarm to the appearance of the stranger and followed his/her steps very attentively (in a couple of occasions she even spat at the stranger, a mildly aggressive behavior). With this scenario the results changed dramatically: in the 7 trials conducted with a stranger (always in separate days and interspersed with normal trials), Dona pointed *both* to the keys and the food at the beginning of the trial, *before* the giver gave any sign of not being able to retrieve the keys. She was now acting as if she understood that the giver could not possibly know where the keys were and therefore had to be directed to them. Note also that she pointed to both the keys *and* the food—pointing only to the keys would have been inappropriate.

To make sure that the subject was reacting to the lack of knowledge of the giver about the new location of the keys, and not that they were in an unusual location, we conducted a number of control trials, the most important of which was the following: in some normal trials, the giver, after giving the food to Dona, did not return the keys to the usual location but instead placed them in an unusual hiding place. Now, in the next trial, the keys lay hidden in an unusual place, but the giver knew where they were and so it was not necessary to point to them. Indeed, the orang did not point to the keys in these trials. She was not reacting to the unusual location of the object, but to the relation between it and the giver.

It appeared, therefore, that the alarming context of the stranger was capable of activating some sort of computation of the relations between people and objects, one that could be glossed as "knowing" versus "not knowing". To further check the importance of this context, we conducted a few more critical trials with a known person performing the unexpected key transfer. This time it was a person who had been present inside the room—the photographer who was filming the experiment. At the appropriate moment, he/she would unexpectedly leave the camera on the floor and change the key before returning to the camera and resuming the filming. In the six trials conducted, Dona pointed to the keys in four of them: her performance was still good, but worse than when the transfer was made by a complete stranger.

The orangutan was therefore capable of representing the past relations between subjects and objects in order to control her ability to direct the agent toward particular targets in a cooperative context. In a sense, this ability is similar to that found by Hare et al. (2001) in chimpanzees: it involved the computation of relations between agents and targets of action beyond the here and now. In our study the orangutan goes beyond the chimps in that she is able to use this representation not just to guide her own behavior toward an object, but also to control the behavior of another agent by directing him toward the unknown target. In this sense, this appears to be an example of "relevance" in referential communication.

One could be tempted to conclude that the initial failure of our subject to direct the human to the keys before he showed any sign of looking for them in the wrong place was a matter of distraction or partial lack of understanding of the requirements of the situation, and that her subsequent success reflects her true competence. In the line of Hare's (2001) argument, however, the context of suggested deception or mild threat which facilitated her performance may be an indication of a limitation in the kind of representations that activate the "know" category in apes. In fact, if we interpret the stranger context as one with competitive connotations, this would allow us to establish an interesting link with Hare, Call, and Tomasello's (2001) results, except that in our study the competitive context facilitates the activation of a possible mentalistic computation in a *cooperative* task.

More experiments along the lines of those designed by Hare et al. and Gómez and Teixidor can help us understand the generality of these apparent theory-of-mind competences we are uncovering in apes.

Do Nonhuman Primates Have a Theory of Mind?

The answer to this question depends upon how we want to define this ability. If we opt for a definition in terms of representing mental states as internal, unobservable entities in explicit formats (linguistic or propositional), then it is more than likely that nonhumans do not have such a theory of mind. If we define theory of mind from a wider perspective, accepting the plurality of ways in which mental states can be represented and the plurality of mental states themselves (for example, the distinction between overt and covert mental states), then the evidence we have reviewed in this chapter suggests that theories of mind may be present in different ways in some primate species.

From an evolutionary and developmental point of view, this second perspective makes better sense, among other things because it is capable of accommodating the first alternative: the possibility that some explicit forms of mentalistic understanding have emerged only in human evolution.

One possibility is that nonhuman primates only represent overt mental states like attention and intentions in the form of schemas like "Danny is watching me" or "Marc is trying to get that banana," whereas covert mental states like knowing and believing remain beyond the nonhuman mind. However, the results of Hare et al. (2001) and Gómez and Teixidor (1992) suggest that apes may at least be capable of representing something similar to knowing versus ignoring. Does this mean they can represent unobservable mental states? To some extent they probably can, in the same sense that they can represent a hidden object as being behind a barrier or even imagine what might have invisibly happened to that object (as in Piagetian tasks of invisible displacement; see chapter 3). But here the object and the hiding event are only circumstantially invisible: in other occasions they are visible. What the primate does is to understand the *permanence* of objects in the world whether they are currently perceivable or not. At the very least, nonhuman primates must be able to do something similar with overt mental states like attention and intentions—to *conserve* them through superficial transformations, that is, to understand that if a chimpanzee tried to reach a banana one minute ago, he might still have this intention (perhaps *inside* him), even if it is not visible now. Similarly, if a person was observed witnessing something (how the banana was moved from A to B), the chimpanzee may conserve the relationship between the person and the location of the object, so that later he will be able to predict that the person will find the object there.

The Plurality of Mentalistic Understanding

We need not assume that an ape's view of complex social events is similar to the sort of language-mediated descriptions we have in our minds when thinking of a human interaction. Probably apes' representations are much less articulated, perhaps less extended in time (both past and future), and based on a different set of core mental states.

For example, although chimpanzees and other primates may lack a notion of misrepresentation (false belief), what they understand about intentions, attention, and knowledge may be enough to guide their social behavior in a way that surprisingly resembles in its general outline and even in some of the details our own Machiavellian maneuvers. Some people (Povinelli, 2000) believe this resemblance is only superficial, in that only humans, with a brand new set of advanced cognitive abilities, can truly interpret behavior in a mentalistic way. However, the "primitive" cognitive mechanisms that apes use for understanding seeing, attending, and intending in their "overt mental-state" versions may be at the root of all mentalistic representation. The gist of an episode of Machiavellian conflict may be present in a chimpanzee's understanding of what is going on. But the details, the extension into the past and the future, and some higher-order ramifications ("I think she may have told him about my suspicion that he knew I was trying to impress him the other day") may be absent or more limited in nonhuman primates.

This perspective—the plurality of mentalistic representations—is especially interesting in relation to a central problem of developmental cognitive science: the explanation of disturbances like autism. Persons with autism have been reported to have special difficulties with mentalistic representations of other people (Baron-Cohen, 1995). A minority of people with autism do manage to understand the basics of what a mental state is and how it works at a theoretical level. They appear to understand especially well the notion that a mental state is something inside someone's head (Swettenham et al., 1996). Even they, however, still have difficulty understanding the *gist* (and many details) of social events in real life. Recent evidence suggests that their difficulties may start with the ability to pay attention to the right information in social scenarios, especially attending to people's eyes and spontaneously following their gaze and gestures to the targets of their attention (Klin et al., 2002). Some of these mentalistic deficits may have to do not with representing other persons' mental states as internal and unobservable entities, but with the ability to detect the basic connection between people and the objects of their attention, and the ability to articulate their abstract mentalistic notions into outlines of who is trying to do what to whom and with what final goal. Chimpanzees and other primates may have some rudimentary versions of these basic mentalistic schemas for making sense of the social world. People with autism may have special problems with these more primitive, and at the same time more basic representations whose essence lies not in the internal and unobservable nature of the mind, but in a more basic property of the mental world—what philosophers call *aboutness* or intentionality (Lycan, 1999). According to this view, something is mental when it *points* to something else, or when it is *about* something else, that is, when it needs to be complemented by a content that is not part of itself. For example, one always *looks at something*, or intends something, or thinks of something. In that sense, the representation of the external behaviors of a subject attending to or intending something can be mentalistic if it portrays him/her as being *about* something (Gómez, in press).

Conclusion: Windows to the Mind

One of the most characteristic and distinct features of primates is their faces with frontally convergent eyes and complex system of muscles, many of which appear to have evolved for the sake of supporting expressive behaviors (Huber, 1931). The combination of emotional expressions and direction of gaze makes of the primate face a window through which many of the mental states of primates can be "advertised" and read by other primates. This trend toward the externalization of emotions and intentions in the social theater is the evolutionary background against which we must understand the peculiar collection of abilities known as theory of mind which is so central in human social life.

Current evidence suggests that primates perceive other primates' behaviors as intentional, in the sense that they may see each other as being connected with particular targets in particular ways. As in the domain of object cognition, there may be interspecific differences in the particular categorizations and in the ways in which intentional and attentional information is processed. Humans appear to have evolved new, powerful forms of computing mental states, but these have not replaced their more basic kinds of mentalistic understanding. Rather, humans probably conserve and may even have evolved new forms of overt mentalism (just as language has not replaced forms of nonverbal communication, but integrated and evolved with them). Understanding intention, attention, and perhaps some forms of knowledge may be a relatively widespread component of the primate mind (at least the ape mind) for understanding other primates.

9

Social Learning, Imitation, and Culture

A characteristic of primates is their extended infancy, a period during which they enjoy an equally prolonged dependence on adults who must provide them with support and protection. Monkey infants spend the first months of their lives carried around by their mothers and exploring the world under close maternal surveillance and in close proximity to other members of their group. Ape infants spend more than 3 years in such close dependence, and later they may still keep very close to their mothers for several years. This means that the initial contact of primate infants with both the physical and the social worlds occurs in the company of their mothers and other members of their social group. This inevitably conditions what aspects of the world they experience and perhaps how they experience them. Primate development is to a large extent *socially mediated.*

Lev Vygotsky on Apes, Speech, and Culture

The distinctive role of social mediation in human cognition was the cornerstone of one of the most influential and original theories in developmental psychology—the cultural-historical theory of Lev Vygotsky. The Russian psychologist worked during the 1930s. He wrote extensively and enthusiastically about Köhler's research with anthropoids, emphasizing how his findings of chimpanzee tool use demonstrated the unquestionably biological roots of intelligence (Vygotsky, 1930). He also emphasized that human intelligence went beyond its biological roots by a most peculiar method—the socialization of individual cognitive development. The human mind, in Vygotsky's view, is not only a product of the evolutionary history of the species (its innate adaptations) and the way in which individuals develop these adaptations in a particular environment during their ontogeny, but also a product of the *social history*—the *culture*—of the groups in which individuals develop. During their history, these groups have accumulated knowledge and behavior patterns that constitute both an artificial environment (the objects fabricated by a particular culture) and a corpus of knowledge (how to use those objects) that the new members of the group have to acquire. According to Vygotsky, social learning is not only a convenient way of sharing the knowledge accumulated by a culture, but also a force that shapes human intelligence in a special way, making it different from the cognition of even the highest primates. From the beginning the cognitive development of human infants is *mediated* by the adults that surround them, and this mediation produces a unique synthesis between natural and cultural cognition, whose result is the unique intellect of humans—an unprecedented combination of biological and cultural-historical evolution.

To illustrate these ideas here is one of Vygotsky's own investigations. Soon after learning about Köhler's experiments with chimpanzees, the Russian psychologist set out to reproduce these with children of different ages. He and his collaborators (Vygotsky, 1930) confronted children with practical problems that required using a stick to reach a toy or moving a chair to climb on it and have access to a goal. The result was that in many respects children behaved like chimpanzees; they provided similar solutions and made similar errors, but with one very important difference. From the beginning human children *talked* during their attempts to solve the problems and tried to recruit the help of the adults who were observing them; they acted as if they expected such help and did not realize that they had to solve the problem on their own. In relation to the first feature—talking during their problem-solving activities—Vygotsky believed that just as children and chimpanzees can use a stick to control an object, older children (but obviously not chimpanzees) can use their speech as a cognitive tool to control their thought and behavior: they tell themselves what to look for or what to do next while trying to solve the problems. But as the study of younger children revealed, this regulatory function of speech has its origin in the social speech children direct to the adults when trying to recruit their help, and the speech the adults direct to children when trying to help them. Vygotsky's point was twofold: from the beginning, children confront problems in the company of other humans who will help them in various ways; secondly, a fundamental means for securing help occurs through language and the social use of other signs and symbols that eventually become interiorized and are used by the individual child to regulate his own behavior. For humans, tool use is no longer a matter of individual intelligence but a social activity impregnated by culture and social mediation. This "cultural-historical" line of psychological development was, in Vygotsky's view, specifically human, and the main reason why human intelligence is superior to the intelligence of other apes. Apes have intelligence, but humans have intelligence and culture, and the combination of both yields the unique forms of human cognition.

This sociocultural view of human development has been continued and extended by authors such as Bruner (1975), especially in relation to language acquisition, and, more recently, Tomasello (1999). Tomasello's theory is especially interesting because he, like Vygotsky, explicitly compares nonhuman primate and human cognition and concludes that it is *cultural learning* and its associated cognitive abilities (for example, imitation and theory of mind) that set human cognition apart.

The question we will explore here is whether and to what extent culture is a uniquely human form of adaptation. Or is the combination of intelligent and cultural adaptations a common pattern of primate development?

Social Learning and Cultural Adaptations

The term "culture" is notoriously difficult to pinpoint in a definition (Ingold, 1994). Gibson (2002) has proposed that it has two main meanings. In a broad sense culture refers to ways of acting or thinking (customs) that are transmitted and kept within a group through social learning. In a narrower sense, the term is used to refer to the distinctive corpus of explicit *symbolic* representations of ways of acting and thinking that characterize a particular community (Gibson, 2002). In this restricted sense, there is little doubt that culture is uniquely human—explicit symbolic products including language are produced only by humans. In the broader, more inclusive sense of the term, cultural adaptations may be more widely shared in the animal world.

The key question for culture in the broad sense is to what extent nonhuman primates can transmit and retain adaptive behaviors through social learning. We know from the discussion in previous chapters that many primate species are able to discover novel adaptive behaviors (for example, how to use some tools to obtain food from otherwise inaccessible sources). But when one member of a primate group has made such a discovery, does he alone benefit from it, or can the other members somehow learn the new skill from its discoverer? Moreover, can primates retain a good, adaptive discovery within a group across generations (will the youngsters learn the skill from their elders?), thereby achieving a truly cultural adaptation?

For many years it was thought that cultural adaptations were exclusively human. Even Köhler—the man who showed the scientific community that chimpanzees have discovered how to use tools in an intelligent way—thought that any form of culture was beyond the chimpanzees' mental abilities (Köhler, 1927). This is why the discoveries made by field primatologists in the 1950s and 1960s came as a surprise. According to these, the rudiments of culture as a form of adaptation might be present in monkeys and apes.

Washing Potatoes in Koshima Island

One of the first and most famous cases described occurred in Japan, amidst a small troop of Japanese monkeys living on the island of Koshima. When Japanese primatologists first tried to study this troop, they found that the monkeys, shy of humans, would remain in the forested mounts and elude them. To solve this problem, the primatologists offered food to the monkeys, leaving it in relatively open areas where they could be observed. The trick worked, and, little by little, the monkeys started to eat the provisioned food and accept the presence of their human observers (Kawai, 1965).

One of the foods they were given was sweet potatoes. These were dirty with soil. From the beginning the monkeys were in the habit of wiping the potato clean with one hand while holding it with the other before eating. They probably were used to doing something similar with some of their natural food items.

One day, one of the monkeys, a young female named Imo, did something different: she took a pile of potatoes to a nearby creek and placed one potato in the water, rubbing it in the usual way but with the innovation of keeping it in the water. She did this several times that day, and repeated it during the next days. This innovative (and presumably more effective) way of cleaning the potatoes became part of her behavioral repertoire. This innovation of Imo would have remained just one more example of the plasticity of individual primate behavior save for the events that followed during the next years.

One month later, a close playmate of Imo also started to wash potatoes in the water. Four months later, Imo's mother and another female were also observed washing potatoes. Little by little the habit spread within the colony and 5 years after Imo washed the first potato in the Island of Koshima, 80 percent of the young (2 to 4 years) monkeys were doing it. Four years later, almost three quarters of all the Koshima monkeys were washing potatoes in the water. During those years the habit itself changed: the fresh water of the stream was abandoned in favor of the salty water of the sea. In fact, at some point the potatoes given to the monkeys were no longer dirty and needed no washing; however, the "sea-washing" habit persisted, apparently now seasoning the potatoes, which perhaps was accidentally discovered when the monkeys first used sea water to perform their potato washing. Many monkeys would now dip the potato in the sea water, take a bite, and then dip the exposed part of the potato, bite again, and so on. Potato washing had become potato dipping.

The Japanese researchers who made this discovery suggested that what they had documented was the establishment of a "precultural" behavior in a primate community. First, one monkey discovered a new type of behavior with an adaptive value; then this new behavior was gradually adopted by other members of the group: first by those who spent more time with the initial innovator, then by other individuals, usually those who were relatives or friends of those already into the potato-washing technique (Kawai, 1965; Hirata et al., 2001). During the first years of potato washing, this process of diffusion always occurred from younger to older monkeys. But something remarkable happened as soon as Imo and the other females who were juveniles at the time of the discovery of potato washing became mature and had their own babies: all the babies of mothers who practiced potato washing became potato washers almost as soon as they had the motor skills necessary to perform the action. As Kawai (1965), one of the Japanese primatologists who first reported this finding, says, potato washing had become a natural behavior within the community and its new members acquired it as naturally as any other behavior proper to their group.

Japanese researchers observed many other examples of precultural acquisition and propagation of habits in different communities of macaques. Some were simpler; for example, learning to eat strange new food items like caramels, or learning to enter the sea. Others were as complex as potato washing; for example, learning to throw handfuls of rice mixed with sand into the sea water as a way of separating the rice and perhaps seasoning it (incidentally, this too was first discovered by the same young monkey, Imo, who invented potato washing). Most of these new habits had something in common: they had been precipitated by human intervention, mostly by the practice of giving the monkeys new food items (sweet potatoes or cooked wheat) in unusual places (at the beach).

How did the monkeys of Koshima become potato washers? One natural assumption would be that the mechanism of propagation had to be some form of imitation: Imo's friend saw how she washed potatoes and copied the behavior of rubbing them in the water. Other individuals would do the same, and most certainly the babies who looked at their mothers washing potatoes would have no problem imitating what they saw. At that time, imitation was thought to be a natural form of behavior among primates, and it appeared to be at the root of this remarkable series of events that led to the establishment of a new subsistence habit from the discovery of a single individual.

Yet Kawai and his colleagues cautiously stated that the mechanisms of diffusion of the behavior were unknown, although they were convinced that they involved some form of social learning because of the diffusion pattern: the second acquirer was Imo's friend, then her mother, then another friend, and then the habit started in other members of the kins to which Imo's friends belonged. Finally, the new generations of monkeys appeared to learn it from their mothers.

Kawai (1965) provided a description of how infants acquired potato washing. Babies are with their mothers when these wash the potatoes in the sea. In their first weeks of life babies feed exclusively on their mothers' milk, but they cling to them when the mothers engage in potato washing. Thus infants are exposed to sea water from very early on, but initially all they do is to occasionally splash the water with their hands. Later (at 6 months) babies start picking up potato pieces accidentally dropped by their mothers in the water and eat them. They watch their mothers eat the potatoes and dip them, but they do not try dipping themselves until after 1 year of age. All monkeys acquire this behavior between 1 and 2.5 years of age. As Kawai points out, these observations do not really clarify the precise mechanism whereby the babies acquired the habit. However, some textbook and popular accounts (Jolly, 1972; Napier and Napier, 1985) favored an explanation in terms of observational learning through active imitation.

Tool-Using Traditions in Chimpanzees

A more spectacular and completely natural case of precultural traditions is that of chimpanzees and their tool-using skills. In the 1960s Jane Goodall (1968, 1986) observed that wild chimpanzees of the Gombe reserve in Tanzania engaged in a remarkable behavior: they approached termite mounds, opened holes in them with their hands, and through those holes they inserted long leaf stems or thin twigs (sometimes they had brought these from some distance); then, after a time, they took out the twigs and these emerged covered with termites. The chimps quickly took the termites to their mouths and ate them. Termite fishing turned out to be a characteristic activity of the Gombe chimpanzees. They engaged in this remarkable way of feeding for only a few weeks every year, during the rainy season, when the termites are active in their nests. Sometimes they appeared to anticipate the advent of the season, when they started inspecting the termite mounds. Almost all Gombe chimpanzees, of all ages and sexes, practiced termite fishing and some other subsistence activities that require the use of tools, like digging for ants.

Goodall's discovery was important because, for the first time, it documented in a systematic field study what until then had been only rumored or anecdotally reported—that tool use is a natural behavior of wild chimpanzees. Shortly afterwards it was found that other groups of chimpanzees in other African regions also used tools, but different tools and for different purposes. For example, in the Taï Forest of the Ivory Coast chimpanzees use stones as hammers to crack open very hard nuts, whose fruit they then consume (Boesch and Boesch-Achermann, 2000). Gombe chimpanzees also eat nuts, but they either crack them open with their molars or hit the nut with their hands against a tree trunk or a rock. They never use stones as hammers (which greatly limits the sort of nuts they can crack open).

The import of these observations went beyond the corroboration of tool use as a natural behavior of chimpanzees. The local variations in the kinds of tools used suggested that this could be a rudimentary manifestation of material culture: acquired skills that are not the product of phylogenetic or straightforward ontogenetic adaptations, but of individual discovery kept and transmitted socially within particular communities. Gombe chimpanzees discovered and kept termite fishing by means of twigs and stems, whereas Taï chimpanzees discovered and kept stone hammering of nuts.

These chimpanzee technologies were observed when they already were well-established habits, but the assumption was that they would have been the product of some cultural propagation process comparable to the one Japanese primatologists had involuntarily provoked and witnessed among the monkeys of Koshima.

Of course, if termites were only available at Gombe and nuts and stones were only available at Taï, it would not be surprising that each type of behavior was seen only locally, and this would have nothing to do with culture and social learning. Yet even though the same kinds of termites and nuts are available to many chimpanzee communities, only some of them exploit them by the above techniques. This is why researchers were convinced that some sort of cultural transmission was at play here (McGrew, 1992).*

Further studies of chimpanzees have not only confirmed the existence of these local technologies, but also uncovered many other tool-using behaviors that appear to be characteristic of particular chimpanzee communities: digging for ants, using squeezed leaves as sponges to obtain water, honey dipping, and so on. Some cultural habits go even beyond the realm of tool use, such as leaf clipping as a form of social interaction or peculiar grooming techniques (McGrew, 1992; Menzel, 1973a; Wrangham et al, 1994). In a recent systematic survey, Whiten et al. (1999) recorded as many

---

* Tomasello (1990) warns against this deduction, arguing that one can never be sure that the superficial ecological similarity does not conceal hidden dissimilarities that we have not been able to detect so far.

as 39 distinct cultural adaptations distributed among 7 chimpanzee communities. Each community had a set of characteristic behavior patterns, some unique to the group, others shared with some other communities. None of these patterns was universal to all chimpanzees, although the ecological conditions that would support them were available either to all communities or at least to some of those that did not possess the pattern. The authors claim that this is strong evidence for different chimpanzee cultures consisting of sets of idiosyncratic acquired adaptations that are socially transmitted from generation to generation in each community. Chimpanzees would be showing not just precursors of cultural processes, but genuine examples of culture. Recently, a similar claim has been made for orangutans, including some tool-using behaviors (van Schaik et al., 2003).

These cultural claims do not go undisputed. The main source of concern raised by cognitive scientists is the issue of what are the cognitive mechanisms at work in these apparent processes of social transmission of adaptations. Let's have a closer look at how young chimpanzees learn some of the skills proper of their community.

How Young Chimpanzees Learn to Use Tools in the Wild

Goodall (1968, 1973) describes in some detail the prolonged process of learning the termite-fishing techniques. During their first year, young chimpanzees watch intently while their mothers fish the termites and may eat some occasional termite that accidentally falls; they can occasionally pick up from the ground the twigs or stems discarded by their mothers and play with them. During their second year, chimps continue to observe their mothers, but now they engage in activities like taking wide grass blades and shredding their edges or biting the ends of long leaf stems, all of which are potential components of the preparation of tools for termite fishing. They never try to fish for termites as yet.

Between 2 and 2.5 years of age, young chimps start to insert stems and sticks in the termite holes their mothers have just used, but they do so with inadequate tools and technique (they select the same kind of twigs and stems as adults but too short). Although they use an adequate grip and usually insert the tool in the right hole (just vacated by the adult), their insertion is too shallow, they don't keep the twig in long enough, their withdrawal movement is too jerky, and their "fishing" sessions are very short. The result is that they catch virtually no termites at all (less than 10 percent of their insertions results in the consumption of at least 1 insect).

Interestingly, despite such an extremely low rate of reward for their efforts, the young chimpanzees do not abandon their practice, and during the second half of their third year of life, their ability to select appropriate tools and their skill in using them improves considerably. They now choose longer sticks (although usually too flexible and occasionally too thick); they tend to commit the error of inserting the shorter end, but now they usually slide their hands up and press the stick further in, like adults do. They have also learned to withdraw the stick more slowly, but not yet to avoid excessive friction with the edges of the hole, so that most of the time they wipe off the termites they had initially caught. It is only at 4 years of age that chimps show some effective mastery of the adult technique and get plenty of insects as a result of their efforts. Goodall mentions that only one of the 4-year-old youngsters she studied failed to develop a mature termite fishing technique: he was an orphan who had lost his mother at the age of 2.

Goodall concludes that young chimps develop the skill of termite fishing by a combination of "processes of [individual] learning and imitation" (Goodall, 1968, p. 210). Inoue-Nakamura and Matsuzawa (1997) have reported a similarly slow process in the development of nut-cracking skills among infant chimpanzees at Bossou, Guinea, that again appears to suggest that chimpanzee infants might use a mixture of individual and social learning for acquiring these feeding skills.

In sum, wild monkeys and chimpanzees appear to be capable of transmitting acquired skills from generation to generation. This suggests that they are capable of protocultural or, in the bolder interpretations (Whiten et al., 1999), fully cultural adaptation. The cognitive mechanisms responsible for the process of skill transmission are assumed to be a mixture of both individual and social learning. The social learning factor was traditionally thought to occur through imitation—an ability that was supposedly widespread among monkeys and apes.

Criticisms of Primate Culture

In the late 1980s a number of laboratory experiments started to cast doubts upon the traditional assumption that monkeys and apes are good imitators. In one experiment Visalberghi and Fragaszy (1990) found that capuchin monkeys confronted with soiled food and a water basin developed food washing behaviors in only a few minutes time, without any imitation. Moreover, naïve monkeys who were allowed to watch other monkeys who had already begun washing did not directly copy this behavior: observing the models simply increased the probability that they would place and handle the food in the water, but did not lead to the washing actions themselves; these appeared only after a period of individual exploration similar to that displayed by the monkeys who had discovered food washing on their own, and therefore could be better described as being the result of an individual discovery.

Tomasello et al. (1987) found that when captive chimps who did not know how to use a rake to retrieve out-of-reach food were exposed to a conspecific who knew how to use it, they did try to use the rake to retrieve the food, but they did not copy the precise movements—the "technique"—used by the demonstrator. They handled the rake in their own way, and did not copy the successful model even when their own attempts were unsuccessful and copying would have been beneficial. Tomasello suggested that this was indeed a case of observational learning, but not imitation, because the critical behavior was not in fact copied. He proposed that what the chimpanzees were doing should rather be termed *emulation*, that is, the reproduction of the *effect* that they had seen other chimpanzees achieving but using their own *means*. From the demonstration they had learned that the goal could be reached with the rake, but not how to do so. This they had to discover on their own, by individual learning.

Tomasello's suggestion was that in our everyday language we confuse under the term "imitation" processes that psychologically are very different. In imitation—he proposed—we reproduce the very movements of an action; in emulation, in contrast, we try to reproduce the result of an action but use our own means. He proposed that chimpanzees might be only capable of emulation, whereas humans can engage in genuine imitation (Tomasello, 1990, 1999)—a superior form of social learning, the one upon which true cultural adaptations are based. In his view, therefore, chimpanzees can learn observationally, but not through the imitative processes that had been assumed.

A more radical criticism came from the psychologist Benet Galef (1992). He pointed out that the process of propagation of potato washing among the Koshima monkeys was so slow that its rate of transmission did not appear to increase as the number of proficient monkeys (and therefore of potential models) increased. If the ma-caques were learning socially—Galef reasoned—the more models available, the more likely that the behavior would be acquired by other members of the community. Yet the rate of progression in the diffusion of the technique remained constant over the years independently of the existing number of skillful monkeys. This led to an uneasy conclusion: perhaps the monkeys were not really learning the new behavior from one another, but discovering it in-dividually through their own exploration, just as the first mon-key who used the technique did. This would be very different from the way in which human cultural adaptations are socially trans-mitted.

Galef made similar criticisms of chimpanzee "cultures." He em-phasized that the slowness of infant learning (4 years before any ef-fective termite fishing is demonstrated by the Gombe chimpan-zees) should be taken as evidence of a gradual individual learning of the skill, rather than an imitation of the mother's behavior, which should lead to much quicker learning.

Forms of Observational and Social Learning

The debate that followed the above criticisms had the important consequence of prompting an analysis in depth of the notion of social learning and the different mechanisms that can subserve this function. The dichotomy between imitation and individual learning is too simplistic. The social milieu may influence what individuals learn and discover in more subtle ways. For example, in the case of chimpanzees, Goodall's observations showed that the process of learning termite fishing is indeed slow: young chimps try at first very clumsily and rather unsuccessfully to get termites; the same is true of young Taï chimps when they first try to crack nuts. It takes them several years of trials, errors, and (more rarely) successes to master the skill. One could be tempted, like Galef, to conclude that the skills are the result of strictly individual trial-and-error learning.

A closer analysis of the situation suggests otherwise. To begin with, young chimpanzees are exposed to termite mounds at all because their mothers take them there (as they take them to any other place they go). Even if termite fishing itself were the result of individual learning during these exposures, this learning would never (or very rarely) occur without the termite fishing of the mothers. There is therefore a first, fundamental way in which a habit may affect its own reproduction in other members of a group without having to rely on direct imitation or any other form of observational learning.

Technically, this phenomenon is known as social exposure, and it ranks very low in the lists of social-learning processes elaborated by psychologists (see, for example, Avital and Jablonka, 2000, for a description of social-learning mechanisms), because it does not appear to require any specialized cognitive skill; it is just an accidental result of the interaction between individual learning skills and the nature of the mother-infant bond in primates. But this accidental exposure to relevant elements of the environment and its concomitant effects on learning may in fact be one of the evolutionary advantages of the close mother-infant relationships of primates.

Moreover, it is very likely that the young chimpanzee is bene-fiting not only from his general exposure to the termite mound area. He may also have his attention selectively drawn toward the objects and the parts of the objects that his mother is manipulating: the termite mound itself, the twigs that she is using, the holes in the mounds through which the twigs are inserted, and, of course, the termites on the twigs and in his mother's mouth. This selective direction of the infant's attention could further increase the proba-bility that the young chimp eventually acts upon similar objects and targets so that he eventually learns termite fishing by himself, as it were, again without having to resort to any kind of direct imitation of the others' actions. Psychologists call this effect *stimulus enhance-ment*, as a way of emphasizing that the subject's attention is at-tracted to particular stimuli in the environment by the actions of others, but he doesn't learn anything at all about the actions them-selves or their effects. He has to discover these on his own.

If, additionally, the young chimpanzees were able to learn some-thing about the effects of their mothers' actions (for example, that termites can be taken out of the mounds with the sticks), then they would be using what Tomasello called "emulation"—a higher so-cial-learning skill, but still one that does not rely on copying the ac-tions of the mother.

Chimpanzees and other primates have been credited with the ability to learn socially by means of any of the above mechanisms, but some psychologists (Tomasello, 1999) believe that only humans have developed a specialized cognitive ability for imitation that al-lows them directly to learn how to perform actions by watching how others perform them. Imitation would be the jewel in the crown of social learning and, for Tomasello, the source of true cul-ture. But is imitation in this sense really uniquely human?

Imitation Experiments with Chimpanzees

Tomasello himself partially revised his position about the imita-tive abilities of chimpanzees following a series of experiments in which he and his associates (see Tomasello, 1999, for a review) compared the performance of 18 to 30-month-old human children, captive mother-reared chimpanzees, and captive human-reared (or "enculturated") chimpanzees in a task in which they had to imitate a series of novel actions performed with objects by a human model. Surprisingly, they found that the human-reared chimpanzees (but not the mother-reared ones) imitated as much or even more than the human children (in a delayed imitation task). Tomasello's suggestion was that chimpanzees can imitate only if they have benefited from a special process of education during their development with humans—a process of enculturation. Interactions with humans change the attention and action patterns of the young chimpanzee, shaping them into a typically human pattern. Hand-rearing would literally create a new cognitive ability that otherwise would remain absent or very underdeveloped in the uncultivated chimpanzee. Here Tomasello is extending the ideas of Vygotsky about the power of adult mediation in cognitive development to nonhuman primates. The application of a regime of human mediation to some nonhuman primates would be able to change the minds of these apes, conferring or somehow awakening abilities that otherwise would not be manifest. (Premack, also in a partially Vygotskian vein, claimed similar effects for the process of language training of apes; see chapter 5.)

The claim that only human-reared chimpanzees can imitate is disputed by other researchers. For example, Whiten et al. (1996) tested captive chimpanzees with a task in which they had to gain access to a reward placed inside a plexiglas box locked with different mechanisms. A person demonstrated how to open the mechanisms. Some chimpanzees saw a particular sequence of actions (for example, a bolt was opened by poking it out with a finger), and other chimpanzees saw a different sequence with exactly the same part of the object that achieved the same goal (the bolt was twisted out with two fingers). The chimpanzees were then allowed to try to open the box by themselves. Whiten and colleagues' reasoning was that if the chimpanzees only attended to the effects ("the bolt can be taken out"), then the way in which they tried to reproduce those effects should bear no resemblance to the particular method demonstrated to them. Some chimpanzees did produce actions of the type they had seen demonstrated (twisting the bolt to take it out). A control group of human children showed more imitation than the chimpanzees, but the chimpanzees appeared to achieve some degree of imitation in the strict sense of reproducing aspects of the modeled action. This tendency has been further confirmed in similar experiments by Whiten (2000).

Tomasello (1999) suggests, however, that the small degree of imitation found by Whiten could have been actually produced by emulation processes (trying to reproduce the twisting movement of the bolt, rather than the action that provoked it).

On the other hand, Whiten (2000) has found clear evidence of imitation of bodily gestures and actions performed outside a problem-solving context by captive chimpanzees who had been taught to play a game of "Do as I do." The game consists of teaching the chimpanzee that he will receive a reward by doing exactly the same action as the human model (touching his nose, for example). At the beginning, the experimenter may need to help the chimpanzees by molding the correct action on their hands, but they eventually learn to match what the model does. Once this is achieved, the chimpanzees are confronted with entirely new actions not used during the training phase (for example, touching their ears, grasping their index fingers). The chimpanzees did reproduce the new actions and therefore appeared to be able to imitate movements outside a problem-solving context.

Tomasello (1999) found the same ability for gestural imitation in an orangutan who had been taught this game. But when the same ape was placed in the context of a problem-solving situation which could only be solved by imitating the form of the action performed by the demonstrator, he failed to do so, even when he was instructed to "do as I do." His ability to imitate seemed to be disconnected when he was in a problem-solving mode!

In sum, researchers have produced some consistent evidence that imitation, in the narrow sense of copying the structure of an action, can be demonstrated among chimpanzees and orangutans, although it is not clear that they routinely use it to copy actions and techniques directly, even in situations where doing so would be advantageous.

All in all, it appears that social learning does play a role in the transmission of chimpanzee technological traditions, and therefore these can be considered as a form of cultural adaptation in the broader sense. Chimpanzees have demonstrated their ability to acquire behaviors from others in well-controlled experiments in captivity. Whether they do this by copying the actions themselves, or by rediscovering them while trying to reproduce the observed effects, or by a mixture of both methods is not yet clear. The theoretical debate, therefore, is not so much about whether they show social or observational learning, but about the cognitive mechanisms they use to learn from others. Current evidence supports Goodall's original suggestion that these mechanisms can be best described as a mixture of observational and individual learning.

Reconsidering the Mechanisms of Social Learning and Cultural Transmission

A common assumption in the debate about primate culture is that a hierarchy can be established among various mechanisms of social learning, with imitation at the very top. Current evidence suggests that chimpanzees and other apes have some access to the top mechanism in the hierarchy, but imitation does not seem to be their preferred means of observational learning. But is this hierarchical view—and its corollary assumption that humans preferentially use the top ability, imitation—correct?

Do Children Ape?

Want and Harris (2002) have recently tried to apply the fine-grained distinctions made by primatologists to the study of social learning in human children. In a review of existing evidence about the de-

velopment of the ability to imitate tool use in children, they come
to a surprising conclusion. Children do not appear to progress
from less to more complex forms of social learning. On the contrary, they first show signs of literal and blind imitation of actions
(what Tomasello, 1999, has recently called "mimicry"), whereas
emulation is a relatively late achievement in their development (in
fact, Want and Harris consider that currently there is no satisfac-
tory evidence that children engage in forms of emulation!). That is
to say, children appear to move from relatively ineffective imitation
to emulation, as if their early imitative abilities could not be recruited later to help in the learning of tool use.

Moreover, in their own study about the ability to learn to solve a
complex problem (retrieving a toy from inside a transparent tube
by inserting a stick; see Chapter 4), Want and Harris (2001) found
that 3.5-year-olds learn when they are shown both the correct *and*
the incorrect strategy, but not if they are shown the correct strategy
only, as if they were watching others' behavior primarily to learn
about the causal structure of the task, instead of rushing to copy
successful actions.

Whiten and colleagues (1996) reported that imitation could
sometimes interfere with the correct solution of a problem (opening puzzle boxes), as some children would reproduce unnecessary
actions from the model that were irrelevant for the solution of
the problem. Finally, in a recent experiment, Horowitz (2003) gave
human adults demonstrations of how to open the plexiglas box
Whiten and colleagues used for their experiment and then measured their ability to imitate, using exactly the same coding and categories as in the original study. The surprising result was that although the human adults solved the problem very quickly, they
used imitation very little; their imitative reactions resembled more
those of chimpanzees than those of children 3 to 4 years old in
Whiten and colleagues' study! This appears to confirm Want and
Harris' (2002) conclusion that as humans grow older they resort
less to imitation.

All in all, there is a feeling of dissatisfaction with the current
state of affairs in relation to the issue of the role of imitation in so-

cial learning. Several researchers are proposing a reconsideration of the problem along the lines of abandoning sharp distinctions between learning mechanisms and embracing a more integrative view of the function of social learning (Whiten, 2000; Carpenter and Call, 2002; Byrne, 2002).

A possible view is that social learning and cultural transmission are normally achieved by the simultaneous use of different skills, including individual exploration, goal-directed intelligent behavior, action and attention following, scene and event perception, and imitation in the narrow sense of copying action. The actual abilities used on each occasion may vary within the same species or even within the same individual, depending upon the task and the context. Humans themselves may resort to variable combinations of skills during their social learning, with imitation in the narrow sense being just one more and not necessarily the most frequently used.

The myth of imitation as the social learning mechanism of choice for humans was illustrated with a remarkable field study. Geza Teleki (1974), one of the early students of chimpanzees at Gombe, once tried an unusual experiment: instead of checking whether chimps would be able to imitate a task modeled by him, he decided to find out if he could learn termite fishing by watching and copying an accomplished chimpanzee fisher. Much to his surprise, Teleki miserably failed to get any termites during the first weeks of his self-imposed apprenticeship. He discovered that termite fishing involves more than simply introducing a probe through a hole: there are optimal tools, optimal times, and optimal movements to be performed. Even the very first, apparently simple step—locating the entrance in the termite mound and clearing it—proved to be exceedingly difficult. He couldn't detect any tell-tale cues as to where the entrances were. Despite being a *Homo sapiens*, or as Meltzoff (1988) suggested, *Homo imitans*, Teleki was unable to acquire termite-fishing skills by imitation. Imitation merely put him in the situation of discovering by himself the actual intricacies of the skill. He had to grope, try and fail, and think carefully about the visible and the hidden mechanisms at work before he got his first termite. When it comes to the cultural transmission of technical skills, there may be no substitute for the individual formation of the skill (even given sophisticated ways of transmission such as language and explicit instruction).

The cultural learning debate, as posed in the last years, may have been seriously misguided and rooted upon a quasi anecdotal misconception of human social learning as essentially imitative in the narrow sense. Imitation of actions is just one more process at play in cultural transmission, and one that may have originally evolved not as an adaptation for more effective transmission of skills, but as a mechanism for interaction and communication (Byrne, 2002).

The Paradox Of Mirror Neurons

The "solitary learning" or "low-level social learning" explanations proposed by critics of the cultural interpretations of primate traditions may be implausible for another reason. The idea that non-human primates, when watching others do things with objects, may be paying attention only to the objects and their transformations (as strict stimulus-enhancement notions or some versions of emulation assume) is in conflict with some recent neurophysiological discoveries. Using sophisticated recording techniques, researchers studying the activity of single neurons in primate brains have discovered that some neurons appear to respond to surprisingly complex aspects of the world. Rizzolati and Gallese (see Gallese, 2003), for example, discovered neurons sensitive to actions performed upon objects (for example, the action of grasping an object), but not to exactly the same object shown in isolation, nor to exactly the same action of grasping but without an object, nor to the sight of the hand and the object without actual contact. Those neurons appear to be sensitive to the action of "hand-grasping-an-object." This suggests that, contrary to the assumptions of stimulus enhancement, the adult primate brain may not respond to objects separately from the actions performed upon them. Actions-upon-objects might be the default representational unit of primate minds when confronted with the manipulative behavior of other individuals.

There is more. Some of the neurons that are activated by the sight of another monkey grasping an object are also activated when the monkey himself is performing such action (even if he is prevented from seeing himself doing it). Primates not only may perceive in terms of actions upon objects, but they may be doing this in terms of the representations they use to organize their own actions. Gallese and Rizzolati gave these neurons the appropriate name of "mirror neurons."

Although it is still early days to assess the true significance of "mirror neurons," one possibility is that the ability to compute crossmodal translations between visually perceived actions and their proprioceptive representations (the core mechanism for imitation in the narrow sense) is a primitive component of primate brains. Why then would action imitation be so rare among monkeys and apes? According to Gallese (2003), the original evolutionary pressure behind mirror neurons may not be imitation, but rather the function of understanding the behavior of others in intentional or goal-directed terms (the mind-reading or theory-of-mind function). Japanese monkeys watching other monkeys washing and eating potatoes would be not only seeing potatoes in the water and potatoes in the mouth of another monkey. They see the other grasping the potato and placing it in the water, and then eating it, and, at some representational level, they see this because they themselves *could* do it. They see this thanks to their ability to read the visual input with the vocabulary of goal-directed actions provided by their mirror neuron system.

Nevertheless they don't appear to be ready immediately to generate an imitative action using this same system. They might need to produce the relevant actions to a large extent through individual learning, even though a part of their motor system might be primed to perform such actions. Why this paradox? We should start by wondering why monkeys would seek to reproduce what they see other monkeys doing. If we think of the everyday life of monkeys, would it make sense for a subordinate monkey to copy the actions of a dominant that threatens him, or take a piece of food, or mount a female as he sees a dominant doing so? It makes sense that while the subordinates understand the actions of the dominant, they do not automatically reproduce them. The same is true of the dominant contemplating the submissive behavior of a subordinate: it would be maladaptive for him to be primed to reproduce the subordinate's behavior. If the neural system used to understand the actions of others consists of mirror neurons that translate sight into action schemas, then the primate brain must have a powerful inhibitory system that insulates these action plans from the executive machinery that would launch them. The ability to reproduce what one sees others doing may seem at first glance to be an impressive adaptation, but only if you have a firm control upon what you imitate or not and under which circumstances you do so.

Perhaps the evolution of imitation has more to do with the evolution of these executive mechanisms than with the evolution of a specialized ability to analyze contemplated actions as motor programs. The notion of an executive mechanism has also the advantage of being compatible with the view that social learning depends upon the articulation of a plurality of cognitive mechanisms.

This would explain why apes can be trained to participate in "do as I do" games, or why they might be able to use some information about the actions of others in some problem-solving contexts, or why they sometimes spontaneously appear to engage in imitations of others outside problem solving (De Waal, 1982, 2001), or why "enculturated" apes are as good as human children in tests of complex imitation with objects. Rather than develop an imitative ability, these apes may be displaying a modified articulation of their existing abilities.

This is not incompatible with the possibility that a more refined capacity for imitating actions has evolved in humans, but probably for purposes other than learning new ways of object manipulation. For example, Byrne (2002) suggests that some of our imitative abilities might be primarily designed to deal with gestures and other social signals for purposes of social interaction. Such an ability might be secondarily recruited by humans for helping in the learning of some manipulative skills.

The question of whether social learning and cultural adaptations are present in nonhuman primates has followed a pendulum trajectory: from an initial conviction of human uniqueness we moved to an apparent demonstration of cultural behaviors in monkeys and apes (the studies on Japanese macaques and chimpanzees in the 1950s and 1960s). Human uniqueness returned when the operation of sophisticated social learning mechanisms was questioned, and now we seem to be moving to an acceptance that the unique way in which humans exploit social learning and cultural adaptation is not the result of a quantum leap in evolution, but an extension of an adaptive trend deeply present in primates (which in turn may have even deeper roots in the animal world).

Teaching

A better candidate to unique human adaptation for cultural transmission is teaching, that is to say, behaviors adapted to facilitating social learning by others. Teaching appears to be very rare among nonhuman primates. Goodall never observed chimpanzee mothers trying to help their offspring to learn termite fishing. No teaching behaviors were reported for Japanese macaques either. The only evidence suggestive of teaching among wild apes comes from observations by Christophe Boesch (1991) with Taï chimpanzees. Mothers of young chimpanzees who have started to try to crack nuts may leave appropriate wooden or stone "hammers" on anvils or tolerate that their infants snatch good hammers from them. Because this only happens with infants who are starting to learn how to crack nuts (and it comes at a cost to mothers, who will be able to crack fewer nuts for themselves), Boesch argues that such maternal behaviors might be stimulating and facilitating the nut-cracking skills of their offspring—a primitive form of teaching. Two possible instances of demonstrative teaching were also observed by this scientist: one mother repositioned an incorrectly placed nut on an anvil and then let her offspring continue with her cracking attempts; another took an incorrectly held wooden "hammer" from her offspring's hand, very slowly placed it correctly in her own hand, and cracked six nuts open. Then she left the hammer. The young chimp picked it up again and holding it now in exactly the same position her mother had held it, now successfully cracked the nuts.

The rarity of these behaviors makes it difficult to decide about their significance. Were they chance occurrences that gave the wrong impression of instructive behaviors? Or were they genuine "didactic sparks" by the mothers that failed to find their way into their routine behaviors, let alone into the behavioral repertoire of the community of chimpanzees?

There is no doubt that in humans teaching behaviors have become a cornerstone of effective social learning and cultural transmission. But are they a specific evolutionary adaptation for cultural transmission, or a secondary result of adding other cognitive skills, such as an advanced theory of mind, to social learning?

Apes in the House: Domestication and Enculturation

The implication of the studies we have reviewed is that adult mediation is inevitably present among primates. This mediation may be unintentional and largely the responsibility of the immature learner, who must find a way to benefit from the example provided by its elders, but it may enable the acquisition of cultural adaptations. But is there any evidence that nonhuman primates may experience something akin to a *cultural shaping* of their minds in the way Vygotsky implied for human children?

We have referred several times to a persistent finding: apes that have been reared by humans, and especially apes that have been trained in the use of artificial symbols, tend to perform better in a number of tests (identifying relations, imitation, joint attention, conservation, and so on). Premack (1983) emphasized the role of learning an abstract code of representation as the explanation for the feats of linguistically trained chimpanzees, whose minds would have been *upgraded* by the acquisition of this new representational format. More recently, Tomasello (1999) has emphasized the "socialization of attention" and cognition in general as the explanation for higher achievements (by human standards) of human-reared apes. Although the two approaches emphasize very different factors, in fact from a Vygotskian perspective they are complementary. Vygotsky's view was that adult mediation was optimally achieved through the use of signs and symbols, especially speech and language. In his view, higher cognitive processes—the processes that differentiate humans from other apes—could only be created through this sociocultural mediation. The possibility that, at a reduced scale, the mind of an ape can be upgraded by giving him, on the one hand, a regime of socially controlled attention and interactive experiences with humans, and on the other, a new, more explicit form of representing the world, would confer dramatic support to the Vygotskian notion that higher cognition can be created through cultural processes of development that change the nature of cognitive ontogeny.

Indeed, one of the features that Vygotsky considered to be distinctive of human children when confronted with practical problems—expecting and actively seeking the help of adults—is actually a characteristic of captive apes tested by humans. Köhler (1927) reported begging behaviors and other attempts to recruit the experimenter's help as the greatest nuisance in his efforts to test chimpanzee intelligence. And, as we saw in chapter 7, Gómez (1990, 1991) reported that gorillas used joint attention and gestures as a way of appealing for the help of humans in a variety of tasks. It appears that it is in the nature of apes to be open to and even actively request some forms of that human mediation which, according to Vygotsky, is at the root of cultural learning and cultural development.

Vygotsky coined the term "zone of proximal development" to refer to what children cannot do on their own but can do with the help of an adult (for example, building a tower with the behavioral "scaffolding" provided by the helping adult). An interesting question is to what extent apes who appear to develop new skills under the guidance of humans are demonstrating a "zone of proximal evolution," in the sense of showing us in what direction ape minds might evolve under new evolutionary pressures.

Conversely, the possibility exists that these supposedly "enculturated" apes are giving the impression of possessing new cognitive skills only because of their greater familiarity with problems and testing procedures, without any Vygotskian impact upon their minds.

Moreover, even if it were demonstrated that ape minds are significantly changed with enculturation and symbolic training, this might not mean that Vygotsky was right in assuming that social and semiotic mediations are the developmental processes through which higher cognitive skills are constructed in modern humans. Perhaps the modern human mind is more biologically prepared to discover things on its own and needs only a minimum of such adult mediation (as Chomsky suggests for language acquisition in humans; see next chapter). But in any case, the presence of such a dramatic developmental effect in apes would indeed offer us important clues about the processes of cognitive evolution and development.

Conclusion: The Social Cradle of Primate Cognition

Can nonhuman primates acquire, transmit, and keep in their repertoire adaptive patterns of behavior by means of social learning processes? We propose that the unambiguous answer is that they indeed can do so. Suggestions that the transmission of feeding techniques in Japanese macaques or tool-using skills in chimpanzees are better explained as the outcome of individual learning appear to be based upon a misunderstanding of what is involved in social learning, which usually combines individual discovery and processes of social facilitation. There is no doubt that in humans these sociocultural processes of development have become much more complex thanks to the suite of cognitive abilities that humans bring to the task.

Contrary to Vygotsky's assumption, however, social mediation—in a broad sense of the term—might not be an exclusive characteristic of humans, but a more general feature of primate development. Primate infants are dependent on their parents for a prolonged period of time. An increased importance of social learning appears to be the inevitable by-product of this developmental style. Primates have not invented social learning: it is present in many other mammals and in birds (Box and Gibson, 1999; Avital and Jablonka, 2000), but the way in which they make use of it suggests that in some cases they have become capable of achieving cultural adaptations.

Primate development is crucially dependent upon processes of social learning. Whether these processes qualify as "culture" depends upon the definition of culture we choose to use, and defining culture has proved to be a most difficult enterprise even among anthropologists (see, for example, Ingold, 1994). The debate about primate and animal cultures hinges on issues of content (what constitutes culture—behaviors, symbolic representations, beliefs, languages?) and issues of process (what counts as genuine cultural transmission—imitation, emulation, any form of observational learning?).

In this chapter we have adopted a broad definition of cultural adaptations, one that accepts behavior as a proper content of cultural transmission, and a combination of different cognitive mechanisms as the best explanation of how cultural transmission occurs. It is in this solid evolutionary matrix of socially mediated development that human cultural learning abilities are situated. Far from being a radical departure from the way other primates develop, human cultures fit well the primate pattern of socially constrained development, but within the framework of the cognitive abilities that humans bring to the task of social learning: language and other symbolic systems, complex patterns of joint attention, perhaps an enhanced ability for representing and reproducing actions, and certainly the assistance the apprentice receives by means of teaching.

The essential continuity in the function of social learning and some of its mechanisms should not be taken to deny the spectacular novelties in the way humans achieve this function within their own cognitive landscape. Vygotsky may have been right in assuming that the interaction of language, thought, and social mediation may bring about new kinds of minds capable of singular cognitive feats. What Vygotsky did not expect was that perhaps it is possible to find traces of this extraordinary developmental mechanism in the interaction between adult human minds and developing ape minds. Hand-reared, domesticated apes, and especially those who are trained into the use of symbols, may be able to show some simple rudiments of that higher-order ways of thought that Vygotsky considered to be the trademark of human cognition.

10

Consciousness and Language

Many believe that the most complex achievements of primate cognitive evolution, perhaps exclusive of the human primate, are the capacity for self-awareness and the closely related ability to produce speech and language. We will consider these in the discussion that follows.

Self-Awareness

This is the ability to be conscious of what one is doing or thinking—the ability to see or feel oneself doing something or thinking of something. In this sense, consciousness implies some ability to represent oneself as one more object (or subject) in the world. But perhaps the most challenging feature of consciousness is its irrepressible *reflexive* nature—that we can be conscious of being conscious, in what appears to be a paradoxical fusion of subject and object of knowledge. This intricacy and the existence of different kinds and levels of consciousness (Neisser, 1988), for which we use the same word, create confusion in our scientific attempts at understanding consciousness, which many consider to be the ultimate challenge of science.

A typical question in comparative cognition is whether humans are the only animal capable of consciousness, or is it a more general trait of primates and animals in general. Consciousness in humans can be voiced, and they can discuss how incomprehensible the phenomenon of consciousness is thanks to their mastery of language. But how can we know whether creatures without language are conscious?

The study of primates has made an ingenious contribution to the problem of objectively assessing the question of self-awareness in nonverbal creatures. Gordon Gallup (1970), an American psychologist, once noticed that chimpanzees who were confronted with mirrors would take advantage of them to manipulate parts of their faces, which, of course, they could ordinarily not see. This may seem natural to humans, but students of animal behavior (or simply pet owners) know that typically animals react to their own reflection on a mirror by engaging in the sort of social response they would produce in front of a conspecific: they can threaten and even attack the mirror, or try to appease it, exactly as they would do with another animal.

It is not only a problem of confusion and lack of familiarity with the mechanism of mirrors. Take the case of monkeys. Although initially they react to the reflection of an object as if it were a real object and try to catch it on the mirror surface, they eventually learn to turn around and find the real object, or use its reflection to retrieve the object from a hiding place. When it comes to their own reflection, however, no matter how much experience they are given with mirrors, they are never able to "find themselves" with their help. In time the monkey may stop reacting to the image of the "other monkey," but still shows no evidence, by exploring parts of his own body, that he realizes the image in the mirror is of himself (Anderson, 2001).

Gallup's chimpanzees, by contrast, used the mirror to inspect their faces and the inner part of their mouths; this suggested that they realized that they were watching an image of themselves. Now Gallup's point was that this is something you realize only if you have the capacity of being aware of yourself, that is, of representing yourself as one more object out there in the world that can be the target of your own attention; this indeed is very close to any basic definition of self-awareness.

Gallup's challenge was how to go beyond these suggestive observations, and he came up with a simple but brilliant idea.* Chimpanzees who were experienced with mirrors were given an anesthetic
and, while they were asleep, a person marked one of their eyebrows
(and sometimes also a visible body part, like a hand) with a special
type of red paint (that could look like blood or a bruise, but that
was completely odorless and insensitive to tact once dry). When
the chimps recovered consciousness their reactions were carefully
observed, first without any mirror present, and then with a mirror.
During the phase without a mirror the chimps readily inspected
any red spots visible to them (on their hands), but never touched
their eyebrows. As soon as the mirror was introduced, the chimpanzees started to inspect their marked eyebrows with their hands
while watching themselves in the mirror (Gallup et al., 1971; Gallup, 1983).

Gallup's conclusion was that chimpanzees were clearly recognizing themselves in the mirror, and this can only happen if they
have self-awareness—the ability to conceive themselves as individual entities in the world. He, in fact, suggested that this self-awareness must also imply some consciousness of themselves as psychological entities, but this part of his interpretation has been subject
to greater debate.

The importance of Gallup's finding was underscored when the
same experiment was conducted with other animals: they all failed
the test. All monkey species tested so far have been unable to show
self-recognition in a mirror when tested with this standard procedure, even after receiving very extensive experience with mirrors
and some additional help. Some authors argued that monkeys have
a tendency to experience eye contact as threatening and this could
put them at a disadvantage with a mirror test, because inevitably
they will be facing all the time another monkey directly and stubbornly staring at them. This might upset them so much that they
would become incapable of discovering the truth: that the ruth-
lessly aggressive monkey opposite them is oneself!

* It is only fair to mention that the mark experiment was discovered almost simultaneously and with complete independence by a developmentalist (Amsterdam,
1972), although it became famous through Gallup's work.

This criticism has been addressed by Anderson (2001) in an elegant experiment in which the angle of the mirrors was changed so as to make it impossible that the monkeys experienced eye contact with their own reflection. Cebus confronted with these tilted mirrors showed less social response to the reflections, but no evidence of self-recognition. On the other hand, monkeys exposed to mirrors can become very proficient at using them to solve problems, like finding pieces of food underneath a cover in the outer part of their cages by looking at their reflection in a mirror opposite the cage. But surprisingly, monkeys don't appear to be able to "find themselves" in the mirror. A possible explanation is that they lack the ability to represent themselves explicitly—that is, consciousness.

In contrast, chimpanzees, orangutans, bonobos, and humans (the latter from 18 to 24 months of age) are capable of mirror self-recognition and therefore can be credited with some explicit form of self-awareness.

The Strange Case of Gorillas

It came as a surprise that gorillas, the other great apes, were generally unable to pass the spot mirror test. Only one individual gorilla passed a version of this test—Koko, one of the apes who was taught sign language and reared and tested in an enriched human environment (Patterson and Cohn, 1994). Diverse theories have been offered to explain the lack of success of gorillas. Gallup himself suggested that gorillas might simply have a different cognitive profile that doesn't include the capacity for self-awareness because of their own peculiar evolution. Other authors (Patterson and Cohn) favor the view that there could be a performance problem specific to gorillas that makes this test inadequate to measure their real capacity for self-awareness, hence the success of Koko, a gorilla reared in atypical conditions. An alternative explanation would be to accept a lack of spontaneous self-awareness in gorillas but a latent ability to acquire it that is activated only when gorillas are "enculturated."

Recently, Inoue-Nakamura (2001) has reported signs of self-recognition in gorillas comparable to those of other apes, but only in the form of self-directed behaviors in front of a mirror (touching parts of their bodies they cannot see otherwise). She did not conduct a mark test, and this leaves open the question of why gorillas should fail this test if they really are aware of themselves and understand the mechanism of mirrors.

Conditions for Mirror Self-Awareness

Not all chimpanzees and apes (gorillas apart) can pass the mirror test. A number of factors are crucial for passing it. First, a minimum extent of experience with mirrors appears to be necessary (Gallup, 1983). Chimpanzees (and humans) initially don't understand the bizarre device which is a mirror: typically, younger children and naïve apes or completely naïve humans react by assuming that there is someone else in the mirror, and they try to touch it or look for it behind the reflecting surface. In a matter of days, though, they appear to understand the workings of the mirror and give evidence of recognizing their own image.

The age of the chimpanzees is also an important factor. Povinelli and colleagues (1993) found that it is rare that chimpanzees pass the spot test before 4.5 years of age (although other researchers [Line et al., 1992] claim 2.5 years as the crucial age for chimpanzee mirror self-recognition). On the other hand, only about 26 percent of older chimpanzees (above 16 years of age) pass the test. The optimal age window for passing it (76 percent of successful subjects) is between 8 and 15 years, when chimps are well beyond their childhood.

Using other, less stringent measures of self-recognition (mainly the production of self-directed behaviors while watching a mirror versus social or exploratory behaviors), but at the same time giving her subjects only a relatively brief exposure to the mirror (one session of 30 to 40 minutes), Inoue-Nakamura (2001) has found that chimpanzees first produce self-directed behaviors at 3.5 years of age. Prior to this age, they either explore the mirror or produce social responses.

In a longitudinal study with an infant chimpanzee (between 76 and 87 weeks of age) who was exposed to mirrors on a daily basis during 3 months spending 10 minutes per day, the same author found that self-directed behaviors emerged at week 82 (at about 1.6 yrs.), coinciding with a sharp decline in social and exploratory behaviors. This is much earlier than she found in her other study, but at the same time it seems that experience with a mirror has no effect until the chimpanzee has reached a certain age; after that, a small amount of exposure to the mirror may be enough for the first self-directed behaviors to emerge. The experimenter's conclusion is that mirror self-recognition depends, on the one hand, on the maturation of some cognitive abilities, but on the other hand also on the amount of experience with mirrors. She bases this conclusion in part upon a cross-cultural study she conducted with some African tribesmen, a culture in which there are no mirrors. Children of this tribe show signs of self-recognition when confronted with a mirror (perform self-directed behaviors) only at 42 months, in contrast with the 18 months in typical Western cultures where mirrors are frequent everyday items.

Self-directed behavior may be a less reliable indicator of self-recognition than the mark test, but using this measure with a variety of primate species, Inoue-Nakamura has found that primates other than apes still fail to show spontaneous signs of self-recognition (self-directed behaviors in front of the mirror).

The Social Nature of Oneself

An interesting discovery is that chimpanzees who have been reared in isolation are not able to pass the mirror test regardless of the amount of experience with mirrors they are given (Gallup et al., 1971; Gallup, 1983). Paradoxically, social experience appears to be a prerequisite for what superficially would appear to be a prototypically individual condition—self-awareness. Yet this finding fits theories of consciousness according to which self-awareness, like other higher cognitive abilities, has deep social roots (Vygotsky, 1930). This finding also favors an interpretation of mirror self-recognition as an ability that does not depend merely upon the recognition of oneself as a physical object, but upon a more elaborate representation of oneself as an agent or subject among other agents or subjects. Both things—being with other people and being confronted with one's own reflection—have something in common. Looking into a mirror at one's own image inevitably produces an eye-contact or mutual-gaze experience (with oneself); being among others leads, among other things, to a repeated experience of eye contact and mutual gaze. In both cases eye contact means that one is a target of attention, of others' or of one's own. Perhaps the kind of self-awareness necessary for mirror self-recognition is one that arises out of the experience of being a target of attention. It is as if the others' attention directs our own attention to ourselves (Gómez, 1994). On the other hand, the failure of monkeys and other animals to achieve mirror self-recognition means that ape and human minds must have something that allows them to benefit from mutual attention in this special way.

Criticisms and Disputations

What kind of self-awareness does the spot test measure, namely, what sort of self-awareness is necessary to be able to recognize oneself in a mirror? Gallup initially thought that his test measured a higher-order type of consciousness, one that would imply the ability not only to be aware of oneself as a physical entity among other entities of the world, but also an ability to be aware of one's own psychological being—something very similar to having a theory of one's own mind. It has been pointed out, however, that mirror self-recognition may only imply an ability to be aware of oneself as a physical entity, an awareness of one's own body that need not include an awareness of one's own mind (Povinelli, 2000).

This possibility is somewhat reinforced by circumstantial evidence. Human children show mirror self-recognition at around 18 months of age, somewhat earlier than they start talking about their own mental states, and much earlier than they are able to pass typical tasks of mental-state understanding like the false belief test (at 4 years). Also, children with autism, who are typically impaired in their ability to think about mental states, have an intact ability to recognize themselves in mirrors (Dawson and McKissick, 1984).

An extreme version of this interpretation is that apes are merely learning to use mirrors to explore invisible parts of their own bodies, just as they learn to use them to locate hidden targets in the environment. After all, they are used to exploring visible spots on their bodies; perhaps mirrors are just allowing them to explore and locate spots in parts of their bodies that normally they only perceive tactually or proprioceptively. In this sense the mirror test would be just "about perception of the body, which all primates are likely skillful at with no special training or experiences" (Tomasello and Call, 1997; p. 337). The difficulty with this suggestion is that it does not explain why monkeys, who are also good at exploring their own body and can even be trained to use mirrors to touch hidden parts of themselves (Anderson, 2001), cannot pass the mark test and do not show spontaneous self-directed behaviors when confronted with mirrors.

Available evidence suggests that whatever is required to pass the mirror test, it is not simply a combination of the ability to recognize one's body plus the ability to use the mirror as a tool to direct one's behavior. Monkeys appear to be able to do both things; they probably can also tell the difference between themselves and other monkeys in social situations (so they can probably tell which hand is about to reach a piece of food—theirs or the other individual's). At some level, monkeys must possess some representation of themselves and their bodies as opposed to other selves and bodies (see Neisser, 1988, for a discussion of levels of awareness). The mirror test must be measuring something else; perhaps an ability to represent oneself mentally, in a more explicit format that could truly reflect a step in the direction of more abstract self-awareness.

The mirror spot test, therefore, may not be the ultimate test of consciousness in its most intricate manifestations, but Gallup might be right that it measures a cognitively complex level of self-awareness—one that among primates might be characteristic of the ape evolutionary line.

Conclusions

The mirror test is primarily a test of self-awareness. It is not clear, however, which self subjects are required to become aware of to pass it. Led by humans' sharp conceptual distinction between the bodily self and the mental self, much discussion has been devoted to whether the test requires awareness of the former or of the latter. A reasonable case can be made that awareness of oneself as a mental entity is not necessary. This need not imply that a simple ability to perceive one's body is enough. The sharp divide between the performance of apes (with the puzzle of gorillas) and the performance of monkeys makes this discovery crucial, though unexplained. A possible explanation is that some form of awareness acquired through social interaction (specifically the experience of being a target of social attention) is responsible for the ability to recognize oneself in a mirror and, therefore, to recognize oneself as a subject. In this sense, mirror self-recognition could indeed be related to theory of mind, but not necessarily to the abstract ability that makes use of metarepresentations; rather, to the more basic skills related to the understanding of intention and attention that we discussed in Chapter 8.

The Gift Of Language

Language is the most distinctive of human abilities and one of the most fascinating objects of study of developmental cognitive science. Although a distinctively human capacity, it has always been a favorite topic in evolutionary cognitive science: the origins of language are one of the great mysteries of science. One of the reasons is that, at first sight, language appears to stand singularly alone as a capacity that only the human primate possesses, but at the same time it is such a complex cognitive object that it is difficult to believe that it is not the culmination of a long evolutionary process.

In Chapter 7 we discussed some aspects of primate communication, paying special attention to those that could bear a closest relationship with language. Some remarkable similarities exist, but they are strangely distributed among nonhuman primates. For example, apes appear to be capable of some forms of referential communication with gestures comparable (but not identical) to those seen in young human children just before the emergence of language or during its very early stages. Yet the ability to produce analogues of words has been found not in any of the ape species, but in the phylogenetically much more distant vervet monkey. If only the ability for referential calls and referential gestures occurred in the same primate species (preferably an ape species), we would be in a better position to begin understanding the evolutionary origins of language. But this is not the case, and more radical approaches to gain insight into the evolution of language have been launched. Among them, the boldest and most remarkable has been the attempt to teach human language to captive apes.

Speech and Language

Although language (or speech in its voiced manifestation) is usually referred to as the language *faculty* or *ability*, it is in fact a complex system composed of different parts or subsystems. To master a language one has to acquire its phonology (the sounds out of which words are made), its lexicon (the words and their meanings, also known as "semantics"), and the rules of grammar to compose complex sentences by combining individual words (also known as "syntax"). Language is made of an exquisite integration of these (and perhaps other) different subsystems. And, as any person learning a second language knows, the subsystems can be relatively dissociated: for example, you may know the syntax of French or Spanish very well, but have a very restricted vocabulary, so that you have to keep looking up the meanings of individual words in a dictionary. Or you may have a good knowledge of syntax and a good vocabulary, but a poor phonology, so that your pronunciation of the words is imperfect or even incorrect. Indeed, adults learning a second language may find it very difficult to acquire all three components perfectly. Typically, phonology is a component that may remain imperfect forever, no matter how many years you practice the language.

One of the greatest mysteries of human cognitive development is that this extremely complex system that is language is perfectly acquired by children in their first few years of life without any apparent effort, without special teaching, without consulting a grammar. Everything works out as if babies come into the world with some sort of ready-made ability to quickly learn any language, even more than one language at the same time and without confusion (Chomsky, 1968; Pinker, 1994).

The nature of this ability (or set of abilities) for learning language is the subject of much debate in developmental cognitive science (Karmiloff and Karmiloff-Smith, 2001). Some authors—inevitably associated with the name of Noam Chomsky, the linguist who revolutionized the study of language in the 1950s—believe that language is a biological capacity exclusive of the human brain and whose development comes strictly determined. Rather than being acquired by children, language *grows* in them provided they are placed in a minimally adequate environment (among people speaking a particular language). To use the popular phrase coined by Steven Pinker (1994), language would be a human *instinct*. Unfortunately, this very condition (the need to be exposed to a language to develop one) convinces other people that language is not an instinct at all but something that needs to be carefully acquired by children in the context of elaborate linguistic and social interactions with human beings (Tomasello, 1995, 1999). Children may possess some predispositions for language, but they have to make use of those predispositions to acquire this complex set of skills.

What admits of little discussion is that, whatever the nature of the human ability to acquire language, it does not appear to exist in nonhuman primates. Language, in its full splendor with syntax, words, phonology, and its ability to generate an infinite number of new sentences, is only seen in humans. Or at least this appears to be the case at face value.

Teaching Language to Apes

One idea is that language is uniquely human not as a biological adaptation, but as a cultural discovery—an ability that was invented and kept by humans thanks to their intelligence. We have evidence of continuity between humans and other primates in many aspects of intelligence (as we saw in the first half of the book); therefore some authors have reasoned that perhaps we could teach other intelligent primates some of our linguistic skills.

Some early attempts at exploring the learnability of language by apes showed that they do not spontaneously acquire spoken language when they are reared within a human family like children (as some adventurous researchers such as the Kelloggs and Hayes did, the latter even actively trying to teach their chimpanzee Vicky to speak [Kellogg and Kellogg, 1933; Hayes, 1951]). Some researchers thought that this inability could be mainly attributed to a problem with the phonological component of language: chimpanzees are not equipped with the anatomical structures necessary to produce the sounds of human speech. The psychologists R. and B. Gardner (1969) thought of a simple way of circumventing this potential difficulty: to teach them sign language like the one used by deaf people in which words are produced with manual gestures. (Contrary to what was once thought, signed languages are not primitive forms of communication: they have all the properties of any spoken human language, even a "phonology" of hand movement components; Pinker, 1994.)

The Gardners "adopted" a one-year-old baby chimp called Washoe and trained her intensively, encouraging her to use signs to communicate with them (for example, requiring her to make a "hug" sign [a sort of embracing sketch done with the arms] before being taken in arms, or a "drink" sign [taking thumb to mouth] when she wanted to drink). Most of the time they had to mold the required sign morphology on Washoe's hands. After a few years of relentless training, the results were spectacular: in contrast to the chimps who had failed to acquire spoken words, Washoe had learned to produce and understand almost 100 manual signs to refer to different actions and objects. Moreover, she not only used the individual signs appropriately, but she also spontaneously started to combine two or more signs in ways that resembled the first word combinations of human children (Gardner and Gardner, 1969, 1974).

Language acquisition in human children follows a relatively stable and predictable pattern of development, despite huge individual differences in rate and speed. First, children start acquiring elements of phonology, then they produce communicative sounds (not yet recognizable words) and gestures (such as pointing); then, toward 12 to 18 months, they produce their first words, but typically they only say one word at a time. Shortly after this, they start making their first combinations of two words in what most people think are their first rudimentary sentences; finally, word combination explodes and very soon complete sentences are produced, so that the basics of language seem to be already in place at around 4 to 5 years of age (Karmiloff and Karmiloff-Smith, 2001).

The Gardners' findings with Washoe suggested that although chimpanzees do not develop any phonological components of language, they can, when given enough training, acquire not only the individual words explicitly taught to them in the manual modality, but also spontaneously produce some rudimentary "sentences." It was as if her training had unleashed some sleeping linguistic ability in Washoe.

The Gardners conducted a number of formal tests to assess what Washoe and three other chimpanzees, later incorporated into the project, had learned. For example, they gave them "blind" vocabulary tests in which slides depicting objects were projected on a screen; a human, who could not see the projected object, asked the chimpanzees "What?" using a manual sign, and the chimpanzees answered with another manual sign—the name of the object. They gave the correct name in about 80 percent of the trials. Moreover, when they committed errors, they tended to do so by confusing one thing with another belonging to the same category, for example, calling a dog "cat" or "cow," but never "shoe" or "apple." These errors are especially interesting because they appear to indicate that the chimpanzees were really assigning some conceptual meaning to the signs they had been artificially taught. Other studies too indicate that primates classify objects according to categories (Chapter 5). They might be learning their artificial signs as labels associated with those concepts.

A further similarity between Washoe and human children was the phenomenon known as "overgeneralization." When young children begin to use new words, for example "dog," it is common that they apply it to a wider number of referents than the correct ones (after a period when the opposite may happen: using it too restrictively to refer to a particular dog). So they may call a cat "dog" or use the name for any other four-legged furry animal, and only progressively learn to restrict the word to its proper meaning. Something very similar happened with Washoe's initial use of signs.

The implication of these findings was that phonology might be a cognitive (or perhaps just an anatomical) specialization of humans, but the ability to use symbolic words and at least some simple grammar to combine them into more complex meanings might not be specifically human. Words had to be very explicitly taught to the chimpanzees (in contrast to human babies who learn them almost automatically), but they appeared to learn their words in a meaningful way and, more impressively, they spontaneously started to produce combinations of these words, as if a modest, but genuine form of language could emerge out of a relatively sophisticated ape mind once it is given the head start of words in an appropriate and encouraging environment.

The first reports of these findings caused a sensation among cognitive scientists. Thus Roger Brown (1970), one of the leaders in the field of child language acquisition at the time, after examining the transcriptions of Washoe's productions and comparing them with his own transcriptions of human children, concluded that Washoe appeared to have reached at least the first stage of language development—one in which words are combined into very simple grammatical combinations using semantic categories like agent-action ("Greg tickle," to request tickles from Greg) or object-subject ("milk Washoe" to ask for milk) in the *telegraphic* speech characteristic of the first linguistic steps of children.

Other projects followed suit, teaching sign language or alternative nonverbal languages (with plastic chips or abstract designs on a computer screen) to chimpanzees and other great apes (Premack, 1976; Rumbaugh, 1977; Patterson and Linden, 1981). The results were essentially the same as those reported by the Gardners. Great apes appeared to have a surprisingly neglected ability for acquiring some rudiments of language when given the right kind of intensive tuition. Of course, their acquisitions were only rudiments—a limited vocabulary and very simple sentences—but that was enough to make of it a sensational discovery.

The ape language studies came to the light at a very special moment in the history of the study of child language development. Only a few years earlier, the linguist Noam Chomsky had proposed his revolutionary theory of language in which the innate abilities of children played a fundamental role (Chomsky, 1968). For Chomsky, language was a specific biological ability, not only in the sense of being exclusive of humans, but also in the sense of being different from any other human cognitive skill. The grammatical structures of language were so special and so complex from a cognitive point of view that they were thought to require specific computational structures different from, for example, those used for object manipulation or object perception. Being so complex, grammar cannot possibly be learned from scratch in only a few years, as human children routinely do. Chomsky's suggestion was that in the human brain there must be an "organ" for language that is innate and unique to humans (Chomsky, 1968; Pinker, 1994).

The discovery of a hidden ability for language in chimpanzees went directly against this view. If you can teach language to an ape, then language cannot be based upon a mysterious human-specific ability. To be sure, one could still argue that humans do have some specializations for language (phonological abilities, a better developed ability for learning words, and a much more complex grammar), but the core of language—the ability to use words and combine them into sentences—would be a more general property of several primate brains, even if some of them appeared to need a stronger head start than others.

Children of Herodotus

At the same time as these groundbreaking discoveries were being made with chimpanzees and other apes, some surprising findings were observed among deaf children born to hearing parents who were committed to an oralist education, that is, who did not teach them a sign language but waited until the children were old enough to be taught oral language through special educational means. The consequence was that in their first few years of life these children were not exposed to the model of a language, and therefore scientists were in a position to study a humane version of the experiment that, according to the Greek historian Herodotus, an Egyptian king eager to know which was the original language of humanity carried out with a couple of unfortunate children whom he reared in complete isolation to avoid their exposure to any language (Goldin-Meadow, 1979). Like any otherwise healthy normal children, the deaf children of the modern-day study engaged in communication with their parents using the nonlinguistic means at their disposal, notably gestures and facial expressions. But, in contrast to the average hearing children, these deaf children started to develop a repertoire of unusual gestures invented by themselves, which appeared to be symbols to refer to the important things of their everyday life, like their toys or their favorite activities.

The (relatively) untutored human mind, placed in a situation of social interaction in a world of objects but without any exposure to a proper language, was producing symbols on its own, as if the symbolic ability was so inevitably inscribed in the human brain that it could not be prevented from emerging even in these relatively impoverished conditions. Moreover, these children were capable of combining their spontaneously invented symbols and other gestures, like pointing, into primitive sentences that, once analyzed, appeared to be comparable to those of hearing children when they start to produce their first spoken word combinations. The deaf children, deprived of a model of language, were apparently forming the same sort of primitive sentences as the intensively trained chimpanzees. Superficially, the sentences of the enriched chimpanzees and those of the linguistically deprived children appear to be extraordinarily similar:

Children:
Cookie GIVE
ball GIVE ball
GIVE that GIVE
GIVE GIVE 'toy'
TAKE-OFF glasses TAKE-OFF glasses TAKE-OFF glasses

(In lower case, objects identified with pointing gesture; in upper case, manual symbols invented by the child. From Goldin-Meadow, 1979.)

Chimpanzee (Nim Chimpsky)
TICKLE ME
EAT NIM EAT
PLAY ME NIM
BANANA NIM BANANA NIM
EAT DRINK EAT DRINK

(From Terrace [1979]).

One of their common features is that many sign combinations consist of repetitions of the same sign, so that even if a long string of signs was produced, the actual sentence was very simple.*

Why would apes need special training to reach a level of linguistic competence comparable to that of completely untrained, to some extent linguistically deprived, children? A possible answer is that human children are probably equipped with some special adaptations (not necessarily innate abilities, but developmental de-

---

* More technically, this is reflected in the fact that the MLU (mean length of utterance) of the deaf children did not continue to grow (Goldin-Meadow, 1979), as neither did the MLU of the linguistic apes (Terrace et al., 1979).

vices) that put them in the linguistic track from the beginning, whereas apes need to be artificially given abilities to start moving along that track. But are the strings of signs produced by the chimpanzees (and the deaf children) really linguistic sentences?

The Paradox Of Nim Chimpsky

The simpler explanation for the apparent similarity between chimpanzees and children is that the similarity is just that—mere appearance. Herbert Terrace (1979), a convinced behaviorist opposed to the nativist and species-specific views of Chomsky and his followers, enthusiastically joined the efforts to teach language to apes, launching his own project with a male chimpanzee, named Nim Chimpsky in equivocal homage to the person whose theories were going to be shattered by the ape evidence. Terrace essentially confirmed the results obtained by the Gardners and others: a chimpanzee does acquire manual signs and uses them in combination when he interacts with humans who actively teach him. However, when Terrace started to conduct detailed analyses of the structure of the signs and the ways and conditions in which they were produced, he came across a number of unexpected discoveries (Terrace et al., 1979).

For one thing, the sign combinations of Nim Chimpsky consisted fundamentally of strings of repeated signs. Like Washoe, Nim produced increasingly longer combinations of signs, but when one attended to the actual number of different things referred to by the symbols used in each string, it emerged that he produced very few combinations beyond two signs. The mean length of his combinations did not grow at all during his years of training, whereas it is a well established and robust fact that the mean length of word combinations* in children learning spoken or sign languages steadily increases during the first years of development, and it is considered to be a good measure of grammatical development

---

* MLU is measured in morphemes or units of meaning, not necessarily corresponding to separate words.

(Brown, 1973). Apparently, Nim's grammar did not develop beyond the two-word stage.

But were his two-sign combinations at least comparable to those of human children? When Terrace analyzed Nim's combinations, he found that they were not produced at random: Nim was using systematic patterns of signing. Children do the same, and this is taken as evidence that they are using some sort of rudimentary grammar. But after examining videotapes of how Nim produced his systematic combinations, Terrace came across an unexpected, but in his view fundamental, discovery. Very frequently, Nim's signs were directly prompted by the humans who were interacting with him. Nim was reproducing signs his caretaker had produced, or made new signs in answer to a question or prompted by some gesture from the caretaker. When Nim's signs were put together in a transcript, they looked like a sentence, and one had the strong impression that Nim was imposing an organization upon his signed output. In Terrace's view, however, this organization did not come from Nim, but from his caretakers, who were inadvertently "shaping" Nim's sequence of signing.

Furthermore, Terrace's team discovered that the content of most of Nim's combinations was just requests for food or things he wanted people to do for him. There were no comments or communication other than attempts at obtaining rewards from people. Terrace—an experienced animal behaviorist—and his colleagues came to the conclusion that his subject probably wasn't even producing individual symbols to *refer* to objects or targets. His signs were mere operant movements emitted with the sole goal of obtaining food, much like circus chimps that are deliberately taught to do things that appear to be human (cycling or taking tea dressed in clothes) but are mere tricks patiently trained in advance; except that in the case of Nim, the trick training had been unwitting (Seidenberg and Petitto, 1979).

They suggested that their conclusions extended to the other ape projects as well. The ape mind was incapable of syntax (as this minute analysis demonstrated), and, in all probability it was also incapable of using signs as truly symbolic words.

Most cognitive scientists found Terrace's arguments very compelling. Some felt even "cheated" by the previous evidence, as was Roger Brown (1986), who rectified his previous conclusions and returned to the view that language, even in its early manifestations, can only be seen in humans. The authors of the other projects protested that the performance of their subjects was not actually comparable to that of Nim, because their training procedures were different (Nim, according to them, had been subject to a rather strict behaviorist training schedule with little regard for the social side of language use). A bitter debate followed, in which scientific objectivity was not always well served. But for many, if not most, cognitive scientists, Terrace's conclusions were the end of the ape language debate: one more argument in favor of the view that language is evolutionarily discontinuous because not even intensive training can induce proper language in a nonhuman primate mind. Even so, a few surviving projects dealing with the linguistic apes claim that the evidence has been misinterpreted or that new, post-Terrace evidence is available that suggests genuine linguistic abilities in apes.

It is noteworthy that the fate of the "Herodotus" (deaf) children was very different. Subsequent investigations have kept and extended the claims that their sign combinations present evidence of grammar and other linguistic properties (Goldin-Meadow and Mylander, 1990).

Project Kanzi: New Studies on Language Acquisition by Apes

A team led by Sue Savage-Rumbaugh, one of the pioneers in the first wave of ape language research in the 1970s, accepted Terrace's methodological criticism. They concluded that not only was Terrace right that there was no proof of grammar formation in the productions of chimpanzees, but there was no proof of symbol making. The acquisitions of the first generation of linguistic apes could be explained as mere conditioned responses produced with the aim of obtaining rewards from their caretakers. These authors suggested, though, that the cause of this poor learning was not the inability of apes to learn language, but an erroneous method of teaching based upon behaviorist paradigms of administering rewards paired with desired responses. Savage-Rumbaugh and her collaborators (Savage-Rumbaugh, 1986) decided that the criticisms could be overcome by changing the teaching regime of the ape subjects and addressing less ambitious goals. Thus they started a new project with chimpanzees with a focus on teaching real symbols, instead of simple conditioned responses.

Working with two chimpanzees, they developed a number of new methods, more interactive and avoiding direct rewards. They tried to imitate the situations in which human children learn their first words: highly repetitive interactive routines in which the words are inserted. They claimed that with these methods it was possible to teach genuine symbolic labeling skills to their chimpanzee subjects. To support this claim, they conducted some interesting experiments like the following (Savage-Rumbaugh et al., 1980). They trained their chimps to classify real objects into two different trays: one for food, the other for instruments (keys, spoons). When the chimps were proficient in doing this, they gave them "lexigrams" (the plastic chip words they had been learning in other situations) and asked them to classify these chips. The chimpanzees were able to place the lexigrams for food in one tray, and those for instruments in another. Apparently, they were capable of treating the lexigrams in terms not of themselves but of the real objects they were intended to represent. This would be a remarkable approximation to what we understand by a "symbol." There is therefore the possibility that what linguistic apes learn are some sort of "symbols," not simple conditioned responses linked to immediate rewards.

In later projects, Savage-Rumbaugh and her team have revisited the issue of grammatical abilities in linguistic apes in a longitudinal study with bonobos, the species of ape that they believe could be a closer cousin of humans than common chimpanzees. They were trying to teach a bonobo mother the use of lexigrams much in the same way as they had taught the chimpanzees of their second project: by means of simple interactive tasks. Their hope was that this bonobo would turn out to be a cleverer apprentice than common chimpanzees. Much to their disappointment, this was not the case. The bonobo mother proved to be a rather obtuse student of lexigrams. Accidentally, though, they discovered something extraordinary. The bonobo mother had attended her tutoring in the company of her very young son, Kanzi, who never participated in the teaching sessions in a direct way. But when Kanzi was tested, he turned out to have learned a lot of lexigrams by observing the training sessions of his mother. Given this unexpected success, the researchers decided to continue their project with Kanzi, using the same sort of informal, relaxed learning environment and relying primarily upon the apparently excellent observational learning skills of their pupil.

One of the highlights of project Kanzi was evidence of his speech comprehension skills (Savage-Rumbaugh et al., 1993). The apparent ability of Kanzi to understand spoken English was another accidental discovery in the project. As a way of keeping the interactions as natural as possible, the humans interacting with Kanzi spoke all the time in English. The participants in the project had the impression that he was able to understand a lot of the things he was being told. This in itself may not be especially remarkable; after all, many pets appear to understand a lot when we talk to them. Most of the time, however, what they understand is the tone of voice, or perhaps they have learned to associate the sound of a word or sentence to a particular situation (going for a walk, getting food, being reprimanded, and so forth).

Savage-Rumbaugh and colleagues (1993) claimed that Kanzi's understanding was genuine linguistic understanding, that he was able to segment the sentences into words and even to analyze parts of their grammatical structure. To test this, they conducted a series of experimental tests with preset sentences under controlled conditions, in which the person uttering the words was not visible and the people with Kanzi could not hear what he was being told. The sentences were all new commands that Kanzi had never heard before, and they were carefully constructed so as to reveal if there was any genuine grammatical understanding: for example, "put water in milk" was contrasted with "put milk in water" as a way of determining if Kanzi was attending only to the individual words or also to the particular positions the words occupied in the sentence. A further interesting twist of this study is that the performance of Kanzi in these tests was compared with the performance of a two-year-old human infant, who was given exactly the same sentences under similar controlled conditions.

The results were spectacular. Kanzi, at 8 years of age, performed as well or even better than the human infant in almost all types of sentences, revealing a capacity to understand spoken English that might be based upon a grammatical understanding broadly comparable to that of a two-year-old human child. And all that as the product of a largely incidental learning.

Some experts in the field of human language acquisition (Bates, 1993) have declared their conviction that these results do reveal *some* understanding of grammar in the bonobo. Such a discovery fits the theoretical positions of these authors: Bates believes language is an ability created in the course of evolution out of the combination of several cognitive skills, some of which may be present in other apes. The special environmental conditions given to Kanzi tapped some of the relevant skills and put them together in the right way to achieve a genuine language. Tomasello (1994) believes that language is a cultural product, and it is the culture—rather than the nature of the chimpanzee—that creates some language in him. Savage-Rumbaugh herself believes that language is in the nature of the chimpanzee and that there is nothing fundamentally different in the mind of Kanzi when compared to the minds of wild bonobos.

Opponents argue that apparent language comprehension can be achieved by a number of cognitive means other than grammar; thus, even conceding Kanzi's comprehension skills, there is still no proof that he is using the sort of grammatical computations that are used by humans (Pinker, 1994). With the perspective of the years passed since the acrimonious debate triggered by Terrace and colleagues' criticisms of ape language, and given the potentially significant findings by Savage-Rumbaugh's team, it is tempting to revisit the case of the first generation of "linguistic" apes. Did they really learn only some sort of circus trick? A cornerstone of Terrace and his colleagues' (1979) criticism was that the apes produced long strings of signs but most of the time they consisted of repetitions of one or two elements, so that their grammatical complexity did not grow at all. But this is not exclusive of chimpanzees: as we mentioned earlier, the deaf children who invented their own sign language did exactly the same (Goldin-Meadow, 1979). In addition, although many of Nim's utterances were imitations of his caretakers, a substantial part of his productions (53 percent) contained completely new signs. Moreover, although to a lesser extent than Nim, young children also produce a high number of utterances that repeat the words other people have just said (Terrace et al., 1979). Perhaps the early words of young children that are learning or inventing languages are not so radically different from the signs of trained chimpanzees; but maybe this is because the children are not yet using language either.

Faking Language

What linguistic apes are doing may not be "genuine" language, in the sense that the underlying representations and brain computations they use are not the same as those used by humans. Specially trained apes would be acquiring a *simulation* of human language, but not the real thing. At the same time, the apes' ability to put up a simulation of language may have something to do with the evolution of genuine language itself.

For example, Derek Bickerton (1995) has suggested that linguistic apes employ a "protolanguage"—a cognitively much simpler version of adult human language. And, according to him, what very young children do in their first stages of linguistic development and what the deaf children of the "Herodotus" study develop on their own initiative are also protolanguages, not genuine grammatical languages.

Probably it would be erroneous to assume that all these protolanguages are identical. It would make evolutionary sense that they are different versions of precursors to human language, perhaps none of them identical to the true precursors that our hominid ancestors may have gone through at some point in our evolution. The protolanguages that we can induce in contemporary apes can give us only indirect information about that missing cognitive link. After all, the simulation of the emergence of language in present-day apes itself occurs under the aegis of an existing linguistic ability. The missing linguistic link we need to speculate about is a cognitive system and a social environment capable of producing a protolanguage without an already existing genuine language.

Deaf children teach us that the modern human mind can create a protolanguage in the absence of a model language, but with the benefit of rich social interaction and communication with its own kind. The ape mind, even with rich social interaction and communication with humans, cannot create a protolanguage—it also needs intensive training or structured exposition to linguistic models. The linguistic training of apes must be providing good simulations of some of the skills that are already hard-wired in the modern human mind and that therefore were part of the early evolutionary acquisitions that put humans on the track of language. One such skill, perhaps the most necessary to teach to an ape, is the use of symbols. As we have seen throughout this book, symbolic training appears to have widespread consequences for the cognitive skills of apes in different domains. In fact, as Tomasello pointed out, symbolic training is frequently accompanied by a cognitive socialization *à la* Vygotsky, and in practice it is difficult to separate the effects of the symbols from the effects of the interactions (if they can be separated at all in principle). In this interpretation apes are brought into what Vygotsky called a *zone of proximal development* that allows them to achieve things their minds would not be able to attain without the aid of their artificially learned symbols and the social support of humans. These achievements, although superficially similar to those of human children, may in fact be computationally different. Paradoxically, however, this flexibility of ape minds may be offering us an insight into the sort of evolutionary process that is capable of promoting new cognitive skills.

The zone of proximal development might in fact be a zone of proximal evolution: the first steps of our ancestors into linguistic territory may well have been nonlinguistic and supported by abilities originally designed for other purposes—clumsy simulations of what would much later become true linguistic skills. But if those clumsy simulations were capable of performing some linguistic functions, they could be creating the sort of selective pressure that would favor new variants of skills better able to perform those newly discovered functions and create new ones; eventually, minds equipped with hard-wired symbol- and grammar-learning skills would emerge by natural selection. But these specific human adaptations for language may have had their origin in a selection process triggered by *exaptations*—faked linguistic skills *avant la langue*.

In conclusion, although linguistic apes are still waiting for a stable and reputable place in the cognitive sciences (pending some difficult verdicts about the nature of their acquisitions), they may have more to offer than the simple conditioned circus performances to which they were once relegated. But what they have to offer may be very different from the humanoid replica that scientists at the other extreme favor. They may be able to teach us a couple of evolutionary lessons about the origins of complex cognitive abilities, if only we could find a way to read and understand those lessons.

11

Learning from Comparisons: The Evolution of Cognitive Developments

A special relationship has always existed between the study of primates and the study of children. During the period of formation of modern developmental psychology as a theoretical science, the main figures in the field (Piaget, Vygotsky) wrote under the influence of state-of-the-art primate studies. Why this special appeal of primates to the developmentalist and the cognitive scientist in general? A possible answer lies in the idea that primates will offer less complex versions of cognitive processes, and understanding these will lead to a better understanding of the structure of the human mind. That was the motivation behind Köhler's pioneering studies with chimpanzees.

This is similar to the motive that leads cognitive scientists to investigate children—the hope that they will find the phenomena of their interest in simpler versions of cognitive processes, and they will be able to understand them better by seeing how they become progressively more complex step by step, piece by piece.

Both children and nonhuman primates appear to offer this possibility of learning about the origins of complex cognition, and this is one of the reasons why primatology and developmental psychology appear to fit together so well.

Other researchers see a different use in primates—a way of identifying what is specifically human in cognitive development. That was, for example, Vygotsky's aim when he repeated some of Köhler's studies with children and concluded that speech and social mediation were the developmental forces that pulled the human primate away from its evolutionary cousins.

Whatever our motivation, when we join these two strategies—studying children and studying primates—and compare different primate minds in their process of development, we are looking at cognition through a double developmental lens, and the results of this may be more complex and difficult to interpret than simply stating what is common or what is specific to one or another primate species. But let us have a look at some of these difficulties.

Representational Minds

A pervasive topic in the book has been the notion that primate behavior is organized through representations. We don't necessarily mean complex mental pictures or descriptions of the environment (although in some aspects, like spatial cognition, something like that might exist). Representations are also responsible for very basic behaviors like picking up an object or finding a suitable approach to a target that cannot be reached in a straight line. As we saw in chapters 2 and 3, young primates progressively acquire representations of objects and how they are placed in the world, and of their own actions in relation to those objects. Some modern accounts have tended to minimize the role of representational change in development, emphasizing that many developmental changes could be explained through the growth of basic cognitive processes like inhibition and working memory (Diamond, 1991). In this view, many aspects of early cognitive development may simply reflect a better ability to put together previously existing representations and use them more effectively to guide actions, rather than attribute development solely to the acquisition of new representations.

As we argued in Chapter 3, this putting together of representations and their selective control through processes like inhibition may precisely imply the sort of representational change that is defended by theories of sensorimotor development. The development of practical intelligence is largely the development of the ability to coordinate behavioral units into complex means-ends sequences, and this can only be achieved with representations of the individual units that have to be combined and the higher-order structures underpinning such combination.

We have insisted that primate intelligence is originally a practical intelligence: a system of representations at the service of organizing actions effectively. To deal with their environments, primates analyze them in units like objects and their relations, subjects and relationships among subjects, and so forth. And then they organize their behavior in an intentional way: primates want things and they are able to keep what they want in mind while executing the necessary steps to achieve it. Different primate species may differ in how many things they can keep in mind and how complexly they can organize their actions in pursuit of their goals. But they appear to share this common view of a world of natural objects distributed in space that can be manipulated and contemplated in relatively flexible ways. These primate views of the world are the product of development.

Developing Minds

One of the more distinctive features of primates is their extended infancies. It takes longer for primates to develop the locomotor skills necessary to displace themselves and manipulate objects than for most other species of animals. And among primates, there are clearly distinct patterns of growth and development. Apes develop their motor skills more slowly than monkeys. For example, chimpanzee babies cannot crawl on all fours until around 4 to 5 months of age, although they can achieve some degree of locomotion by other methods after they are 1 month old. By contrast, rhesus babies can crawl almost from their first days of life if they are given the opportunity and encouraged to do so. Human babies do not crawl until around 9 to 10 months of age.

In the ape line of evolution there is an important leap in the degree of motor immaturity at birth and the delay in the rate of subsequent development. This leap was further extended in the human line, rendering infants even more helpless and slow to develop. This pattern of immaturity has two important consequences: first, certain basic motor and cognitive skills are put together or acquired more slowly. Secondly, infants are more dependent upon their mothers and other adult members of their group for longer periods of time. Both things may have important consequences for cognitive development. In the first case—delayed motor and cognitive development—the same skills may eventually be acquired by monkeys, apes, and humans, but slower acquisition may give rise to different underlying representations. Maybe representations of how to do motor things like grasping or walking can be more detailed and flexible if they are put together more slowly. Or, complementarily, perhaps an effect of motor immaturity is to favor the initial building of perceptual representations with some independence of motor representations. Indeed, a striking finding of developmental psychology in recent years has been that *perceptual* knowledge appears to be acquired earlier than *action* knowledge, as when babies search in the wrong place for objects whose correct location they appear to know perceptually. Children eventually reconcile their perception and action, but we have evidence that similar perception-action gaps can be found in adult monkeys (Hauser, in press).

Nonetheless evolution has also delayed perceptual development, at least in humans. In Chapter 2 we saw how some perceptual landmarks, like the preference for new over known stimuli, occur in humans following the 1:4 rate rule when compared with monkeys. It remains to be investigated if the degree of delay is the same in the motor and perceptual realms, or evolution has widened the developmental gap in ape infants, and especially human infants, literally forcing them to watch before they act during their first few months of development.

At the time of writing this chapter, my five-month-old daughter had just started to reach for the objects she saw. She did so very clumsily and had difficulty homing in on the object at the first at-tempt. As for locomotor skills, her state was even more helpless. All she knew how to do was to roll over from supine to face down posi-tion, and she frequently got into trouble when doing this: one of her arms was trapped under her body and she didn't know what to do to release it. She needed our help to return to the supine posi-tion. However, there was something that she really did well (apart from crying, that is): *looking*. She knew how to move her eyes and her head to watch events in the world. These usually involved peo-ple moving around, and she had a surprising ability to follow these sometimes extended and complex movements. We don't know, of course, what she made of what she saw, although, if developmental psychologists are to be believed, she might have been learning a lot about the world of objects and people just from watching it.

When I met my first baby gorillas, they were admittedly some-what older than my daughter is now, about 6 to 8 months old. But the very different way in which they behaved cannot be explained by this small difference: they were capable of moving completely on their own, not only by walking on all fours on the ground, but also by climbing on boxes or chairs, not to mention on people. They were of course able to grasp the things they saw without hesi-tation, and take them to their mouth or do other things with them. They were certainly interested in watching things, but they did not seem to be watching as "full time" as a human baby; they were busy *doing* things during a good part of their time.

It took several months for my daughter to be able to move on her own for even a fraction of the gorillas' range of movement. But in the meantime she learned many things about objects and about the world. Scientists don't know yet if, at this early stage, these things are really different from what the gorillas know or are essentially the same but perhaps represented in slightly different formats, with slightly different emphases (maybe the gorillas are more concerned with what objects and space allow them to do; maybe young human babies are more focused on what other people do with objects— just to put forward a speculation). Perhaps one of the points of de-laying ape and human motor maturity is to allow for the lengthening and strengthening of a separate strain of perceptual knowledge. Perhaps knowledge acquired through perception, without immediate connection to action, is more "declarative," more amenable to explicit handling later in development. We don't have yet enough data about what non-human primates know perceptually to decide among these possibilities. Finding out about these things is one of the future tasks of the comparative study of cognitive development.

Developing What Is Already There

If you compare the changes in shape that happen to a newborn primate until it becomes adult, they are important but do not affect the essential structure of their bodies. Except for a few changes brought about by puberty, there is nothing in the adult body that was not present in the baby body. But a comparison of the behavioral repertoire of a newborn primate with the behavioral repertoire of an adult primate reveals dramatic changes. Something very fundamental has happened between birth and adulthood that has completely changed the behavioral (and, we assume, the cognitive) landscape of the grown-up body.

The behavioral changes from birth to adulthood might be carefully preprogrammed in the newborn brain: they might consist of the unfolding of predetermined abilities in a process of maturation. Even if such processes of maturation do exist, they are only a part of what happens in development, not the whole story, at least in the case of primates. Rather than simply unfolding what comes programmed for them, primates appear to be forced to reconstruct on their own things that, paradoxically, may well be specified in their genes. Instead of coming with a set of pre-programmed movements that they can carry out with their bodies from the beginning, primates are given the limbs, their interconnections, probably quite a complete set of subcortically organized postural patterns, and then they are left to slowly discover what they can do with their bodies (moving to places, grasping objects, climbing, walking). What would be the point of making primates rediscover the things that a part of their brain might already know how to do? A possible explanation is that this discovery occurs in a different part of their brain, let's say in the cortical areas, and the cortical representations thus formed are of a different nature than the subcortical ones. They are likely to be less detailed (for example, they probably don't contain a detailed description of the instruction necessary to carry out a movement, but just the "idea" of that movement), but in turn they may be more explicit and available for flexible combination with other similar representations,* especially for the sort of intelligent means-ends coordination that allows primates to solve problems in innovative ways.

One of the main points of development is precisely this—forcing primates to acquire representations of what in a certain sense they already know.** This apparently redundant process may have the crucial function of allowing motor behavior to be under the control of flexible representations and thus become *intelligent* behavior. Development is, in part, a voyage of discovery of what the species brain already knows, but its final destination is an individual's intelligence.

Continuity and Discontinuity in Cognitive Evolution

A persistent problem of comparative research is the lack of agreement about the empirical discoveries in the study of primate minds. As we have seen throughout this book, more frequently than not researchers disagree about what primates are capable of doing and understanding. Some people believe that the results of observational and experimental studies demonstrate a clear continuity between human and primate cognition—that under superficial behavioral differences (absence of language in non-humans) exist

* People familiar with the theories of Annette Karmiloff-Smith (1992) may recognize the parallel between the process I'm describing here and her ideas about representational redescription. The re-representations I am describing here, however, occur at the level of what she identifies as "procedural" knowledge. My tenet is that, in the same way that there are different levels of explicit knowledge, there are also different levels of procedural knowledge, some more explicit than others.

** In a sense, they are "remembering" what they know, as the Greek philosopher Plato, the first nativist, liked to put it.

commonalities (some language can be taught to apes). Other people, in contrast, believe that underlying superficial behavioral similarities (tool use or gaze following) there are profound cognitive differences (no causal or mental understanding).

This divergence of interpretations is not new. It has been present from the very beginning of comparative research. It is similar to the dispute between nativists and empiricists in developmental psychology. After almost a century of intense empirical research, the same basic disagreement remains among scientists of different persuasions.

When a theoretical discrepancy proves so resistant to empirical findings, this is a clear sign that the problem lies in the conflicting theories themselves: both sets must be only partially adequate and fail to encompass the whole nature of the phenomenon. It is like the proverbial controversy among blind people who struggle to identify the beast they are touching: one claims it is a snake, the other claims it is a hippopotamus; in fact it is an elephant, but one person is touching its trunk, the other its legs. Each fails to get a complete picture yet both stubbornly keep their convictions based on their undisputable but fragmentary pieces of evidence.

Let us try to address the issue of the continuity/discontinuity and similarity/dissimilarity debate by using an example borrowed from an area different from cognition. If we compare the anatomy of hands and faces among primates, claiming similarity and disparity are both legitimate approaches. The hand of the chimpanzee is at once the same and different from the hand of a human (see p. 10). It is a *hand* (hence the similarity), but it is a *chimpanzee hand* (hence the difference). What is scientifically more important—the similarities or the differences? That depends entirely upon the nature of the question you wish to address. If you are interested in understanding the articulation of five fingers into an organ capable of a range of basic grips, the similarities between different examples of hands will be more important; but if you are trying to understand certain fine-grained precision grips or the ability to play the piano, the differences may prove to be more relevant.

Discontinuity extremists may feel inclined to contend that, given the differences, a chimpanzee hand should not be considered a proper hand at all; whereas continuity extremists might claim that, given the obvious similarities, we should be speaking of "hands" without further distinctions. Both assertions would be absurd and scientifically sterile.

Perhaps this anatomical example is too simple (and the continuity too obvious) to be applied to the realm of behavior and cognition. Let us discuss a more complex case, halfway between anatomy and behavior—human bipedalism. This is a quintessentially human trait that consists of a complex set of anatomical and physiological adaptations. There is no question that humans have evolved a specific ability to walk on two legs and that this has occurred as part of a series of dramatic adaptive changes, some of which are obvious and visible even to the naked eye. Is bipedalism uniquely human among primates? An inspection of the anatomical adaptations of humans suggests so (Fleagle, 1999).

And yet, when one watches the behavior of chimpanzees and other primates in the wild, it turns out that occasionally they may walk on their legs (very clumsily and for short periods of time). Limited bipedalism appears thus to be a natural behavior of apes. Moreover, this occasional bipedalism is possible thanks to the use of a number of specific anatomical and physiological adaptations that are not selected specifically for that purpose. One theory (Crompton, 2001) is that this sporadic ground bipedalism is, paradoxically, a by-product of apes' adaptations to life in the trees. Relatively erect postures are very convenient for climbing and moving up and down among the branches of a tree. This is usually done with the help of at least one hand that firmly grasps a branch (much as we must do to navigate our way up or down the steep stairs of a two-story London bus on the move). These adaptations happen also to be occasionally useful on the ground (for example, for transporting an object or obtaining a better view of the environment), where apes can manage to walk upright without the help of the hands for a number of meters.

Can chimpanzees walk on two legs? The answer can only be "yes," unless we want to claim that those wild or captive chimps who move from A to B on their two legs are not actually displacing themselves at all, and that sight is just a figment of our imagination. *Are* chimpanzees therefore bipedal? Answering this question with a "yes" is more difficult. It depends upon what we mean by *being* bipedal. Chimps are not bipedal in the same sense as humans are. Chimpanzees, if you insist, are to some extent "ambipedal," but bipedalism for them is a secondary consequence of their adaptations to a wider range of locomotion. Human ancestors seized upon some similar set of locomotor adaptations that was probably present in our common ancestors and evolved specific adaptations to become full-time bipeds (losing in the process some other locomotor possibilities).

It would be foolish to deny that chimp bipedal walking is genuine; as foolish as pretending that there is nothing new or distinctive in human bipedalism and that it can be fully understood from chimpanzee bipedalism. The structures underlying chimp and human bipedalism are partly similar and partly very different, and the behavior of walking itself is also similar and different. There is no doubt about the specificity of human bipedalism, but there is also no doubt about its continuity with ape locomotion, including their occasional bipedalism. This is a genuine case of evolutionary continuity between apes and humans. Our theoretical troubles in dealing with this fact are our own fault, not a problem of insufficient data or the youth of a discipline.

Something similar happens with the cognitive abilities we have been discussing in this book. Primate minds are different versions of the same mind: depending upon what aspect we want to understand, we may have to focus more upon the similarities or the differences, but both are there. Deciding to concentrate upon similarities does not make the differences disappear, and concentrating upon the differences does not eliminate the similarities.

Apes Are Not Ancestors of Humans

Everybody knows that apes are not the ancestors of humans, but our evolutionary "cousins." Present-day apes and humans are descended from the same ancestral primate which is now extinct. This means that the evolutionary distance that separates humans from apes is not simply 5 million years of evolution, but 5 + 5 million years of independent evolution, meaning the time humans have been evolving on their own and the time apes have been evolving on their own. This, however, is frequently forgotten in shorthand discussions, and we tend to discuss ape abilities as precursors (the ancestral forms) of human abilities (for example, chimpanzee tool use as a precursor to human tool use). But chimpanzee tool use cannot possibly be a precursor to human tool use; if anything, we can speculate that chimpanzee tool use may be similar to the tool-using skills that our common ancestor had. We may suppose that chimpanzees' cognitive skills have changed relatively little in relation to those of our common ape ancestor. Even so, chimpanzees are not a direct mirror of our ancestral minds, but a reflection distorted by those 5 million years of independent evolution. Even if we assume that humans are the apes that have changed the most, we should still be prepared to treat chimpanzee behaviors not as the ancestral forms that were transformed into human behaviors, but as a different version of the kind of creature that could evolve from that unknown ape ancestor.

Think of the well-known game of whispering a message into someone's ear along a chain of people. Usually, when the message reaches the final person, it has changed in a surprising way. In evolution we are in a situation in which we don't know what was the original "message": we just know different versions achieved through different chains of ancestors. Chimpanzees, gorillas, orangutans, bonobos are all transformations of the same original message from which humans were formed, but they are not necessarily more faithful copies of that message.

The temptation to think of ape cognition as a version closer to the original ancestor than human cognition is probably based upon the irresistible impression that ape abilities are less complex but lean in the "same direction" as human cognition—an undeveloped version, a precursor to the complexity of the human mind. It is this impression which partly explains the special connections between primate and child studies: the child mind is a precursor to the adult mind in the developmental span of a lifetime, while the ape mind would be a precursor to the human mind in the developmental span of evolution.

Here too let us keep in mind that ape minds are not precursors to human minds, as monkeys' minds are not precursors of ape minds. A better formulation is to consider the ontogeny of the ape mind as an evolutionary *co-cursor* of the ontogeny of the human mind. "Co-cursor" means that it is not an earlier version of development that was modified into the human version, but a different version of what a primate cognitive development might be.

The Scope of Practical Cognition

This being the case, what can we learn from comparing primate minds? For one thing, we can learn about the diversity of the cognitive mechanisms that make up minds. This can be especially important for understanding the human mind itself. We are frequently under the illusion that our mind works in a certain way of which we are fully aware, especially when it comes to intelligence and higher cognitive functions. We think that our intelligence is fundamentally made up of awareness and language. This may not always be the case.

For example, take intentional communication. Many scientists believe that a communicative intention is a special kind of intention with an especially complex cognitive structure. A plain intention is, let us say, wanting the waiter to give us a spoon for our coffee. A communicative intention—the one that would drive our request for the spoon—involves *wanting* the waiter to *realize* that we *want* a spoon. What makes this intention so complicated is that we have to be aware of three different mental states that are put together in an embedded relationship: a complicated exercise in what we called theory of mind.

Careful analysis reveals that a true communicative intention may be even more complicated. Think, for example, of the following possibility. You are terribly shy and the waiter is terribly rude. You don't dare to address him to ask for your spoon, yet you need it. You come up with the following solution: you wait until the waiter is passing by your table and then carry out a little pantomime pretending that you are looking for a spoon or something to stir your coffee. But you carefully avoid looking at the waiter. Your hope is that he will notice this and then give you the spoon without your having to ask him. In effect, you *want* the waiter to *realize* that you *want* a spoon (what we concluded earlier might be a communicative intention), but you are not entering into overt intentional communication with him; on the contrary, you are carefully avoiding it. What is then a true communicative intention? If in the above example you want the waiter to realize that you want the spoon, but you don't want him to realize that you want him to realize that, then the step that you avoid must be what is necessary for an intention to be communicative: *wanting* the waiter to *realize* that you *want* him to *realize* that you *want* a spoon—an intention with 5 levels of embedded theory-of-mind computations!

Our logical analysis, based upon explicit propositional representations, leads us to conclude that when we are doing something apparently as simple as asking for a spoon, we are in fact engaging in a virtuoso exercise of mental awareness with no fewer than 5 embedded mental states (Gómez, 1994; Sperber, 1994). Surely there must be something wrong with this analysis. What is wrong is that we are trying to describe a cognitive function (what is technically known as "ostension" [Sperber and Wilson, 1986]) with a sophisticated cognitive mechanism that, despite its sophistication, is in fact unable to compute this particular function. Ostension (showing that you have an intention to communicate something) is neither achieved nor detected by representing the internal mental states of other people, but by computing something as basic as what in Chapter 7 we called *attention contact.* As we suggested in that chapter, attention contact is based upon representations of *external* mental states expressed in patterns like gaze or eye contact.

Of course, in human communication we combine representations of attention contact with representations of the internal states of other people. Hence we may speculate about whether the waiter is deliberately ignoring our attempts at calling his attention, perhaps because he is still angry because the other day we did not give him the tip he appeared to expect, and so forth. But the only way in which we can achieve ostension and enter into intentional communication is by using the distinct mechanism of attention contact. We will immediately know when the waiter finally decides to pay attention to us, thanks to something different from our inference of his internal mental states.

Forms of detecting, avoiding, and provoking attention contact appear to be pervasive among primates. In many monkey species they might be closely linked to systems of aggression and submission, but in ape species they appear to work in a relatively flexible way to regulate different kinds of social interactions, among them some forms of referential communication (see chapters 7 and 8).

One lesson from primates is, therefore, that some capital functions of our human cognitive life may be based upon representations that are resistant to linguistic or propositional descriptions, and that certainly are not achieved by means of them. Note that this is not to deny that the explicit and abstract representations of human minds achieve important cognitive functions: it is just to remind ourselves that these higher-order cognitive functions are just peaks of complex cognitive icebergs that we will not understand with limited notions of explicit cognition.

Exaptive Minds

In evolutionary cognitive science, we are used to think of mental skills in terms of adaptations for specific tasks. In the course of evolution organisms have developed different mental tools, each exquisitely adapted to perform certain functions (see Hauser, 2001). For example, primates in general have developed a notion of object permanence that allows them to keep track of objects in the world; some monkeys have developed representational systems of alarm calls to avoid predators more effectively; chimpanzees have developed sophisticated object-manipulation skills that allow them to use a variety of tools. Just as primate bodies have evolved distinct morphological adaptations (hands, eyes, faces), their minds must have evolved distinct cognitive adaptations.

Nevertheless, when primates are confronted with especially unusual problems, they may come up with solutions that, rather than the product of adaptations, we should describe as *exaptations*. In evolution, an adaptation is a feature that has acquired a certain form because of its efficiency in performing a particular function. For example, the primate hand became designed by the function of grasping. However, sometimes a feature that was originally selected for a certain function may coincidentally happen to be capable of performing a new, unexpected function. A somewhat whimsical example is the case of the human nose; it happens to be ideally suited for performing the function of supporting spectacles, although it was not selected by evolution for that purpose. Noses are not adapted for the function of carrying eyeglasses: they are *exapted* into that function.

Of course, the point about eyeglasses is that these were designed by humans to fit the existing properties of noses. But can exaptations occur naturally, that is, can some adaptations for function X become unexpectedly useful in dealing with function Y? Some biologists such as the late Stephen Jay Gould (Gould and Vrba, 1982) are convinced that exaptations do occur in nature and much more frequently than we suppose, but we may confuse them with adaptations.

Behavioral and cognitive exaptations occur very frequently in primates who are placed in conditions of captivity. In these radically new conditions (for one thing, they do not have to look for food because they receive their daily allowance, but they are not free to move and are forced to depend upon humans), they have to cope with a number of new functions using their existing cognitive and behavioral abilities. And they are relatively good at coming up with solutions to their new problems. For example, as we saw in chapter 7, captive apes readily develop forms of referential communication with their human caretakers that may not be part of their usual repertoire in the wild. They don't need to be painstakingly taught these forms of communication. They come "naturally" to them when they are placed in these artificial captive conditions.

Apes can also develop new forms of object manipulation. The

more dramatic case is that of captive gorillas and orangutans: in captivity they routinely develop complex tool-using behaviors; in the wild they are rarely observed using tools (especially gorillas). Some people are inclined to dismiss these innovative patterns as aberrant behaviors provoked by captivity and, therefore, of no evolutionary interest. Theirs would be a narrow conception of evolution in which species are considered to be fixed products optimally adapted to their fixed environments. But evolution is anything but a static process. The fundamental engine that drives evolution is the ability of particular individuals to survive the inevitable changes that sooner or later occur in their environments. One way of doing this is precisely by *exapting* existing abilities adapted to a particular function to deal with the new functions that an environmental change may demand. Tool-using captive gorillas are a demonstration that, if they needed to, wild gorillas might be able to exploit food resources that are only accessible through tools. Chimpanzees have already done so, probably to their evolutionary advantage.

Exaptive Stupidity

A consequence of this exaptive view of evolution is that exapted abilities may not be optimally designed to perform the tasks they are innovatively being used for. Exaptation may produce clumsiness and stupidity. For example, referential communication of apes with humans can be very clumsy and rudimentary. Some apes come up with a bizarre hand-taking gesture to orient humans to objects, when an extension of their own arm would do a better job. This could be because they are recruiting adaptations originally designed for object manipulation to create forms of directing humans to targets (see chapter 7), while at the same time using their joint-attention adaptations to make genuine communicative gestures out of those contact gestures. Human babies, in contrast, appear to be better designed for engaging in referential communication: all babies develop very naturally a pointing gesture with their extended index finger that is ideally adapted for referential signaling. Only some apes, occasionally, develop something similar to that

(Menzel, 1999; Gómez, 1992). But babies also have cognitive adaptations for reference, like the inclination to engage in protodeclarative gestures directing others to targets of attention instead of targets of action. Apes engage in protodeclarative gesturing even more rarely than they engage in index finger pointing (if at all).

Apes have to invent gestural reference laboriously, using cognitive and behavioral means that in some cases are far from well adapted to the task; human babies, in contrast, come naturally to referential behaviors and, no wonder, follow a longer and more elaborate referential career.

In sum, one of the consequences of primates' reliance upon cognitive development as a way of generalized adaptation is their ability to explore new cognitive territories. Captive primates are dramatically forced to do so, but the processes of exaptation we witness in these artificial cases may be essentially the same that primates have to use in nature when natural environmental changes occur. Sometimes exaptations of existing abilities may be enough to keep the primates adapted to their changed environments; other times exaptations may be a transitory solution for survival that acts like an evolutionary bridge into new abilities, when random genetic changes happen to be better adaptive to the new conditions and put their fortunate owners in a position to exploit the new functions better than the members of the old species can do with their exaptations. Yet even in cases where the successful new adaptations may completely replace the exaptations, the first evolutionary step toward the new adaptation was through the exaptive use of the older. Moreover, in some cases the exaptation may be creating new functions and therefore new selection pressures, such that the mutations that eventually create the new adaptation would not have been selected had they occurred in the absence of the exaptation.

For example, in the case of reference, modern apes might be giving us an idea of the sort of processes that may have operated in promoting the evolution of specific adaptations for referential functions. Perhaps the first hominids that separated from the ape line into the human line were capable of rudimentary forms of reference, and these rudimentary forms moved them into a vast new cognitive territory that they could not possibly fully conquer with their existing cognitive tools. The conditions for selecting "natural-born referencers" were, however, set by those acts of exaptation.

The lesson from comparative primate research is, in this case, that a view of the mind as a fixed collection of cognitive adaptations is wrong: it must be replaced with a wider view of the mind as a dynamic *articulation* of cognitive abilities, which, as a whole, is capable of going beyond its specific adaptations.

A particularly extreme example of this might be the case of "linguistic" apes. The ability of the primate mind to produce exaptations can be stretched to surprising extremes when infant apes are reared and trained by humans in special circumstances. Great apes that are hand-reared and taught artificial ways of communication may develop behaviors and ways of representing the world that may be very different in many respects to those developed by wild apes, although, as we have seen throughout the book, the precise nature of what they have achieved remains controversial.

To conclude, perhaps the more important lesson we can extract from comparative primate research is that primate minds are in a very profound sense *developed* minds. The forms of cognition that characterize primates cannot be constructed in any other way except through development. Development is the most effective tool of evolution to produce cognition, and primate minds perhaps are literally the most *developed* in nature.

References

Amsterdam, B. K. 1972. Mirror self-image reactions before age two. *Developmental Psychology*, 5, 297–305.

Anderson, J. R. 2001. Self and others in nonhuman primates: A question of perspective. *Psychologia*, 44, 3–16.

Anderson, J. R., and Mitchell, R. W. 1999. Macaques but not lemurs co-orient visually with humans. *Folia Primatologica*, 70, 17–22.

Antinucci, F. 1990. The comparative study of cognitive ontogeny in four primate species. In: *"Language" and intelligence in monkeys and apes: Comparative developmental perspectives* (ed. S. T. Parker and K. R. Gibson), pp. 157–171. Cambridge: Cambridge University Press.

Astington, J. W. 1994. *The child's discovery of the mind.* Cambridge, Mass: Harvard University Press.

Avital, E., and Jablonka, E. 2000. *Animal traditions: Behavioural inheritance in evolution.* Cambridge: Cambridge University Press.

Bachevalier, J. 2001. Neural bases of memory development: Insights from neuropsychological studies in primates. In: *Developmental cognitive neuroscience* (ed. C. A. Nelson and M. Luciana), pp. 365–379. Cambridge, Mass.: MIT Press.

Baillargeon, R., Spelke, E. S., and Wasserman, S. 1986. Object permanence in five-month-old infants. *Cognition*, 20, 191–208.

Bard, K. A. 1992. Similarities and differences in the neonatal behavior of chimpanzee and human infants. In: *The role of the chimpanzee in research* (ed. G. Eder, E. Kaiser, and F. A. King). Basel: S. Karger.

Barkow, J., Cosmides, L.,, and Tooby, J. 1992. *The adapted mind.* Oxford: Oxford University Press.

Baron-Cohen, S. 1995. *Mindblindness: An essay on autism and theory of mind.* Cambridge, Mass.: MIT Press.

Bates, E. 1979. *The emergence of symbols: Cognition and communication in infancy.* New York: Academic Press.

Bates, E. 1993. Comprehension and production in early language development. *Monographs of the Society for Research in Child Development*, 58, 222–242.

Bates, E., Camaioni, L., and Volterra, V. 1975. The acquisition of performatives prior to speech. *Merrill-Palmer Quarterly*, 21, 205–226.

Beck, B. 1980. *Animal tool behavior.* New York: Garland.

Bickerton, D. 1995. *Language and human behaviour.* London: UCL Press.

Birch, H. G. 1945. The relation of previous experience to insightful problem-solving. *Journal of Comparative Psychology*, 38, 267–383.

Boesch, C. 1991. Teaching in wild chimpanzees. *Animal behaviour*, 41, 530–532.

Boesch, C., and Boesch-Achermann, H. 2000. *The chimpanzees of the Taï Forest: Behavioural ecology and evolution.* Oxford: Oxford University Press.

Bogartz, R. S., Shinskey, J. L., and Schilling, T. H. 2000. Object permanence in five-and-a-half-month-old infants? *Infancy*, 1, 403–428.

Bower, T. G. R. 1974. *Development in infancy.* New York: Freeman.

——— 1979. *Human development: A primer.* New York: Freeman.

Box, H. O., and Gibson, K. R. 1999. *Mammalian social learning: Comparative and ecological perspectives. Cambridge:* Cambridge University Press.

Boysen, S. T., and Kuhlmeier, V. A. 2002. Representational capacities for pretense with scale models and photographs in chimpanzees (*Pan troglodytes*). In: *Pretending and imagination in animals and children* (ed. R. W. Mitchell), pp. 210–228. Cambridge: Cambridge University Press.

Branch, J. E. 1986. Spatial localization by chimpanzees (*Pan troglodytes*) after changes in an object's location via seen and unseen rotations. Ph.D. Thesis. *Georgia Institute of Technology.* University Microfilms International.

Bremner, J. G. 2001. Cognitive development: Knowledge of the physical world. In: *Infant development* (ed. G. Bremner and A. Fogel), pp. 99–138. Oxford: Blackwell.

Brennan, W. M., Ames, E. W., and Moore, R. W. 1966. Age differences in infants' attention to patterns of different complexities. *Science*, 151, 354–356.

Bretherton, I., McNew, S., and Beeghly-Smith, M. 1981. Early person knowledge as expressed in gestural and verbal communication: When do infants acquire a "theory of mind"? In: *Infant Social Cognition* (ed.

M. E. Lamb and M. R. Sherrod), pp. 333–373. Hillsdale, N.J.: Lawrence Erlbaum.

Brown, R. 1970. The first sentences of child and chimpanzee. In: *Psycholinguistics* (ed. R. Brown), pp. 208–231. New York: Free Press.

———— 1973. *A First Language.* Cambridge, Mass.: Harvard University Press.

———— 1986. *Social psychology. 2nd ed.* New York: Free Press.

Bruner, J. S. 1972. Nature and uses of immaturity. *American Psychologist,* 27, 1–22.

———— 1975. From communication to language—a psychological perspective. *Cognition,* 3, 255–287.

Bryant, P. E., Jones, P., Claxton, V., and Perkins, G. M. 1972. Recognition of shapes across modalities by infants. *Nature,* 240, 303–304.

Bühler, K. 1918. *Die geistige Entwicklung des Kindes.* Jena: Fischer.

Butler, R. A. 1965. Investigative behavior. In: *Behavior of nonhuman primates* (ed. A. M. Schrier, H. F. Harlow, and F. Stollnitz), pp. 463–493. New York: Academic Press.

Butterworth, G. 1991. The ontogeny and phylogeny of joint visual attention. In: *Natural theories of mind: Evolution, development and simulation of everyday mindreading* (ed. A. Whiten), pp. 223–232. Oxford: Blackwell.

Byrne, R. W. 1995. *The thinking ape.* Oxford: Oxford University Press.

———— 2002. Imitation of novel complex actions: What does the evidence from animals mean? *Advances in the Study of Behavior,* 31, 77–105.

Byrne, R. W., and Byrne, J. M.E. 1993. Complex leaf-gathering skills of mountain gorillas (*Gorilla g. beringei*): Variability and standardization. *American Journal of Primatology,* 31, 241–261.

Call, J. 2000. Representing space and objects in monkeys and apes. *Cognitive Science,* 24, 397–422.

———— 2001. Object permanence in orangutans (*Pongo pygmaeus*), chimpanzees (*Pan troglodytes*), and children (*Homo sapiens*). *Journal of Comparative Psychology,* 115, 159–171.

Call, J., and Rochat, P. 1996. Liquid conservation in orangutans (*pongo pygmaeus*) and humans (*homo sapiens*): Individual differences and perceptual strategies. *Journal of Comparative Psychology,* 110, 219–232.

———— 1997. Perceptual strategies in the estimation of physical quantities by orangutans (*Pongo Pygmaeus*). *Journal of Comparative Psychology,* 111, 315–329.

Call, J., and Tomasello, M. In press. What chimpanzees know about seeing revisited: An explanation of the third kind. In: *Joint attention* (ed. C. Hoerl, N. Eilan, T. McCormack, and J. Roessler). Oxford: Oxford University Press.

Carey, S., and Xu, F. 2001. Infants' knowledge of objects: Beyond object files and object tracking. *Cognition*, 80, 179–213.

Carpenter, M., and Call, J. 2002. The chemistry of social learning. *Developmental Science*, 5, 22–24.

Carpenter, M., Nagell, K., and Tomasello, M. 1998. Social cognition, joint attention, and communicative competence from 9 to 15 months of age. *Monographs of the Society for Research in Child development*, 63.

Cheney, D. L., and Seyfarth, R. M. 1990. *How monkeys see the world.* Chicago: Chicago University Press.

——— 1991. Reading minds or reading behaviour? Tests for a theory of mind in monkeys. In: *Natural theories of mind: evolution, development and simulation of everyday mindreading* (ed. A. Whiten), pp. 175–194. Oxford: Blackwell.

——— 1999. Mechanisms underlying the vocalizations of nonhuman primates. In: *The design of animal communication* (ed. M. Hauser and M. Konishi). Cambridge, Mass.: MIT Press.

Chomsky, N. 1968. *Language and mind.* New York: Harcourt Brace.

Cosmides, L. 1989. The logic of social exchange: Has natural selection shaped how humans reason? Studies with the Wason selection task. *Cognition*, 31, 187–276.

Cowey, A., and Weiskrantz, L. 1975. Demonstration of cross-modal matching in rhesus monkeys, *Macaca mulatta. Neuropsychologia*, 13, 117–120.

Crockford, C. and Boesch, C. 2003. Context-specific calls in wild chimpanzees, *Pan troglodytes verus:* Analysis of barks. *Animal Behaviour*, 66, 115–125.

Crompton, R. 2001. The evolution of bipedalism. *School of Psychology Seminar Series, University of St. Andrews.*

D'Amato, M. R., and Van Sant, P. 1988. The Person concept in monkeys (*Cebus apella*). *Journal of Experimental Psychology: Animal Behavior Processes*, 14, 43–55.

Darby, C. L., and Riopelle, A. J. 1959. Observational learning in the rhesus monkey. *Journal of Comparative and Physiological Psychology*, 52, 94–98.

Davenport, T. R. K., and Menzel, E. W. 1960. Oddity preference in the chimpanzee. *Psychological Reports*, 7, 523–526.

Davenport, T. R. K., and Rogers, C. M. 1970. Intermodal equivalence of stimuli in apes. *Science*, 168, 279–280.

Davenport, T. R. K., Rogers, C. M., and Russell, I. S. 1973. Cross-modal perception in apes. *Neuropsychologia*, 11, 21–28.

Dawson, G. and McKissick, F. 1984. Self-recognition in autistic children. *Journal of Autism and Developmental Disorders*, 14, 383–394.

De Waal, F. 1982. *Chimpanzee politics: Power and sex among apes.* London: Jonathan Cape.

De Waal, F. 1989. *Peacemaking among primates.* Cambridge, Mass.: Harvard University Press.

De Waal, F. 2001. *The Ape and the Sushi Master. Cultural reflections by a primatologist.* London: Allen Lane.

DeLoache, J. S. 1995. Early understanding and use of symbols: The model. *Current Directions in Psychological Science,* 4, 109–113.

Deruelle, C., Barbet, I., Delpy, D., and Fagot, J. 2000. Perception of partly occluded figures by baboons (*Papio papio*). *Perception,* 29, 1483–1497.

Diamond, A. 1990a. The development and neural bases of memory functions as indexed by the AB and delayed response tasks in human infants and infant monkeys. In: *The development and neural bases of higher cognitive functions* (ed. A. Diamond), pp. 267–317. New York: The New York Academy of Sciences.

———— 1990b. Developmental time course in human infants and infant monkeys, and the neural bases of inhibitory control in reaching. In: *The development and neural bases of higher cognitive functions* (ed. A. Diamond), pp. 637–676. New York: The New York Academy of Sciences.

———— 1991. Neuropsychological insights into the meaning of object concept development. In: *The epigenesis of mind. Essays on biology and cognition* (ed. S. Carey and R. Gelman), pp. 67–110. Hillsdale, N.J.: Lawrence Erlbaum.

———— 1995. Evidence of robust recognition memory early in life even when assessed with reaching behaviour. *Journal of Experimental Child Psychology,* 59, 419–456.

Dickinson, A., and Balleine, B. W. 2000. Causal cognition and goal-directed action. In: *The evolution of cognition* (ed. C. Heyes and L. Huber), pp. 185–204. Cambridge, Mass: MIT Press.

Doré, F. Y., and Dumas, C. 1987. Psychology of animal cognition: Piagetian studies. *Psychological Bulletin,* 102, 219–233.

Doré, F. Y., and Goulet, S. 1998. The comparative analysis of object knowledge. In: *Piaget, evolution, and development* (ed. J. Langer and M. Killen), pp. 55–72. Hillsdale, N.J.: Lawrence Erbaum Associates.

Dunbar, R. 2000. Causal reasoning, mental rehearsal, and the evolution of primate cognition. In: *The evolution of cognition* (ed. C. Heyes and L. Huber), pp. 205–219. Cambridge, Mass: MIT Press.

Etienne, A. S. 1976. L'étude comparative de la permanence de l'objet chez l'animal. *Bulletin de Psychologie,* 327, 187–197.

Fabre-Thorpe, M., Delorme, A., and Richard, G. 1999. Perception des dimensions globale et locale de stimuli visuels. Singes et hommes face au monde visuel: La catégorisation. *Primatologie*, **2,** 111–139.

Fagot, J., and Deruelle, C. 1997. Processing of global and local visual information and hemispheric specialization in humans (*Homo sapiens*) and baboons (*Papio papio*). *Journal of Experimental Psychology: Human Perception and Performance*, 23, 429–442.

Fagot, J., Deruelle, C., and Tomonaga, M. 1999. Perception des dimensions globale et locale de stimuli visuels chez le primate. *Primatologie*, 2, 61–77.

Fagot, J., Tomonaga, M., and Deruelle, C. 2001. Processing of the global and local dimensions of visual hierarchical stimuli by humans (*Homo sapiens*), chimpanzees (*Pan troglodytes*), and baboons (*Papio papio*). In: *Primate origins of human cognition and behavior* (ed. T. Matsuzawa), pp. 87–103. Berlin: Springer.

Falk, D., and Gibson, K. R. 2001. *Evolutionary anatomy of the primate cerebral cortex.* Cambridge: Cambridge University Press.

Fantz, R. L. 1956. A method for studying early visual development. *Perceptual and Motor Skills*, 13–15.

——— 1965. Ontogeny of perception. In: *Behavior of nonhuman primates* (ed. A. M. Schrier, H. F. Harlow, and F. Stollnitz), pp. 365–403. New York: Academic Press.

Farroni, T., Csibra, G., Simion, F., and Johnson, M. H. 2002. Eye contact detection in humans from birth. *Proceedings of the National Academy of Sciences*, 99, 9602–9605.

Ferrari, P. F., Kohler, E., Fogassi, L., and Gallese, V. 2000. The ability to follow eye gaze and its emergence during development in macaque monkeys. *Proceedings of the National Academy of Sciences*, 97, 13997–14002.

Filion, C. M., Washburn, D. A., and Gulledge, J. P. 1996. Can monkeys (*Macaca mulatta*) represent invisible displacement? *Journal of Comparative Psychology*, 110, 386–395.

Fleagle, J. G. 1999. *Primate adaptation and evolution.* London: Academic Press.

Fobes, J. L., and King, J. E. 1982. Measuring primate learning abilities. In: *Primate Behavior* (ed. J. L. Fobes and J. E. King), pp. 289–326. New York: Academic Press.

Fodor, J. A. 1979. *The language of thought.* Cambridge, Mass.: Harvard University Press.

——— 1983. *The modularity of mind.* Cambridge, Mass.: MIT Press.

Fossey, D. 1983. *Gorillas in the mist.* New York: Houghton Mifflin.

Frith, U. 2003. *Autism: Explaining the enigma.* 2nd. ed. Oxford: Blackwell.

Fujita, K. 2001. What you see is different from what I see: Species differences in visual perception. In: *Primate origins of human cognition and behavior* (ed. T. Matsuzawa), pp. 29–54. Berlin: Springer.

Galef, B. G. J. 1992. The question of animal culture. *Human Nature*, 3, 157–178.

Gallese, V. In press, 2003. The manifold nature of interpersonal relations: The quest for a common mechanism. *Philosophical Transactions of the Royal Society of London.*

Gallup, G. G. 1970. Chimpanzees: Self-recognition. *Science*, 167, 86–87.

———— 1983. Towards a comparative psychology of mind. In: *Animal cognition and behavior* (ed. R. L. Mellgren), pp. 473–510. Amsterdam: North-Holland.

Gallup, G. G., McClure, M. K., Hill, S. D., and Bundy, R. A. 1971. Capacity for self recognition in differentially reared chimpanzees. *The Psychological Record*, 21, 69–74.

Garber, P. A. 2000. Evidence for the use of spatial, temporal, and social information by primate foragers. In: *On the move. How and why animals travel in groups* (ed. S. Boinski and P. A. Garber), pp. 261–298. Chicago: University of Chicago Press.

Gardner, B. T., and Gardner, R. A. 1974. Comparing the early utterances of child and chimpanzee. In: *Minnesota symposia on child psychology. Vol. 8* (ed. A. Pick), pp. 3–24. Minneapolis: University of Minnesota Press.

———— 1969. Teaching sign language to a chimpanzee. *Science*, 165, 664–672.

Gibson, K. R. 2002. Customs and cultures in animals and humans: Neurobiological and evolutionary considerations. *Anthropological Theory*, 2, 323–339.

Goldin-Meadow, S. 1979. Structure in a manual communication system developed without a conventional language model: Language without a helping hand. In: *Studies in neurolinguistics. Vol. 4* (ed. H. Whitaker and H. A. Whitaker), pp. 125–209. New York: Academic Press.

Goldin-Meadow, S. and Mylander, C. 1990. Beyond the input given. *Language*, 66, 323–355.

Gómez, J. C. 1990. The emergence of intentional communication as a problem-solving strategy in the gorilla. In: *"Language" and intelligence in monkeys and apes: Comparative developmental perspectives* (ed. S. T. Parker and K. R. Gibson), pp. 333–355. Cambridge: Cambridge University Press.

———— 1991. Visual behavior as a window for reading the minds of others in primates. In: *Natural theories of mind: evolution, development and simulation of everyday mindreading* (ed. A. Whiten), pp. 195–207. Oxford: Blackwell.

——— 1992. El desarrollo de la comunicación intencional en el gorila [The development of intentional communication in gorillas]. Ph.D. thesis. Universidad Autónoma de Madrid.

——— 1994. Mutual awareness in primate communication: A Gricean approach. In: *Self-recognition and awareness in apes, monkeys and children* (ed. S. Parker, M. Boccia, and R. Mitchell). Cambridge: Cambridge University Press.

——— 1995. *Eye gaze, attention and the evolution of mindreading in primates.* Paper presented at 25th Meeting of the Jean Piaget Society, Berkeley, California, June 1995.

——— 1996a. Non-human primate theories of (non-human primate) minds: Some issues concerning the origins of mind-reading. In: *Theories of theories of mind* (ed. P. Carruthers and P. K. Smith), pp. 330–343. Cambridge: Cambridge University Press.

——— 1996b. Ostensive behavior in the great apes: The role of eye contact. In: *Reaching into thought: The minds of the great apes* (ed. A. Russon, S. Parker, and K. Bard), pp. 131–151. Cambridge: Cambridge University Press.

——— 1997. The study of the evolution of communication as a meeting of disciplines. *Evolution of Communication,* 1, 101–132.

——— 1998. Assessing theory of mind with nonverbal procedures: Problems with training methods and an alternative 'key' procedure. *Behavioral and Brain Sciences,* 21, 119–120.

——— 1999. Development of sensorimotor intelligence in infant gorillas: The manipulation of objects in problem solving and exploration. In: *The mentalities of gorillas and orangutans: Comparative perspectives* (ed. S. T. Parker, R. W. Mitchell, and H. L. Miles), pp. 160–178. Cambridge: Cambridge University Press.

——— In press. Joint attention and the notion of subject: insights from apes, children, and autism. In: *Joint attention* (ed. C. Hoerl, N. Eilan, T. McCormack, and J. Roessler). Oxford: Oxford University Press.

Gómez, J. C., Sarriá, E., and Tamarit, J. 1993. The comparative study of early communication and theories of mind: Ontogeny, phylogeny and pathology. In: *Understanding other minds: Perspectives from autism* (ed. S. Baron-Cohen, H. Tager-Flusberg, and D. Cohen), pp. 397–426. Oxford: Oxford University Press.

Gómez, J. C., and Teixidor, P. 1992. Theory of mind in an orangutan: A nonverbal test of false-belief appreciation? In: *XIV Congress of the International Primatological Society* (August). Strasbourg.

Gómez, J. C., Teixidor, P., and Laá, V. 1996. Understanding the referential and ostensive functions of joint visual attention in young chimpanzees. In: *BPS Developmental Psychology Section Annual Conference* (Sept. 11–13). Oxford.

Goodall, J. 1968. The behaviour of free-living chimpanzees in the Gombe Stream area. *Animal Behaviour Monographs*, 1, 161–311.

——— 1973. Cultural elements in a chimpanzee community. In: *Precultural primate behavior* (ed. E. W. Menzel), pp. 144–184. Basel: Karger.

——— 1986. *The chimpanzees of Gombe.* Cambridge, Mass.: Harvard University Press.

Gopnik, A., and Meltzoff, A. 1997. *Words, thoughts, and theories.* Cambridge, Mass.: MIT Press.

Gould, S., and Vrba, E. 1982. Exaptation: A missing term in the science of form. *Paleobiology*, 8, 4–15.

Guillaume, P., and Meyerson, I. 1930. *Recherches sur l'usage de l'instrument chez les singes.* Paris: Librairie Philosophique, 1987.

Gunderson, V. M. 1983. Development of cross-modal recognition in infant pigtail monkeys (*Macaca nemestrina*). *Developmental Psychology*, 19, 398–404.

Gunderson, V. M., and Sackett, G. P. 1984. Development of pattern recognition in infant pigtailed macaques (*Macaca nemestrina*). *Developmental Psychology*, 20, 418–426.

Harding, C. G. 1982. Development of the intention to communicate. *Human Development*, 25, 140–151.

Hare, B. 2001. Can competitive paradigms increase the validity of experiments on primate social cognition? *Animal Cognition*, 4, 269–280.

Hare, B., Addessi, E., Call, J., Tomasello, M., and Visalberghi, E. 2003. Do capuchin monkeys, *Cebus apella*, know what conspecifics do and do not see? *Animal Behaviour*, 65, 131–142.

Hare, B., Call, J., Agnetta, B., and Tomasello, M. 2000. Chimpanzees know what conspecifics do and do not see. *Animal Behaviour*, 59, 771–785.

Hare, B., Call, J., and Tomasello, M. 2001. Do chimpanzees know what conspecifics know? *Animal Behaviour*, 61, 139–151.

Harlow, H. F. 1959. The development of learning in the rhesus monkey. *American Scientist*, winter, 459–479.

——— 1971. *Learning to love.* Chicago: Aldine.

Harlow, H. F., and Harlow, M. K. 1949. Learning to think. *Scientific American*, 36–39.

Hauser, M. D. 1996. *The evolution of communication.* Cambridge, Mass.: MIT Press.

——— 1997. Artifactual kinds and functional design features: What a primate understands without language. *Cognition*, 64, 285–308.

——— 1999. Perseveration, inhibition and the prefrontal cortex: A new look. *Current Opinion in Neurobiology*, 9, 214–222.

——— 2000. A primate dictionary? Decoding the function and meaning of another species' vocalizations. *Cognitive Science*, 24, 445–475.

———— 2001. *Wild minds. What animals really think.* London: Penguin Books.

———— In press. Knowing about knowing. Dissociations between perception and action systems over evolution and during development. *ANYAS.*

Hauser, M. D., and Carey, S. 1998. Building a cognitive creature from a set of primitives: Evolutionary and developmental insights. In: *The evolution of mind* (ed. D. D. Cummins and C. Allen), pp. 51–106. New York: Oxford University Press.

Hauser, M. D., Carey, S., and Hauser, L. B. 2000. Spontaneous number representation in semi-free-ranging rhesus monkeys. *Proceedings of the Royal Society. B*, 267, 829–833.

Hauser, M. D., Pearson, H., and Seelig, D. 2002. Ontogeny of tool use in cottontop tamarins, *Saguinus oedipus:* Innate recognition of functionally relevant features. *Animal Behaviour*, 64, 299–311.

Hauser, M. D., Santos, L. R., Spaepen, G. M., and Pearson, H. 2002. Problem solving, inhibition and domain-specific experience: Experiments on cottontop tamarins, *Saguinus oedipus. Animal Behaviour*, 64, 387–396.

Hayes, C. H. 1951. *The ape in our house.* New York: Harper and Row.

Hemmi, J. M., and Menzel, C. R. 1995. Foraging strategies of long-tailed macaques, *Macaca fascicularis:* Directional extrapolation. *Animal Behaviour*, 49, 457–464.

Herrnstein, R. J., Loveland, D. H., and Cable, C. 1976. Natural concepts in pigeons. *Journal of Experimental Psychology: Animal Behavior Processes*, 2, 285–302.

Heyes, C. M. 1993. Anecdotes, training, trapping, and triangulating: Do animals attribute mental states? *Animal Behaviour*, 46, 177–188.

———— 1998. Theory of mind in nonhuman primates. *Behavioral and Brain Sciences*, 21, 101–148.

Hirata, S., Watanabe, K., and Kawai, M. 2001. "Sweet-potato washing" revisited. In: *Primate origins of human cognition and behavior* (ed. T. Matsuzawa), pp. 487–508. Tokyo: Springer.

Hobson, P. 1994. Perceiving attitudes, conceiving minds. In: *Children's early understanding of mind* (ed. C. Lewis and P. Mitchell), pp. 71–93. Hove: LEA.

Hood, B. M. 1995. Gravity rules for 2- to 4-Year olds? *Cognitive Development*, 10, 577–598.

Hood, B. M., Hauser, M. D., Anderson, L. and Santos, L. 1999. Gravity biases in a non-human primate? *Developmental Science*, 2, 35–41.

Hopkins, W. D., and Washburn, D. A. 2002. Matching visual stimuli on the basis of global and local features by chimpanzees (*Pan troglodytes*) and rhesus monkeys (*Macaca mulatta*). *Animal Cognition*, 5, 27–31.

Horowitz, A. C. 2003. Do humans ape? Or do apes human? Imitation and intention in humans (*Homo sapiens*) and other animals. *Journal of Comparative Psychology*, 117, 325–336.

Huber, E. 1931. *Evolution of facial musculature and facial expression.* Baltimore: Johns Hopkins University Press.

Hubley, P., and Trevarthen, C. 1979. Sharing a task in infancy. In: *Social interaction and communication during infancy* (ed. I. C. Uzgiris), pp. 57–80. San Francisco: Jossey Bass.

Ingold, T. 1994. Introduction to culture. In: *Companion Encyclopedia of Anthropology. Humanity, culture and social life* (ed. T. Ingold). London: Routledge.

Inoue-Nakamura, N. 2001. Mirror self-recognition in primates: An ontogenetic and a phylogenetic approach. In: *Primate origins of human cognition and behavior* (ed. T. Matsuzawa), pp. 297–312. Tokyo: Springer.

Inoue-Nakamura, N., and Matsuzawa, T. 1997. Development of stone tool use by wild chimpanzees (*Pan troglodytes*). *Journal of Comparative Psychology*, 111, 159–173.

Ishibashi, H., Hihara, S., and Iriki, A. 2000. Acquisition and development of monkey tool-use: behavioral and kinematic analyses. *Canadian Journal of Physiological Pharmacology*, 78, 958–966.

Janson, C. 2000. Spatial movement strategies: Theory, evidence, and challenges. In: *On the move. How and why animals travel in groups* (ed. S. Boinski and P. A. Garber), pp. 165–203. Chicago: University of Chicago Press.

Johnson, M. H., and Morton, J. 1991. *Biology and cognitive development: The case of face recognition.* Oxford: Blackwell.

Jolly, A. 1972. *The evolution of primate behavior.* New York: Macmillan.

Karin-D'Arcy, M. R., and Povinelli, D. J. 2003. Do chimpanzees know what each other sees? A closer look. *International Journal of Comparative Psychology*, 15, 21–54.

Karmiloff, K., and Karmiloff-Smith, A. 2001. *Pathways to language. From fetus to adolescent.* Cambridge, Mass: Harvard University Press.

Karmiloff-Smith, A. 1992. *Beyond modularity: A developmental perspective on cognitive science.* Cambridge, Mass.: MIT Press.

Karmiloff-Smith, A., and Inhelder, B. 1975. "If you want to get ahead, get a theory." *Cognition*, 3, 195–212.

Kawai, M. 1965. Newly-acquired pre-cultural behavior of the natural troop of Japanese monkeys on Koshima Island. *Primates.* 6, 1–30.

Kellman, P. J., and Spelke, E. S. 1983. Perception of partly occluded objects in infancy. *Cognitive Psychology*, 15, 483–524.

Kellogg, W. N., and Kellogg, L. A. 1933. *The ape and the child.* New York: McGraw-Hill

Kendon, A. 1967. Some functions of gaze direction in two-person conversations. *Acta Psychologica*, 26, 22–63.

Klin, A., Jones, W., Schultz, R., Volkmar, F., and Cohen, D. 2002. Defining and quantifying the social phenotype in autism. *American Journal of Psychiatry*, 159, 895–908.

Köhler, W. 1927. *The mentality of apes.* New York, Vintage. (Quoted from the German edition: *Intelligenzprüfungen an Menschenaffen.* Berlin: Springer, 1921.)

Kohts, N. 1923. *Studies on the intellectual faculties of the chimpanzee* [in Russian]. Moscow: Gosudarstvennoe Izdateltsvo.

Langer, J. 1998. Phylogenetic and ontogenetic origins of cognition: Classification. In: *Piaget, evolution, and development* (ed. J. Langer and M. Killen), pp. 33–54. Hillsdale, N.J.: Lawrence Erbaum Associates.

———— 2000a. The descent of cognitive development. *Developmental Science*, 361–388.

———— 2000b. The heterochronic evolution of primate cognitive development. In: *Biology, brains, and behavior. The evolution of human development* (ed. S. T. Parker, J. Langer, and M. L. McKinney), pp. 215–235. New Mexico: School of American Research Press.

Lasky, R. E., Romano, N., and Wenters, J. 1980. Spatial localization in children after changes in position. *Journal of Experimental Child Psychology*, 29, 225–248.

Leavens, D., and Hopkins, W. 1998. Intentional communication by chimpanzees: A cross-sectional study of the use of referential gestures. *Developmental Psychology*, 34, 813–822.

Lefebvre, L., Nicolakakis, N. and Boire, D. 2002. Tools and brains in birds. *Behaviour*, 139, 939–973.

Lewkowicz, D. J., and Lickliter, R. 1994. The development of intersensory perception. Hillsdale, N.J.: Lawrence Erlbaum.

Limongelli, L., Visalberghi, E., and Boysen, S. T. 1995. Comprehension of cause-effect relations in a tool-using task by chimpanzees (*Pan troglodytes*). *Journal of Comparative Psychology*, 109, 18–26.

Lin, A. C., Bard. K.A., and Anderson, J.R. 1992. Development of self-recognition in chmpanzees (*Pan troglodytes*). *Journal of Comparative Psychology*, 106, 120–127.

Lock, A. 1978. The emergence of language. In: *Action, gesture and symbol: The emergence of language* (ed. A. Lock), pp. 3–18. London: Academic Press.

Lorenz, K. 1981. *The foundations of ethology.* Berlin: Springer.

Lorinctz, E., Perret, D. and Gómez, J. C. In press. A comparative study of spontaneous gaze following in rhesus macaques and humans. *Journal of Comparative Psychology*.

Lycan, W. 1999. Intentionality. In: *The MIT encyclopedia of the cognitive sciences* (ed. R. Wilson and F. Keil). Cambridge, Mass.: MIT Press. (pp. 413–415).

Macedonia, J. M., and Evans, C. S. 1993. Variation among mammalian alarm call systems and the problem of meaning in animal signals. *Journal of Ethology*, 93, 177–197.

Marler, P. 1991. The instinct to learn. In: *The epigenesis of mind: Essays on biology and cognition* (ed. S. Carey and R. Gelman). Hillsdale, N.J.: Lawrence Erlbaum.

McGrew, W. C. 1992. *Chimpanzee material culture. Implications for human evolution.* Cambridge: Cambridge University Press.

McKinney, M. L. 1988. *Heterochrony in evolution.* (ed. F. G. Stehli and D. S. Jones). New York: Plenum Press.

Mehler, J., and Bever, T. G. 1967. Cognitive capacity of very young children. *Science*, 158, 141–142.

———— 1968. Reply to Piaget. *Science*, 162, 979–981.

Meltzoff, A. N. 1988. The human infant as *Homo imitans*. In: *Social learning: Psychological and biological perspectives* (ed. T. R. Zentall and B. G. J. Galef). Hillsdale, N.J.: Lawrence Erlbaum.

Meltzoff, A. N., and Borton, R. W. 1979. Intermodal matching by human neonates. *Nature*, 282, 403–404.

Menzel, C. R. 1991. Cognitive aspects of foraging in Japanese monkeys. *Animal Behaviour*, 41, 397–402.

———— 1996. Structure-guided foraging in long-tailed macaques. *American Journal of Primatology*, 38, 117–132.

———— 1999. Unprompted recall and reporting of hidden objects by a chimpanzee (*Pan troglodytes*) after extended delays. *Journal of Comparative Psychology*, 113, 426–434.

Menzel, E. W. 1971. Communication about the environment in a group of young chimpanzees. *Folia primatologica*, 15, 220–232.

———— 1973a (ed.). *Precultural primate behavior.* Basel: Karger.

———— 1973b. Leadership and communication in young chimpanzees. In *Precultural primate behavior* (ed. E. W. Menzel). Basel, Karger: 192–225.

———— 1974. A group of young chimpanzees in a one-acre field. *Behavior of nonhuman primates. Vol. 5.* Ed. M. Schrier and F. Stolnitz. New York, Academic Press.

Menzel, E. W., and Juno, C. 1982. Marmosets (*Sanguinus fuscicollis*): Are learning sets learned? *Science*, 217, 750–752.

Menzel, E. W., and Menzel, C. R. 1979. Cognitive, developmental and social aspects of responsiveness to novel objects in a family group of marmosets (*Sanguinus fuscicollis*). *Behaviour*, 70, 250–279.

Mounoud, P. 1970. *La structuration de l'instrument chez l'enfant.* Neuchatel, Delachaux Niestlée.

Munakata, Y., Santos, L. R., Spelke, E. S., Hauser, M. D., and O'Reilly, R. C. 2001. Visual representation in the wild: How Rhesus monkeys parse objects. *Journal of Cognitive Neuroscience,* 13, 44–58.

Muncer, S. J. 1983. "Conversations" with a chimpanzee. *Developmental Psychobiology,* 16, 1–11.

Myers, R. E. 1978. Comparative neurology of vocalization and speech: Proof of a dichotomy. In: *Human evolution: Biosocial perspectives* (ed. D. A. Hamburg and E. R. McCown), pp. 59–75. Menlo Park: Benjamin/Cummins.

Myowa-Yamakoshi, M., and Tomonaga, M., 2001. Perceiving eye-gaze in an infant Gibbon (*Hylobates agilis*). *Psychologia,* 44, 24–30.

Napier, J. R., and Napier, P. H. 1985. *The natural history of the primates.* London: Cambridge University Press.

Navon, D. 1977. Forest before trees: The precedence of global features in visual perception. *Cognitive Psychology,* 9, 353–383.

Neisser, U. 1988. Five kinds of self-knowledge. *Philosophical Psychology,* 1, 35–59.

Núñez, M., and Rivière, A. In press. Una re-evaluación de la lógica inferencial del paradigma de la creencia. *Infancia y Aprendizaje.*

Oden, D. L., Thompson, R. K. R., and Premack, D. 2001. Can an ape reason analogically? Comprehension and production of analogical problems by Sarah, a chimpanzee (*Pan troglodytes*). In: *The analogical mind. Perspectives from cognitive science* (ed. D. Gentner, K. J. Holyoak, and B. N. Kokinov). Cambridge: MIT Press.

Overman, W. H., and Bachevalier, J. 2001. Inferences about the functional development of neural systems in children via the application of animal tests of cognition. In: *Developmental cognitive neuroscience* (ed. C. A. Nelson and M. Luciana), pp. 109–124. Cambridge: MIT Press.

Parker, S. T. 1977. Piaget's sensorimotor series in an infant macaque: a model for comparing unstereotyped behaviour and intelligence in human and nonhuman primates. In: *Primate biosocial development: Biological, social, and ecological determinants* (ed. S. Chevalier-Skolnikoff and F. E. Poirier), pp. 43–112. New York: Garland.

——— 1993. Imitation and circular reactions as evolved mechanisms for cognitive construction. *Human Development,* 36, 309–323.

Parker, S. T., and McKinney, M. L. 1999. *The evolution of cognitive development in monkeys, apes, and humans.* Baltimore: Johns Hopkins University Press.

Pascalis, O., and Bachevalier, J. 1999. Le développement de la reconnaissance chez le primate humain et non-humain. *Primatologie,* 2, 145–169.

Patterson, F., and Cohn, R. 1994. Self-recognition and self-awareness in Lowland gorillas. In: *Self-recognition and awareness in apes, monkeys and children* (ed. S. Parker, M. Boccia, and R. Mitchell), pp. 273–290. Cambridge, Mass.: Cambridge University Press.

Patterson, F., and Linden, E. 1981. *The education of Koko.* New York: Holt, Rinehart, and Winston.

Pearce, J. M. 1997. *Animal learning and cognition. 2nd ed.* Hove: Psychology Press.

Pepperberg, I. M. 1999. *The Alex studies.* Cambridge, Mass.: Harvard University Press.

Perner, J. 1991. *Understanding the representational mind.* Cambridge, Mass.: MIT Press.

Perret, D. 1999. A cellular basis for reading minds from faces and actions. In: *The design of animal communication* (ed. M. Hauser and M. Konishi). Cambridge, Mass.: MIT Press.

Phillips, W., Baron-Cohen, S., and Rutter, M. 1992. The role of eye-contact in goal-detection: Evidence from normal toddlers and children with autism or mental handicap. *Development and Psychopathology*, 4, 375–384.

Phillips, W., Gómez, J. C., Baron-Cohen, S., Laá, M. V., and Rivière, A. 1995. Treating people as objects, agents or "subjects": How young children with and without autism make requests. *Journal of Child Psychology and Psychiatry*, 36, 1383–1398.

Piaget, J. 1936. *La naissance de l'intelligence chez l'enfant.* Neuchatel: Delachaux et Niestlée.

——— 1937. *La construction du réel chez l'enfant.* Neuchâtel: Delachaux et Niestlée.

——— 1968. Quantification, conservation, and nativism. *Science*, 162, 976–979.

Piaget, J., and Inhelder, B. 1966. *La psychologie de l'enfant.* Paris: Presses Universitaires de France.

Pinker, S. 1994. *The language instinct.* London: Penguin.

Plooij, F. X. 1978. Some basic traits of language in wild chimpanzees? In: *Action, Gesture and Symbol: The emergence of language* (ed. A. Lock), pp. 111–131. London: Academic Press.

——— 1979. How young chimpanzee babies trigger the onset of mother-infant play—and what the mother makes of it. In: *Before speech: The beginnings of human communication* (ed. M. Bullowa, M.), pp. 223–243. Cambridge: Cambridge University Press.

Poucet, B. 1993. Spatial cognitive maps in animals: New hypotheses on their structure and neural mechanisms. *Psychological Review*, 100.

Povinelli, D. J. 1994. Comparative studies of animal mental state attribution: A reply to Heyes. *Animal Behaviour*, 48, 239–401.

———— 2000. *Folk physics for apes.* Oxford: Oxford University Press.

Povinelli, D. J., and Eddy, T. J. 1996a. What young chimpanzees know about seeing. *Monographs of the Society for Research in Child Development*, 61, 1–190.

———— 1996b. Factors influencing young chimpanzees' (*Pan troglodytes*) recognition of attention. *Journal of Comparative Psychology*, 110.

———— 1997. Specificity of gaze following in young chimpanzees. *British Journal of Developmental Psychology*, 15, 213–222.

Povinelli, D. J., Nelson, K. E., and Boysen, S. T. 1990. Inferences about guessing and knowing by chimpanzees (*Pan Troglodytes*). *Journal of Comparative Psychology*, 104, 203–210.

Povinelli, D. J., Reaux, J. E., Bierschwale, D. T., Allain, A. D., and Simon, B. B. 1997. Exploitation of pointing as a referential gesture in young children, but not adolescent chimpanzees. *Cognitive Development*, 12, 423–461.

Povinelli, D. J., Rulf, A. B., Landau, K. R., and Bierschwale, D. F. 1993. Self-recognition in chimpanzees (*Pan Troglodytes*): Distribution, ontogeny, and patterns of emergence. *Journal of Comparative Psychology*, 180, 74–80.

Povinelli, D. J., and Vonk, J. 2003. Chimpanzee minds: Suspiciously human? *Trends in Cognitive Sciences*, 7, 157–160.

Premack, D. 1976. *Intelligence in ape and man.* Hillsdale, N.J.: Lawrence Erdman.

———— 1983. The codes of man and beasts. *The Behavioral and Brain Sciences*, 6, 125–167.

Premack, D., and Premack, A. J. 1983. *The mind of an ape.* New York, Norton.

Premack, D., and Woodruff, G. 1978a. Chimpanzee problem-solving: a test for comprehension. *Science*, 202, 532–535.

———— 1978b. Does the chimpanzee have a theory of mind? *Behavioral and Brain Sciences*, 1, 515–526.

Quinn, P. C. 2002. Category representation in young infants. *Current Directions in Psychological Science*, 11, 66–70.

Redshaw, M. 1978. Cognitive development in human and gorilla infants. *Journal of Human Evolution*, 7, 133–141.

———— 1989. A comparison of neonatal behaviour and reflexes in the great apes. *Journal of Human Evolution*, 18, 191–200.

Roberts, W. A., and Mazmanian, D. S. 1988. Concept learning at different levels of abstraction by pigeons, monkeys, and people. *Journal of Experimental Psychology: Animal Behavior Processes*, 14, 247–260.

Rochat, P. 2001. *The infant's world.* Cambridge: Harvard University Press.

Rumbaugh, D. M. 1965. Maternal care in relation to infant behaviour in the squirrel monkey. *Psychological Report*, 16, 171–176.

—— 1977. Language learning in a chimpanzee: The LANA project. New York: Academic Press.

Sackett, G. P. 1965a. Effects of rearing conditions upon the behavior of rhesus monkeys (*Macaca mulatta*). *Child Development*, 36, 855–868.

—— 1965b. Manipulatory behavior in monkeys reared under different levels of early stimulus variation. *Perceptual and Motor Skills*, 20, 985–988.

—— 1966. Development of preference for differentially complex patterns by infant monkeys. *Psychonomic Science*, 6, 441–442.

Santos, L. and Hauser, M. D. 2002. A nonhuman primate's understanding of solidity: Dissociations between seeing and acting. *Developmental Science*, 5, F1-F7.

Santos, L., Sulkowski, G. M., Spaepen, G. M., and Hauser, M. D. 2002. Object individuation using property/kind information in rhesus macaques (*Macaca mulatta*). *Cognition*, 83, 241–264.

Sarriá, E., and Rivière, A. 1991. Desarrollo cognitivo y comunicación intencional preverbal: Un estudio longitudinal multivariado. *Estudios de Psicología*, 46, 35–52.

Savage-Rumbaugh, E. S. 1986. *Ape language: From conditioned response to symbol*. Oxford: Oxford University Press.

Savage-Rumbaugh, E. S., Murphy, J., Sevcik, R. A., Brakke, K. E., Williams, S. L., and Rumbaugh, D. M. 1993. Language comprehension in ape and child. *Monographs of the Society for Research in Child Development*, 58, 1–221.

Savage-Rumbaugh, E. S., Rumbaugh, D. M., Smith, S. T., and Lawson, J. 1980. Reference: The linguistic essential. *Science*, 210, 922–925.

Scerif, G., Gómez, J. C.,, and Byrne, R. In press, 2003. What do Diana monkeys know about the focus of attention of a conspecific? *Animal Behaviour*.

Schiller, P. H. 1952. Innate constituents of complex responses in primates. *Psychological Review*, 59, 177–191.

Schino, G., Spinozzi, G., and Berlinguer, L. 1990. Object concept and mental representation in *Cebus apella* and *Macaca fascicularis*. *Primates*, 31, 537–544.

Schultz, A. H. 1969. *The life of primates*. London: Weidenfeld and Nicolson.

Schusterman, R. J., Thomas, J. A., and Wood, F. G. 1986. *Dolphin cognition and behaviour: A comparative approach*. Hillsdale, N.J.: Lawrence Erlbaum.

Seidenberg, M. S. and Petitto, L. A. 1979. Signing behavior in apes: A critical review. *Cognition*, 7, 177–215.

Seyfarth, R. M. 1987. Vocal communication and its relation to language. In: *Primate societies* (ed. B. B. Smuts, D. L. Cheney, R. M. Seyfarth,

R. W. Wrangham, and T. T. Struhsaker), pp. 440–451. Chicago: University of Chicago Press.

Seyfarth, R. M., and Cheney, D. T. 1980. The ontogeny of vervet monkey alarm-calling behavior: A preliminary report. *Zeitschrift für Tierpsychologie*, 54, 37–56.

Shurcliff, A., Brown, D., and Stollnitz, F. 1971. Specificity of training required for solution of a stick problem by Rhesus monkeys (*Macaca mulatta*). *Learning and Motivation*, 2, 255–270.

Slater, A. 2001. Visual perception. In: *Infant development* (ed. G. Bremner and A. Fogel), pp. 5–34. Oxford: Blackwell.

Smuts, B. B., Cheney, D. L., Seyfarth, R. M., Wrangham, R. W., and Struhsaker, T. T. (eds.) 1987. *Primate societies*. Chicago: University of Chicago Press.

Snowdon, C. T., Brown, C. H., and Petersen, M. R. 1982. *Primate communication*. Cambridge: Cambridge University Press.

Solomon, T. L. 2001. Early development of strategies for mapping symbol-referent relations: What do young children understand about scale models. Ph.D. Thesis. School of Psychology, University of St. Andrews.

Southgate, V., and Gómez, J. C. 2003. Object understanding in rhesus macaques. *Psycholloquia Seminars*. University of St. Andrews, Department of Psychology.

Spelke, E. S., Kestenbaum, R., Simons, D., and Wein, D. 1995. Spatiotemporal continuity, smoothness of motion, and object identity in infancy. *British Journal of Developmental Psychology*, 13, 113–142.

Sperber, D. 1994. Understanding verbal understanding. In: *What is intelligence?* (ed. J. Khalfa), pp. 179–198. Cambridge: Cambridge University Press.

Sperber, D., and Wilson, D. 1986. *Relevance: Communication and cognition*. Cambridge, Mass.: Harvard University Press.

Spinozzi, G., De Lillo, C., and Truppa , V. 2003. Global and local processing of hierarchical visual stimuli in Tufted Capuchin monkeys (*Cebus apella*). *Journal of Comparative Psychology*, 117, 15–23.

Still, A., and Costall, A. 1991. *Against cognitivism*. London, Harvester.

Swettenham, J., Gómez, J. C., Baron-Cohen, S., and Walsh, S. 1996. What's inside someone's head? Conceiving of the mind as a camera helps children with autism acquire an alternative to a theory of mind. *Cognitive Neuropsychiatry*, 1, 73–88.

Teleki, G. 1974. Chimpanzee subsistence technology: Materials and skills. *Journal of Human Evolution*, 3, 575–594.

Terrace, H. S. 1979. *Nim: A chimpanzee that learned sign language*. New York: Knopf.

Terrace, H. S., Petitto, L. A., Sanders, R. J., and Bever, T. G. 1979. Can an ape create a sentence? *Science*, 206, 891–902.

Theall, L. A., and Povinelli, D. J. 1999. Do chimpanzees tailor their gestural signals to fit the attentional states of others? *Animal Cognition*, 2, 207–214.

Thompson, R. K. R., and Oden, D. L. 1996. A profound disparity revisited: Perception and judgement of abstract identity relations by chimpanzees, human infants, and monkeys. *Behavioural Processes*, 149–161.

——— 2000. Categorical perception and conceptual judgements by nonhuman primates: The paleological monkey and the analogical ape. *Cognitive Science*, 24, 363–396.

Thompson, R. K. R., Oden, D. L,, and Boysen, S. T. 1997. Language-naive chimpanzees (*Pan troglodytes*) judge relations between relations in a conceptual matching-to-sample task. *Journal of Experimental Psychology: Animal Behavior Processes*, 23, 31–43.

Thorndike, E. L. 1898. Animal intelligence: An experimental study of the associative processes in animals. *Psychological Review: Series of Monograph Supplements*, 2, 1–109.

Tinklepaugh, O. L. 1929. An experimental study of representative factors in monkeys. *Journal of Comparative Psychology*, 8, 197–236.

Tomasello, M. 1990. Cultural transmission in the tool use and communicatory signaling of chimpanzees? In: *"Language" and intelligence in monkeys and apes: Comparative developmental perspectives* (ed. S. T. Parker and K. R. Gibson), pp. 274–311. Cambridge, Mass.: Cambridge University Press.

——— 1994. Can an ape understand a sentence? A review of *Language comprehension in ape and child* by E. S. Savage-Rumbaugh et al. *Language, and Communication*, 00, 0–00.

——— 1995. Language is not an instinct. *Cognitive Development*, 10, 131–156.

——— 1999. *The cultural origins of human cognition.* Cambridge, Mass.: Harvard University Press.

Tomasello, M., and Call, J. 1997. *Primate cognition.* Oxford: Oxford University Press.

Tomasello, M., Call, J., and Hare, B. 2003. Chimpanzees understand psychological states—the question is which ones and to what extent. *Trends in Cognitive Sciences*, 7, 153–160.

Tomasello, M., Call, J., Warren, J., Frost, G. T., Carpenter, M., and Nagell, K. 1997. The ontogeny of chimpanzee gestural signals: A comparison across groups and generations. *Evolution of Communication*, 1, 223–259.

Tomasello, M., Davis-Dasilva, M., and Camak, L. 1987. Observational learning of tool-use by young chimpanzees. *Human Evolution, 2,* 175–183.

Tomasello, M., George, B., Kruger, A., Farrar, J., and Evans, E. 1985. The development of gestural communication in young chimpanzees. *Journal of Human Evolution,* 14, 175–186.

Tomasello, M., Gust, D., and Forst, T. 1989. A longitudinal investigation of gestural communication in young chimpanzees. *Primates,* 30, 35–50.

Tomasello, M., Hare, B., and Agnetta, B. 1999. Chimpanzees follow gaze direction geometrically. *Animal Behaviour,* 58, 769–777.

Tomasello, M., Hare, B., and Fogleman, T. 2001. The ontogeny of gaze following in chimpanzees, *Pan troglodytes,* and rhesus macaques, *Macaca mulatta. Animal Behaviour,* 61, 335–343.

Tomonaga, M. 2001. Investigating visual perception and cognition in chimpanzees (*Pan troglodytes*) through visual search and related tasks: From basic to complex processes. In: *Primate origins of human cognition and behavior* (ed. T. Matsuzawa), pp. 55–86. Berlin: Springer.

Torigoe, T. 1985. Comparison of object manipulation among 74 species of non-human primates. *Primates,* 26, 182–194.

Uller, C., Jaeger, R., Guidry, G., and Martin, C. 2003. Salamanders (*Plethodon cinereus*) go for more: Rudiments of number in an amphibian. *Animal Cognition,* in press.

Uller, C., Xu, F., Carey, S., and Hauser, M. D. 1997. Is language needed for constructing sortal concepts? A study with nonhuman primates. In: *Proceedings of the 21st Annual Boston University Conference on Language Development* (ed. E. Hughes), pp. 665–677. Somerville, Mass.: Cascadilla Press.

van Schaik, C. P., Ancrenaz, M., Borgen, W., Galdikas, B., Knott, C. D., Singleton, I., Suzuki, A., Utami, S. S., and Merrill, M. 2003. Orangutan cultures and the evolution of material culture. *Science,* 299, 102–104.

Vauclair, J. 1990. Processus cognitifs élaborés: Étude des représentations mentales chez le babouin. In: *Primates. Recherches actuelles* (ed. J. J. J. J., and J. R. Anderson). Paris: Masson.

Vauclair, J. 1996. *Animal cognition. An introduction to modern comparative psychology.* Cambridge, Mass: Harvard University Press.

Visalberghi, E., and Fragaszy, D. M. 1990. Do monkeys ape? In: *"Language" and intelligence in monkeys and apes. Comparative developmental perspectives* (ed. S. T. Parker and K. R. Gibson). Cambridge: Cambridge University Press.

Visalberghi, E., Fragaszy, D. M.,, and Savage-Rumbaugh, S. 1995. Performance in a tool-using task by common chimpanzees (*Pan troglo-*

dytes), bonobos (*Pan paniscus*), an orangutan (*Pongo pygmaeus*), and Capuchin monkeys (*Cebus apella*). *Journal of Comparative Psychology*, 109, 52–60.

Visalberghi, E., and Limongelli, L. 1996. Acting and understanding: Tool use revisited through the minds of capuchin monkeys. In: *Reaching into thought. The minds of the great apes* (ed. A. E. Russon, K. A. Bard, and S. T. Parker), pp. 57–79. Cambridge: Cambridge University Press.

Visalberghi, E., and Tomasello, M. 1998. Primate causal understanding in the physical and psychological domains. *Behavioral Processes*, 42, 189–203.

Von Grünau, M. and Anston, C. 1995. The detection of gaze direction: A stare-in-the-crowd effect. *Perception*, 24, 1297–1313.

Vonk, J., and MacDonald, S. E. 2002. Natural concepts in a juvenile gorilla (*Gorilla gorilla gorilla*) at three levels of abstraction. *Journal of Experimental Analysis of Behavior*, 78, 315–332.

——— In press. Levels of abstraction in orangutan (*Pongo abelii*) categorization. *Journal of Comparative Psychology*.

Vygotsky, L. 1930. Orudie i znak [Tool and sign in the development of the child]. In: *The collected works of L. S. Vygotsky. Vol. 6: Scientific legacy* (ed. R. W. Rieber), pp. 1–68. New York: Kluwer/Plenum. [Quoted from the Russian edition].

Want, S. C., and Harris, P. L. 2001. Learning from other people's mistakes: Causal understanding in learning to use a tool. *Child Development*, 72, 431–443.

——— 2002. How do children ape? Applying concepts from the study of non-human primates to the developmental study of 'imitation' in children. *Developmental Science*, 5.

Wasserman, E. A., Young, M. E., and Fagot, J. 2001. Effects of number of items on the baboon's discrimination of same from different visual displays. *Animal Cognition*, 4, 163–170.

Weir, A. A., Chappell, J., and Kacelnik, A. 2002. Shaping of hooks in New Caledonian crows. *Science*, 297, 981.

Weiskrantz, L., and Cowey, A. 1975. Cross-modal matching in the rhesus monkey using a single pair of stimuli. *Neuropsychologia*, 13, 257–261.

Westergaard, G. C. 1988. Lion-tailed macaques (*Macaca silenus*) manufacture and use tools. *Journal of Comparative Psychology*, 102, 152–159.

——— 1993. Development of combinatorial manipulation in infant baboons (*Papio cynocephalus anubis*). *Journal of Comparative Psychology*, 107, 34–38.

Whiten, A. 2000. Primate culture and social learning. *Cognitive Science*, 24, 477–508.

Whiten, A., and Byrne, R. W. 1988. Tactical deception in primates. *Behavioral and Brain Sciences*, 11, 233–273.

Whiten, A., Custance, D. M., Gómez, J. C., Teixidor, P., and Bard, K. 1996. Imitative learning of artificial fruit processing in children (*Homo sapiens*) and chimpanzees (*Pan troglodytes*). *Journal of Comparative Psychology*, 110, 3–14.

Whiten, A., Goodall, J., McGrew, W. C., Nishida, T., Reynolds, V., Sugiyama, Y., Tutin, C. E. G., Wrangham, R. W., and Boesch, C. 1999. Cultures in chimpanzees. *Nature*, 399, 682–685.

Wicker, B. 2001. Perception et interpretation du regard: neuroanatomie functionelle chez l'homme et chez le singe. Ph.D. Thesis. Lyon: Université Claude Bernard.

Williams, T. D., and Carey, S. 2000. Development of object individuation in infant pigtail macaques. *Poster presented at the XIth Biennial Meeting of the International Society of Infant Studies*. Brighton, UK.

Woodruff, G., Premack, D., and Kennel, K. 1978. Conservation of liquid and solid quantity by the chimpanzee. *Science*, 202, 991–994.

Wrangham, R. W., McGrew, W. C., Waal, F. de, and Heltne, P. G. 1994. *Chimpanzee cultures*. Cambridge, Mass.: Harvard University Press.

Xu, F., and Carey, S. 1996. Infants' metaphysics: The case of numerical identity. *Cognitive Psychology*, 30, 111–153.

Xu, F., Carey, S., and Welch, J. 1999. Infants' ability to use object kind information for object individuation. *Cognition*, 70, 137–166.

Zimmermann, R. R., and Torrey, C. C. 1965. Ontogeny of learning. In: *Behavior of nonhuman primates* (ed. A. M. Schrier, H. F. Harlow, and F. Stollnitz), pp. 405–447. New York: Academic Press.

Zuberbühler, K. 2000a. Referential labeling in wild diana monkeys. *Animal Behaviour*, 59, 917–927.

———— 2000b. Interspecies semantic communication in two forest monkeys. *Proceedings of the Royal Society of London. B.*, 267.

———— 2000c. Causal knowledge of predators' behaviour in wild diana monkeys. *Animal Behaviour*, 59, 209–220.

Index